Behind the Mask of Hypocrisy: The Hidden Faces of Deception

Behind the Mask of Hypocrisy: The Hidden Faces of Deception: Exposing the Truth Hidden Beneath Religious and Worldly Appearances

Joseph Ngoma and Joseph Habimana Ngoma

Published by Joseph Ngoma, 2025.

BEHIND THE MASK OF HYPOCRISY: THE HIDDEN FACES OF DECEPTION: EXPOSING THE TRUTH HIDDEN BENEATH RELIGIOUS AND WORLDLY APPEARANCES

First edition. November 11, 2025.

ISBN: 979-8232193379

Written by Joseph Ngoma and Joseph Habimana Ngoma.

This book is dedicated first to **Almighty God** —the Creator of Heaven and Earth,the Healer of nations,and the Restorer of broken lives.To You belong all glory, wisdom, and power.You are the Author of truth and the Revealer of mysteries hidden since the foundation of the world.

To my **Christian family**,whose love, faith, and prayers have strengthened me through every season of battle and revelation —your encouragement has been a testimony of God's unfailing grace.

And to **every reader across the world**,may these words awaken your spirit, renew your understanding,and lead you closer to the One who is Truth, Freedom, and Life itself —**Jesus Christ.**

"You shall know the truth, and the truth shall make you free." — *John 8:32*

JOSEPH HABIMANA NGOMA

Disciple of Jesus Christ

2025

Copyright Page

Scripture Notice

Unless otherwise noted, all Scripture quotations are taken from the Holy Bible, King James Version (KJV). References were consulted in Windows HTML Help Format. The KJV text is in the public domain.

First Edition, 2025

Requests for information and permissions should be addressed to:

Joseph Habimana Ngoma

E-mail: habimanangoma@gmail.com

Dedication

"This book is dedicated first to Almighty God — the Creator of Heaven and Earth, the Healer of nations, and the Restorer of broken lives. To You belongs all glory, wisdom, and power. You are the Author of truth and the Revealer of mysteries hidden since the foundation of the world."

To my Christian family, whose love, faith, and prayers have strengthened me through every season of battle and revelation — your encouragement has been a testimony of God's unfailing grace.

And to every reader across the world, may these words awaken your spirit, renew your understanding, and lead you closer to the One who is Truth, Freedom, and Life itself — Jesus Christ.

"You shall know the truth, and the truth shall make you free." — John 8:32

Preface

This book was not written from human imagination but from divine conviction. It was born in the secret place — in moments of prayer, revelation, and deep reflection upon the world's growing deception.

Every page carries a cry from the Spirit: a call for the Church, for nations, and for individuals to remove their masks and return to truth. We live in an age where appearance has replaced authenticity, where religion has replaced relationship, and where performance has replaced purity. But God is raising a remnant — a people who will no longer live for applause, but for alignment with His will.

Behind the Mask of Hypocrisy exposes the hidden faces of deception — in families, churches, governments, workplaces, and even within our own hearts. It does not seek to condemn, but to awaken. It does not point fingers, but turns the mirror toward the soul.

May every reader encounter conviction, revelation, and transformation through these words. May the Spirit of Truth — the Holy Spirit — strip away every falsehood and rebuild in you the image of Christ, the Truth Himself.

"For nothing is hidden that will not be revealed, nor anything secret that will not be known and come to light." — Luke 8:17

Table of Contents

Introduction: The Masked Generation

The Age of Pretending

We live in a generation where truth has become strange and deception has become normal.

A generation that smiles in public but bleeds in secret.

A generation that worships appearance more than substance.

Many have mastered the art of pretending—pretending to love, pretending to believe, pretending to care, pretending to serve God, pretending to be humble—while their hearts are filled with darkness.

This is the **Masked Generation**—a people who wear holiness like makeup, righteousness like costume, and faith like a show. We have learned how to perform goodness but not to live it. We dress in light, but our hearts remain in shadows.

The Definition of Hypocrisy

Hypocrisy is the art of pretending to be what you are not.

It is the sin of wearing the mask of righteousness while living in rebellion.

It is the distance between your lips and your heart.

Jesus said in *Matthew 15:8*,

> "These people draw near to Me with their mouth, and honor Me with their lips, but their heart is far from Me."

Hypocrisy is not just lying to people—it is lying to God. It is living in disguise, acting holy when you are unclean, and speaking truth while practicing deceit. A hypocrite is not just a sinner; he is a sinner pretending to be a saint. He builds an image that God cannot recognize.

In the Greek, the word *hypokrites* means "actor" — one who plays a role on stage. Many today are not living life; they are performing it. They have turned Christianity into a theater of false impressions, and holiness into a show for spectators.

How Hypocrisy Became a Spirit That Rules the World

Once, hypocrisy was just a behavior—but now it has become a spirit, a power that rules the world.

It sits on thrones, walks in pulpits, teaches in classrooms, and even sings in choirs.

It lives in governments that claim justice but practice corruption.

It hides in churches that preach holiness but live in secret sin.

It rules in homes where parents pretend to love while their hearts are full of bitterness.

It disguises itself as kindness, but its motive is control. It smiles while planning destruction.

The spirit of hypocrisy is the spirit of **Satan**, for he was the first deceiver. He pretended to bring wisdom, but his goal was death. Since the Garden of Eden, that same lying spirit has possessed humanity—making people love the mask more than the truth.

In politics, leaders use the name of the people to enrich themselves.

In religion, preachers use the name of God to promote themselves.

In relationships, lovers use words of love to manipulate each other.

Everywhere we turn, the world is choking under the perfume of falsehood.

Hypocrisy has become global—it wears the flag of every nation and the robe of every church.

Why Truth Is Hated in a World That Loves Appearances

We live in a world that honors image more than integrity.

People would rather look right than be right.

They would rather be praised than be pure.

They would rather shine before men than bow before God.

Truth has become offensive because it exposes what people try to hide. It burns masks and shatters illusions. The moment truth speaks, hypocrisy feels threatened. That is why Jesus was hated—He came as light, and light reveals everything that darkness tries to conceal.

The world says, "Be yourself," but it does not mean it. It only accepts you if your "self" fits its standards. So, people create fake versions of themselves to survive.

They smile when they want to scream.

They post holiness on Sunday and live hell on Monday.

They build an image to impress others while losing their souls in the process.

But no man can hide forever. The mask may fool the world, but it cannot fool God.

Jesus' Warning to Hypocrites (Matthew 23)

When Jesus walked the earth, His harshest words were not against sinners but against **hypocrites.**

In *Matthew 23*, He thundered:

> "Woe to you, scribes and Pharisees, hypocrites! For you clean the outside of the cup and the dish, but inside they are full of greed and self-indulgence."

He called them "whitewashed tombs"—beautiful on the outside but full of death inside.

Why? Because God looks beyond the surface. He judges the heart.

Today, those same words echo through time. Jesus still warns the hypocrites of our generation—the politicians who promise peace but sow division, the preachers who shout "Hallelujah" while serving their flesh, the believers who act righteous but harbor hate, jealousy, and pride.

He still says:

> "Woe to you who act righteous to be seen by men! You have your reward already." (*Matthew 6:1–2*)

The warning is clear: hypocrisy may fool men, but it cannot deceive Heaven. God is calling this generation to repentance, to remove the mask and walk in truth.

A Call to the Unmasking

This book is a trumpet in the spirit—a divine alarm for a sleeping generation.

It is not written to condemn but to awaken.

It is not written to shame but to expose, heal, and restore.

The time has come to take off the mask.

To let truth burn every disguise.

To let the Holy Spirit purify our hearts until we become transparent before God.

We must stop performing and start transforming.

We must return to sincerity, humility, and truth.

We must live for God, not for the crowd.

For the mask can make you popular, but only truth will make you free.

> "And you shall know the truth, and the truth shall make you free."
> —*John 8:32*

Part I – The Roots of Deception

Chapter 1: The Origin of Hypocrisy — The First Lie

How Satan Became the Father of Deception (John 8:44)

Before Hypocrisy Entered Earth, It Began in Heaven

Before humanity ever learned to lie, the first lie was born in Heaven.

Before man ever wore a mask, an angel did.

The first act of hypocrisy was not in the Garden of Eden — it was in the heart of **Lucifer**, the most radiant being God had ever created.

Lucifer was not created evil.

He was created *perfect in beauty*, *wise in splendor*, and *anointed to worship.*

He stood in the very presence of God, reflecting divine glory like a mirror of light.

But the day came when the mirror stopped reflecting — and began desiring.

> "You were the seal of perfection, full of wisdom and perfect in beauty...
> You were blameless in your ways from the day you were created
> till wickedness was found in you." — *Ezekiel 28:12, 15*

Lucifer's beauty became his blindness.

He looked at himself and saw glory that was not his — and wanted it.

He desired *to be admired* rather than *to adore, to receive worship* rather than *to give it.*

In that moment, his heart deceived itself.

He became the first being to act — to appear holy on the outside while hiding rebellion on the inside.

That was the **birth of hypocrisy.**

From Light Bearer to Liar

The name *Lucifer* means *"light-bearer."*

But the one who once carried light became the architect of darkness.

He learned how to imitate what he lost.

He could no longer shine with the truth, so he began to shine with deception.

He became, as Jesus called him, **"the father of lies."**

> "He was a murderer from the beginning, not holding to the truth,
> for there is no truth in him.
> When he lies, he speaks his native language,
> for he is a liar and the father of lies." —*John 8:44*

Lucifer became the father of deception because he was the first to **twist truth** into appearance.

He disguised rebellion as revelation.

He covered jealousy with the language of justice.

He made pride sound like progress.

He didn't just fall from Heaven — he fell from **truth**.

That is why deception is not just a sin — it is a nature, a spiritual inheritance from the father of lies.

The Mask of False Light

Satan's deception is dangerous because it **looks like light.**

He does not come with a pitchfork and horns; he comes with charisma and words that sound wise.

He does not destroy through visible evil; he seduces through distorted good.

He presents poison in a golden cup — the same way he tempted Eve in Eden.

> "You will not surely die... you will be like God, knowing good and evil." — *Genesis 3:4–5*

That was not a complete lie — it was a twisted truth.

Eve *did* gain knowledge, but she lost innocence.

She *saw* more, but *became less.*

The serpent offered godliness without God, enlightenment without obedience, power without purity.

This is the same voice that whispers today:
"You can sin and still be spiritual."
"You can live your way and still have God's blessing."
"You can disobey the Word and still be fine."
It sounds enlightened — but it's the oldest lie ever told.
It is hypocrisy in its purest form: *evil pretending to be good.*

The Seed of the Serpent in Humanity

When Adam and Eve believed the serpent's deception, something spiritual happened.

They did not just disobey — they *inherited* a new nature.

The serpent's tongue became man's language.

Humanity learned to hide sin behind leaves, to cover shame with excuses, to blame others instead of confessing truth.

> "Then the man said, 'The woman You gave me...'" — *Genesis 3:12*

The first result of sin was **pretense** — man hiding from God, wearing a mask of fear and guilt.

Since then, every generation has learned to act — to appear righteous, speak kindly, and look spiritual, while the heart remains unchanged.

That is why Jesus said to the Pharisees:

> "You are of your father the devil... for he is a liar and the father of lies." —*John 8:44*

He wasn't just talking about bloodline; He was talking about *spiritual resemblance.*

Those who live in deception carry the same nature as the serpent — a life of performance instead of purity, of words without truth.

Satan's Greatest Weapon: Pretense, Not Power

Satan's most powerful weapon is **not persecution**, but **pretending.**

He knows how to look like light, speak like truth, and appear like an angel.

> "For Satan himself transforms into an angel of light." — *2 Corinthians 11:14*

He deceives nations through systems that appear good,
he corrupts churches through teachings that sound right,
and he destroys souls through temptations that look harmless.

He no longer needs to attack from outside when he can infiltrate from within.

His greatest victories are not in the world's darkness but in the Church's compromise.

His mission is not only to tempt sinners but to deceive believers into thinking they are right with God while living in rebellion.

Hypocrisy is Satan's silent victory — a man living a lie while believing he is in the light.

Truth Is the Only Weapon Against Deception

Every war of deception can only be won by truth.

Satan fell because he rejected truth; we rise when we return to it.

Jesus did not say, "You shall feel the truth" — He said,

> "You shall know the truth, and the truth shall make you free." — *John 8:32*

Truth is not a theory — it is a Person.

It is Jesus Himself.

The only way to defeat the father of lies is to live in union with the **Spirit of Truth.**

When the light of Christ fills the heart, deception cannot hide.

When humility takes root, pride loses power.

When we walk in the Word, the serpent's voice loses its charm.

Summary Revelation

- **Hypocrisy began in Heaven**, in the heart of Lucifer, not on earth.

- **Lucifer became Satan** when pride disguised itself as glory.

- **Deception was born** when appearance replaced truth.

- **The serpent's nature** entered humanity in Eden through a lie that looked like wisdom.

- **Satan's strategy** is not to fight truth but to imitate it.

- **His power lies in pretense**, not in force.

- **Christ's truth** is the cure; only the Spirit of Truth can expose the spirit of lies.

A Closing Reflection

Every time we choose appearance over honesty,
every time we act holy while hiding sin,
every time we twist Scripture to excuse behavior,
we echo the deception of Lucifer.

But every time we humble ourselves, confess the truth, and walk in the light,
we break that ancient curse.

We prove that the Light of Christ still conquers the false light of the enemy.

Lucifer wore the first mask — but Jesus tore it off.

Where Satan lied, Christ revealed.

Where Satan fell through pride, Christ triumphed through humility.

And every believer who walks in truth becomes a living testimony that **deception no longer reigns — truth does.**

The Garden of Eden: The First Mask Worn by Man After Sin

Before there was guilt, there was glory.

Before there was shame, there was shining.

In the beginning, Adam and Eve were **naked**, yet not embarrassed — because their nakedness was clothed with **the glory of God**.

They walked in perfect transparency — with no lies between them, no secrets before God, no separation in their souls.

Nakedness was not weakness; it was *purity*.

They had nothing to hide, because sin did not yet exist.

Their hearts and faces were uncovered before their Creator, and their fellowship was pure, open, and unbroken.

> "And they were both naked, the man and his wife, and were not ashamed." — *Genesis 2:25*

They were not afraid to be seen, because they were covered in light.

But when sin entered, **light turned into darkness**.

The glory lifted, the innocence vanished, and the first emotion that entered the human heart was *fear*.

The Moment the Mask Was Born

The serpent had spoken his lie, and the forbidden fruit had been eaten.

What looked beautiful became bitter.

And suddenly, Adam and Eve saw what they had never seen before — themselves, without glory.

> "Then the eyes of both of them were opened, and they knew that they were naked;
>
> so they sewed fig leaves together and made coverings for themselves." — *Genesis 3:7*

This was more than a physical reaction; it was **spiritual panic.**

For the first time, man felt *exposed* before the God who made him.
And what did he do?
He hid.
He covered.
He pretended.
That was the **birth of the mask.**
The fig leaves became the first human disguise —
a desperate attempt to appear whole while being broken,
to look clean while being corrupted,
to seem confident while trembling inside.
Man tried to hide the very thing God wanted to heal.
Instead of running *to* God, he ran *from* God.
Instead of confessing, he covered.
Instead of repenting, he justified.

From Transparency to Pretending

Sin changed man's nature.

The transparency of the heart turned into the *technology of hiding.*
Adam and Eve began the tragic pattern that continues to this day —
people building walls instead of altars, excuses instead of repentance.
They hid behind **work** — thinking achievement could cover emptiness.
They hid behind **religion** — thinking rituals could replace relationship.
They hid behind **pride** — thinking self-confidence could heal shame.
They hid behind **blame** — shifting responsibility onto others.

> "Then the man said, 'The woman You gave to be with me—she gave me of the tree, and I ate.'" — *Genesis 3:12*

Man's greatest tragedy is not that he sins, but that he hides his sin.

Sin created the fear of exposure — and from that fear came the culture of hypocrisy.

Every hypocrite, at the root, is a *frightened soul* — afraid to be known, afraid to be judged, afraid to be naked before truth.

Adam hid from God among the trees, and ever since, humanity has been inventing new trees to hide behind —

titles, money, religion, fame, relationships, politics, even ministry.

But every mask, no matter how beautiful, begins to rot from underneath.

The Divine Search for the Hidden Heart

God's first question to fallen man was not, "What have you done?" but,

> "Where are you?" — *Genesis 3:9*

God knew where Adam was — but Adam no longer knew where he was spiritually.

Sin had not only separated man from God; it had separated man from himself.

The mask had already begun its work — disconnecting the outer man from the inner truth.

That same question still echoes through generations:

"Where are you?"

Not physically, but spiritually.

Where are you hiding?

Behind what leaves, what excuses, what image, what secret sin?

God still walks in the cool of the day, looking for hearts that will stop hiding and start healing.

He doesn't expose to embarrass — He exposes to embrace.

He doesn't call to condemn — He calls to restore.

Man Covers, God Uncovers

Humanity's instinct is to cover; God's nature is to uncover.

Man hides the wound; God reveals it to heal it.

Man buries the truth; God resurrects it.

> "He who conceals his sins does not prosper,
> but whoever confesses and forsakes them finds mercy." — *Proverbs 28:13*

Repentance is not about perfection — it's about *exposure.*

It is the act of standing before the light and saying,

"Here I am, Lord. I am broken, but I'm Yours."

God cannot heal what we refuse to reveal.

He cannot wash what we continue to cover.

The first mask was made of leaves, but today's masks are made of pride, religion, and false appearances.

Yet the cure remains the same — truth and surrender.

The Restoration of Nakedness — Spiritual Transparency

Through Christ, God invites humanity back to that first garden of intimacy.

Through the Cross, the covering of guilt is replaced by the covering of grace.

In Jesus, we are clothed again — not in fig leaves, but in righteousness.

> "For all of you who were baptized into Christ have clothed yourselves with Christ." — *Galatians 3:27*

True nakedness before God is not physical; it is spiritual transparency — living open before Him, honest before others, and pure before yourself.

It means no more pretending, no more hiding, no more masks.

The first Adam hid from God; the last Adam, Jesus, hung naked on the Cross.

Where the first man covered himself in shame, the Son of Man uncovered Himself in sacrifice.

He bore our nakedness so that we might regain our glory.

Final Reflection

The Garden of Eden was where hypocrisy began — but also where grace was promised.

The same God who asked, "Where are you?" is still calling today.

He is not searching for perfection; He is searching for *honesty.*

Let the fig leaves fall.

Let the masks drop.

Let the light of truth shine on the parts of your soul that have been hiding.

For the path back to Eden begins not with perfection, but with *exposure.* And in that exposure, the glory that was lost will be found again.

The Difference Between Image and Likeness — How We Lost Divine Transparency

When God said,

> "Let Us make man in Our image, after Our likeness" — *Genesis 1:26*

He spoke two dimensions of divine identity into existence — **image** and **likeness.**

These two are not the same; they are the two halves of man's original wholeness.

Image — The Visible Reflection of the Invisible God

The *image* of God is what can be seen, recognized, and represented.

It is man's outward reflection of divine authority and design.

The image is the shadow of Heaven upon human form — the ability to think, create, speak, rule, and bring order.

Image means resemblance.

It means that when creation looked at Adam, it saw something of the Creator.

It is why the psalmist said,

> "You made him a little lower than the angels and crowned him with glory and honor." — *Psalm 8:5*

The image gave man dignity — to stand as God's representative on earth.

But image alone was never enough.

It was meant to be animated by something greater: **likeness.**

Likeness — The Inner Nature That Reflects God's Heart

If the image is the frame, the likeness is the life inside it.

If the image is the lamp, the likeness is the flame.

If the image is the body, the likeness is the breath that gives it light.

Likeness is not physical — it is moral, spiritual, and relational.

It is the capacity to love like God, think like God, forgive like God, and reign like God — in righteousness, not rebellion.

To carry God's *image* is to resemble His form;
to carry His *likeness* is to reproduce His character.
The image makes us **look** like sons;
the likeness makes us **live** like sons.
Without likeness, image becomes imitation.
Without likeness, worship becomes performance.
Without likeness, religion becomes hypocrisy.

The Fall — When the Image Remained but the Likeness Died

When sin entered the human heart, the **image** remained — but the **likeness** was lost.

Man did not cease to exist in God's design, but he ceased to exist in God's nature.

He still had dominion, but he lost discernment.

He still had speech, but he lost truth.

He still had a body that looked like God's design, but a heart that no longer carried God's purity.

Man kept the **form** of godliness but lost the **power** of it.

He still looked divine on the outside, but he became carnal on the inside.

He still spoke in the language of Heaven, but he lived in the logic of hell.

That was the birth of hypocrisy — when **outward resemblance no longer matched inward reality.**

> "Having a form of godliness but denying its power." — *2 Timothy 3:5*

We became actors wearing God's face but living with the serpent's heart.
We began to quote Scripture without conviction,
to build altars without repentance,
to sing about light while walking in darkness.

The Loss of Likeness — The Birth of Deception

The loss of divine likeness is what gave birth to the spirit of deception.

For deception is not simply the telling of lies; it is *living one.*

When man lost likeness, he began to use **truth as a costume**, not as a calling.

He started to worship with words but not with will.

He learned to speak holy while living unholy.

He turned faith into religion, and religion into performance.

> "This people honors Me with their lips, but their hearts are far from Me." — *Isaiah 29:13*

This is the tragedy of fallen man — to still *look like God* but no longer *live like Him.*

The body still bears His image, but the spirit bears the serpent's mark.

The mouth blesses, but the heart betrays.

The face smiles, but the soul schemes.

The hands give, but the motive hides pride.

That is why hypocrisy is not a behavior problem — it is a **likeness problem.**

We lost the divine resemblance of holiness, humility, and truth, and replaced it with performance, pride, and pretense.

The World of Masks — Religion Without Relationship

Today, the same spiritual distortion still rules the world.

We see it in churches, governments, families, and nations —

religious forms without spiritual substance.

Temples without truth.

Worship without holiness.

Preachers without repentance.

Congregations that sing about grace but live in greed.

The modern world has perfected the art of looking divine while living deceitfully.

We have turned faith into fashion, sermons into shows, and pulpits into platforms.

But Heaven is not impressed by the **image** of faith — it looks for the **likeness** of Christ.

> "For whom He foreknew, He also predestined to be conformed to the image of His Son." — *Romans 8:29*

To be restored in God's likeness is to let the Holy Spirit reshape the inner man —

to make us not just believers in name, but disciples in nature.

The Restoration of Likeness — The Work of the Spirit

Jesus did not come to polish our image; He came to restore our likeness.

He came to make us not merely look holy, but to **be holy.**

Through His death and resurrection, He reopened the path back to transparency —

to live once again without masks before the Father.

> "And we all, who with unveiled faces contemplate the Lord's glory,
>
> are being transformed into His image with ever-increasing glory."
> — *2 Corinthians 3:18*

The Spirit of God works from the inside out —

He does not decorate the outer man; He resurrects the inner one.

He restores in us the likeness of Christ — truth in the tongue, love in the heart, humility in the soul, and holiness in the mind.

Only when likeness is restored can image and truth become one again.

Then the outward life will match the inward nature,

and man will once more walk with God in **divine transparency.**

Final Reflection

In Eden, we lost our likeness and began to wear masks.

In Christ, we regain our likeness and remove them.

Sin made us actors; grace makes us authentic.

The mask hides shame, but the Spirit restores shape — the shape of God's heart within man.

To be created in God's image is an honor;

to live in His likeness is a responsibility.

The world is full of images — but Heaven is looking for likeness.

And when He finds a heart that mirrors His nature,

He finds a son, a daughter, and a vessel through which His glory can flow again.

When Truth Was Replaced by Pretense

The greatest tragedy in human history is not merely that man sinned — it is that man learned to **pretend he did not.**

The fall of man was not the end of truth; it was the birth of pretense.

Sin entered through disobedience, but hypocrisy entered through **denial.**

From that moment, humanity has been at war with truth.

Instead of repenting, we began **rehearsing.**

Instead of confessing, we began **covering.**

Instead of returning to God, we began **performing for people.**

Truth was no longer the standard — *appearance became the new god.*

Men began to worship how things looked rather than how things truly were.

The First Actors in Scripture

Cain killed his brother Abel, then looked Heaven in the face and asked,

> "Am I my brother's keeper?" — *Genesis 4:9*
>
> That was not ignorance; that was *pretense.*
>
> He covered murder with indifference, sin with sarcasm.
>
> And from that day, mankind began pretending before God as if He could not see.

King Saul disobeyed the command of the Lord — sparing what God had cursed —

and when confronted by the prophet Samuel, he justified himself, saying,

> "I have performed the commandment of the Lord." — *1 Samuel 15:13*
>
> He thought that *words* could hide *disobedience.*

He valued image over integrity, sacrifice over submission, performance over purity.

The Pharisees rejected the Messiah while calling themselves *keepers of the Law.*

They prayed long prayers but had no love.

They gave large offerings but had no obedience.

They looked holy in robes but were full of pride and death inside.

Jesus looked them in the eyes and said,

> "You are like whitewashed tombs, which outwardly appear beautiful,
> but within are full of dead men's bones." — *Matthew 23:27*

This is what happens when truth is replaced by pretense —
the soul becomes a tomb that looks alive but carries death inside.

When Lies Become More Comfortable Than Truth

The devil does not need to make people evil; he only needs to make them fake.

Whenever truth is replaced by pretense, **Satan reigns** —
for deception is his kingdom, and pretending is his worship.

People love lies because lies allow them to stay *comfortable.*

Lies let you look spiritual without being sanctified.

Lies let you sing without surrendering, preach without purity, and serve without submission.

Lies let you be admired by men while remaining empty before God.

> "They exchanged the truth of God for a lie,
>
> and worshiped and served created things rather than the Creator."
> — *Romans 1:25*

Truth demands change — lies allow performance.
Truth convicts — pretense entertains.
Truth calls you to the cross — pretense leads you to the stage.

Truth purifies the heart — pretense polishes the image.
That is why many would rather build a reputation than build character,
speak of grace but resist repentance,
and quote Scripture but ignore obedience.
Pretense feels safe — but it is the most dangerous prison on earth.
You can live in it your whole life and never know you are bound,
until one day, the light of eternity exposes the darkness of your disguise.

The War Between Truth and Performance

Every soul faces two altars:
one built on truth, and the other built on image.
At one altar, you must die to self;
at the other, you perform to be seen.
One leads to transformation,
the other to hypocrisy.
The modern world has chosen the stage over the cross.

People no longer want prophets who speak truth; they want performers who sound pleasing.

Churches are filled with applause, but empty of repentance.
Men fear being corrected more than being condemned.
This is the war between *Truth and Performance.*
Truth crucifies the flesh; performance glorifies it.
Truth humbles; performance entertains.
Truth heals; performance hides.
But no stage can replace the altar.
No applause can replace anointing.
No image can replace intimacy with God.

> "God is Spirit, and those who worship Him must worship in spirit and in truth." —*John 4:24*

Jesus — The Manifestation of Truth

That is why Jesus came — not as an actor, but as **Truth Himself.**

He did not come to impress the crowd but to expose the lie.

He came to tear the mask of religion, to confront pretense, to awaken hearts that had been numbed by hypocrisy.

He spoke truth that divided nations and offended institutions.

He called sinners to repentance and saints to reality.

He shone light on every shadow and left no room for disguise.

> "For this cause I was born, and for this cause I came into the world:
> to bear witness to the truth." —*John 18:37*

He came to separate the *actors* from the *worshipers,*
the *religious* from the *repentant,*
the *crowd* from the *cross.*
And He declared,

> "You shall know the truth, and the truth shall make you free." — *John 8:32*

Freedom Through Confession, Not Perfection

Freedom is not found in pretending — it is found in **confession.**

You can polish your image for a lifetime and still die in bondage.

You can impress thousands and still be lost.

But one moment of honest repentance can do what years of pretense never will — it can set you free.

Hypocrisy enslaves; truth delivers.

Pretense builds kingdoms of men; truth builds the Kingdom of God.

Pretending will make people like you; truth will make Heaven know you.

> "If we confess our sins, He is faithful and just to forgive us our sins and to cleanse us from all unrighteousness." — *1 John 1:9*

Freedom begins when you stop hiding and start healing.

The world doesn't need more actors; it needs more truth-tellers.

God is not waiting for your perfection — He is waiting for your honesty.

A Call to Return to Truth

The first lie was spoken in the Garden, but the last truth was spoken on the Cross.

When Jesus said, *"It is finished,"* He tore not only the veil of the temple but the mask of man. He opened a way for humanity to return to divine transparency — to walk again in truth, to live again without disguise.

The Holy Spirit is calling this generation to return to honesty before God.

To stop pretending.

To stop acting.

To stop hiding behind the leaves of religion and return to the nakedness of truth.

Because until we remove the mask, we cannot be healed.

Until we confess the lie, we cannot receive the truth.

And until we face who we are, we cannot become who God made us to be.

Key Scriptures:

- *John 8:44* — Satan, the father of lies
- *Genesis 3:7–10* — The first mask in the garden
- *Genesis 1:26* — Image and likeness
- *Matthew 15:8* — Lips without heart
- *John 8:32* — Truth makes free

Chapter 2: The Mask in Religion

The Holiness That Became a Costume

Religion was never meant to be a performance — it was meant to be a **pathway**.

It was the bridge that connected man back to God, the sacred place where truth and worship met in harmony.

But in the hands of hypocrites, that bridge has become a **mask.**

What once carried men into the presence of God now hides them from His face.

Holiness — once a flame that burned within the heart — has become a garment that can be worn and removed at will.

What was meant to reveal the glory of God has become a costume for self-glory.

We have turned the holy altar into a public stage, the sacred song into a show, and the cross into a logo.

> "Having a form of godliness but denying its power." — *2 Timothy 3:5*

The Fall of True Religion

True religion is meant to humble men; false religion makes them proud.

True holiness draws you closer to God; false holiness draws attention to yourself.

When the heart departs from truth, holiness becomes *theater.*

We begin to act righteous instead of being righteous,
to recite Scripture instead of living Scripture,
to appear anointed instead of being surrendered.

The holiness that once burned as *devotion* now shines as *decoration.*

We wear crosses but ignore the crucifixion within.

We lift our hands in worship but never lift our hearts in obedience.

We preach about light but keep our secrets in darkness.

> "This people draws near to Me with their mouth and honors Me with their lips,

but their heart is far from Me." — *Isaiah 29:13*

Religion has become the greatest disguise of sin — a refuge for actors, a hiding place for those who want the benefits of God without the cost of holiness.

The Church as a Stage

The Church, which was meant to be the **pillar and ground of truth** (*1 Timothy 3:15*),

has, in many places, become a **theater of performance.**
The sacred altar has turned into a platform for applause.
Ministers are acting. Congregations are clapping.
The Spirit of God is **grieving.**
We measure success not by souls transformed but by seats filled.
We count followers instead of intercessors.
We glorify gifted speakers but ignore broken spirits.
We pursue excellence on stage while neglecting integrity in secret.
Where there was once weeping, there is now entertainment.
Where there was once repentance, there is now rehearsed emotion.
Where there was once fear of God, there is now fear of losing popularity.
The sanctuary has become a studio.
The shepherds have become stars.
The sheep have become spectators.

And the presence of God, though invited by name, is often absent in power.

The Mask of Modern Holiness

Today, many wear the **name of God** but deny His **nature.**

They preach the Word, but do not live it.
They sing of holiness but walk in compromise.
They teach about humility but crave attention.
They speak of revival but resist repentance.
They stand on altars of light but operate in darkness.
They smile in public but scheme in private.

They use the language of Heaven to promote the ambitions of hell.
This is not holiness — it is *hypocrisy dressed in robes of reverence.*
It is the serpent speaking in the voice of the saint.
And yet, it is not new. The prophets saw it long ago.

> "Her priests do violence to My law and profane My holy things; they do not distinguish between the holy and the common." — *Ezekiel 22:26*

When holiness becomes a costume, **the sacred becomes casual,** and **the casual becomes sacred.**

We lose reverence, we lose discernment, and we lose the presence that once made us tremble.

When God's Spirit Withdraws

The most terrifying moment in any church is not when the crowd leaves — it is when **the Spirit leaves** and no one notices.

When preaching continues without conviction.
When worship continues without repentance.
When programs multiply but the presence is gone.

We have learned how to keep the lights on even when the fire has gone out.

We know how to entertain without anointing,
how to fill time without filling hearts,
how to sing "Come, Holy Spirit" while ignoring His correction.
That is the danger of modern religion —
it looks alive but is dead inside.

> "You have a reputation of being alive, but you are dead." — *Revelation 3:1*

God Is Calling His Church Back to True Holiness

But the mercy of God still speaks.

The Spirit still calls from behind the curtain of pretense, saying:

"Return to Me, and I will return to you." — *Malachi 3:7*

Holiness is not a performance — it is a **posture.**

It is not about being seen; it is about being surrendered.

It is not the perfection of appearance; it is the purity of motive.

True holiness does not begin on the stage — it begins on the altar of the heart.

Holiness is not what you wear — it's what you *bear*:

the character of Christ, the fruit of the Spirit, the fear of God.

It is the fire that burns quietly in secret prayer,

the humility that refuses to be seen,

the obedience that continues even when no one applauds.

A Call to Ministers and the Church

God is raising a new breed of servants — men and women who will wear *truth* instead of *titles.*

They will not entertain; they will intercede.

They will not perform; they will purify.

They will not chase fame; they will chase fire.

This generation does not need another show — it needs a *revival of sincerity.*

The Church must once again tremble before the Word of God.

The pulpit must become a place of tears, not trends.

The altar must become a place of sacrifice, not selfies.

When holiness becomes truth again, power will return.

When repentance becomes real again, miracles will return.

When we remove the costume, the **presence will come.**

A Prayer for True Holiness

Lord, strip away every garment of pretense.

Tear off the costume we have worn in Your name.

Forgive us for acting holy while hiding sin, for performing worship without purity.

Clothe us again, not with robes of religion, but with garments of righteousness.

Let Your Spirit burn away pride, hypocrisy, and self-promotion.

Teach us to honor what is holy, to walk in truth, to tremble at Your Word.

Make Your Church pure again, that Your glory may dwell among us.

> "Worship the Lord in the beauty of holiness;
> tremble before Him, all the earth." — *Psalm 96:9*

Final Reflection

Holiness is not something you can put on; it's something that must grow within.

It is not a costume to impress others — it is a covenant with God.

If we return to that truth, the Church will once again shine with genuine light —

not the spotlight of man, but the fire of Heaven.

Let every robe of religion fall,

let every stage of performance crumble,

and let the Bride of Christ rise again in **purity, humility, and power.**

Religious Leaders Who Preach What They Do Not Live

Jesus warned His disciples,

> *"Beware of the leaven of the Pharisees, which is hypocrisy." — Luke 12:1*

He did not say, "Beware of pagans."
He did not say, "Beware of unbelievers."
He said, beware of the religious.
The Pharisees were not atheists — they were Bible scholars.
They were not idol worshipers — they were temple dwellers.
They knew the Scriptures, but they did not know the ***Spirit.***
They spoke of holiness, yet despised the Holy One standing before them.
They stood in Moses' seat, preaching righteousness,
but their hearts were filled with pride, jealousy, and greed.
They loved titles more than truth.
They loved applause more than repentance.
They loved recognition more than revelation.
Their religion was not a relationship with God; it was a performance before men.

> *"They love to pray standing in the synagogues and on the corners of the streets,*
>
> *that they may be seen by men." — Matthew 6:5*

The Modern Pharisees

Their descendants are still among us —
men and women who preach the Word but do not practice it.
They tell others to pray, but they themselves do not pray.
They speak of fasting, but secretly feast on sin.
They condemn immorality publicly, but entertain it privately.

They preach humility, yet live in arrogance.

They preach generosity, yet manipulate the flock for gain.

They have mastered the art of ***looking anointed*** *while living disconnected from the* ***Anointer.***

They love the platform but despise the prayer closet.

They love microphones but avoid meditation.

They love followers but not faithfulness.

They love honor from men but not holiness before God.

> *"This people honors Me with their lips, but their heart is far from Me." — Matthew 15:8*

They carry Bibles in their hands but not in their hearts.

They preach about the cross but refuse to carry theirs.

They have built churches but not altars, crowds but not disciples, brands but not brokenness.

The Tragedy of a Personality-Driven Gospel

The tragedy of our generation is not the absence of churches, but the absence of truth within them.

We live in an era where people follow ***personalities, not principles.***

They worship preachers more than Christ.

They chase miracles more than holiness.

They honor the vessels more than the God who fills them.

Many now seek emotional experiences instead of spiritual transformation.

They measure anointing by applause, not by obedience.

They measure growth by followers, not by faithfulness.

They measure success by buildings, not by brokenness.

But God is not impressed by numbers — He is moved by truth.

He is not seeking famous voices; He is seeking faithful hearts.

The danger of this generation is that many churches have ***the language of revival*** *but* ***the lifestyle of rebellion.***

We have replaced repentance with reputation,
and righteousness with relevance.

> *"For such are false apostles, deceitful workers, transforming themselves into apostles of Christ.*
>
> *And no wonder! For Satan himself transforms himself into an angel of light." — 2 Corinthians 11:13–14*

The Mask Will Fall

But the day will come when every mask will fall.

God cannot be deceived. He sees beyond the pulpit, beyond the robes, beyond the sermons, beyond the smiles.

The secrets of men will be shouted from the rooftops.

> *"For nothing is hidden that will not be disclosed,*
>
> *and nothing concealed that will not be made known or brought to light." — Luke 8:17*

The Lord will separate the true shepherds from the actors,
the servants from the showmen,
the preachers of truth from the performers of religion.
Many will say,

> *"Lord, Lord, did we not prophesy in Your name, cast out demons in Your name, and do many miracles in Your name?"*
>
> *And He will say,*
>
> *"I never knew you. Depart from Me, you who practice lawlessness." — Matthew 7:22–23*

God is not fooled by eloquence; He searches for ***obedience.***

He is not impressed by charisma; He looks for ***character.***

He does not count how many you lead to the altar if you yourself refuse to bow there.

A Warning and a Call

Every preacher, every teacher, every leader must remember:

To preach truth without living it is to betray it.

To carry the Bible without obeying it is to mock it.

To speak in the name of Christ while living contrary to Him is to crucify Him again before men.

The call to ministry is not a call to performance — it is a call to death to self.

True ministry flows from intimacy, not image.

The true servant of God does not use the pulpit to be seen, but to make Christ seen.

He does not preach for recognition, but for redemption.

> *"It is required in stewards that a man be found faithful." — 1 Corinthians 4:2*

The day of pretending is ending.

God is raising voices that will not flatter kings,

that will not compromise truth for comfort,

that will not exchange holiness for popularity.

The coming revival will not be a show — it will be a shaking.

And only those who are rooted in truth will stand when the spotlight fades and only the presence remains.

Final Reflection

The time has come for every leader to ask:

Do I preach what I live, or do I live what I preach?

Do I serve for the crown, or for the cross?

Do I desire God's approval, or the crowd's applause?

For the day of reckoning is near — and only those who walk in truth will endure.

> *"Not everyone who says to Me, 'Lord, Lord,' shall enter the kingdom of heaven,*
>
> *but he who does the will of My Father in heaven." — Matthew 7:21*

Let us therefore preach with clean lips, live with pure hearts,

and walk with unveiled faces before God —

that our ministry may not be a performance, but a living testimony of the One we proclaim.

Fake and False Christians — Wearing the Name Without the Nature

This is one of the greatest tragedies of our time:

Many people wear the name "Christian," but few carry the ***nature of Christ.***

They call themselves believers, but their fruits deny their confession.

They have the vocabulary of faith but not the victory of faith.

They know the songs of the church, but not the heart of the Savior.

Being a Christian is not about attending church — it is about becoming the church.

It is not about wearing a cross — it is about carrying one.

It is not about saying, "I'm saved," — it is about living as one who has been sanctified.

It is not about speaking in tongues — it is about walking in truth.

The Religion of the Lips, Not the Heart

Jesus warned long ago:

> *"This people honor Me with their lips, but their heart is far from Me."*
> *— Isaiah 29:13*

False Christianity is the religion of the lips — loud in confession, empty in character.

Many have learned how to look holy without being holy,
how to speak faith while living in fear,
how to sing worship songs while serving worldly idols.
They know how to lift their hands, but not how to lift their hearts.
They love to speak about love but refuse to forgive.
They attend every service but avoid every sacrifice.
They want Christ's crown but not His cross.
They want His blessings but reject His boundaries.
They want His grace but despise His government.

> *"Why do you call Me, 'Lord, Lord,' and do not do what I say?" — Luke 6:46*

This is the root of false Christianity —
wanting the benefits of the Kingdom while still bowing to the desires of the flesh.

The Modern Judas Spirit

They are like Judas — walking with Jesus but never transformed by Him.
Judas followed Christ, but his heart followed silver.
He kissed Jesus but betrayed Him in the same moment.
He was close to the Truth, yet still lived a lie.
The Judas spirit is alive today:
Men and women who use the name of Jesus to hide their sin instead of crucify it.
They wear the uniform of faith but fight for the enemy of their souls.
They preach the cross but refuse to carry it.
They sing of freedom while living in chains.
They are Christian in speech but carnal in spirit —
holy in public but hidden in darkness.
They can quote verses online but cannot conquer temptation in private.
They are fluent in "church language" but illiterate in obedience.

When Christianity Becomes Cosmetic

In this generation, many have turned Christianity into a cosmetic faith —
a religion of appearances, a performance of piety.
They have learned how to post Scriptures without practicing them,
how to say "Praise the Lord" without submitting to the Lord,
how to wear purity like perfume but live in secret pollution.
But God is not impressed by the outer display;
He searches the depth of the heart.

> *"Man looks at the outward appearance, but the Lord looks at the heart." — 1 Samuel 16:7*

True faith is not cosmetic — it is ***costly.***
It demands death to self, surrender to truth, and daily obedience.
It is not what you say before people, but what you live before God.
It is not about looking saved — it is about being sanctified.

The Danger of Spiritual Pretenders

You can sit in church and still belong to hell.
You can preach like Peter and still betray like Judas.
You can prophesy like Balaam and still die like a fool.
You can sing like an angel and live like a demon.
The danger of false Christianity is that it feels safe —
it lets you keep your sin while feeling spiritual.
It deceives you into thinking that knowledge equals righteousness,
that ministry equals intimacy,
that activity equals anointing.
But the Lord does not know you by your position in church,
nor by your participation in programs.
He knows you by your ***obedience.***

"By their fruits you shall know them." — Matthew 7:16

Not by their followers.
Not by their preaching.
Not by their style of worship.
But by the fruit of their life.

True Christianity — The Life That Reflects the Cross

True Christianity is not a label; it is a ***lifestyle.***
It is not about how loud you shout, but how deeply you obey.
It is not measured by emotion, but by endurance.
It is not about the noise you make, but the nature you carry.
To be a Christian is to live crucified with Christ —
to die daily to sin and rise daily in righteousness.
It means you no longer live for applause but for approval.

It means your heart becomes His home,
your mind becomes His temple,
your hands become His instruments.

> *"If anyone desires to come after Me, let him deny himself, take up his cross daily, and follow Me." — Luke 9:23*

You are not known by your church membership but by your spiritual character.

Not by your title but by your testimony.

Not by your clothes or your words — but by your fruit.

A Call to True Discipleship

The world does not need more Christians in name — it needs more Christians in nature.

It does not need more preachers who speak truth — it needs more believers who live it.

It does not need more churches full of noise — it needs altars full of repentance.

The mark of a true Christian is not perfection, but transformation.

It is not about never falling, but about always rising again in humility and faith.

True Christians don't just go to church — they become the church.

They don't just wear the cross — they walk the way of the Cross.

> *"If you love Me, keep My commandments." — John 14:15*

Final Reflection

The name Christian is sacred — it means "little Christ."

To wear it without the nature of Christ is to take God's name in vain.

It is better to be an honest sinner seeking God than a fake saint hiding from Him.

For God can forgive the broken, but He resists the proud.

Let every soul examine itself:

Do I just call on Jesus, or do I follow Him?

Do I sing about the cross, or do I carry it?
Do I wear His name, or do I live His nature?
The world is watching, Heaven is recording, and eternity is approaching.
Let us strip off the mask and walk as true disciples —
so that when He returns, He will not say, "I never knew you,"
but "Well done, My good and faithful servant."

The Danger of Serving God with Lips but Not with Heart (Isaiah 29:13)

> "These people draw near to Me with their mouths
> and honor Me with their lips,
> but their hearts are far from Me,
> and their worship is made up only of rules taught by men." —
> *Isaiah 29:13*

These were not the words of a God addressing pagans.

He was not speaking to idol worshipers, nor to nations that did not know His name.

He was speaking to *His own people* —

those who came to the temple, offered sacrifices, and quoted the Scriptures.

They had religion, but not relationship.

They had words, but not worship.

Their lips were loud, but their hearts were silent.

This is the essence of **religious hypocrisy** — to say what you do not live,
to honor God publicly while ignoring Him privately,
to appear holy while the heart is unhealed.

Lip Service Without Life Surrender

You can lift your hands in worship and still hold hatred in your heart.

You can sing about love while secretly despising your brother.

You can cry in prayer while living in rebellion.

You can speak the name of Jesus while refusing His lordship.

> "Why do you call Me, 'Lord, Lord,' and do not do what I say?" —
> *Luke 6:46*

God is not impressed by emotional words; He is moved by obedient hearts.

He does not count how loud your praise is, but how deep your repentance goes.

He does not look at your posture in church, but at your position before His will.

Serving God with your lips is easy —
you only need a voice.
But serving Him with your heart costs everything —
you must surrender your pride, your will, your secret desires.

Professional Worshipers, Empty Hearts

Many have become **professional worshipers** —
experts in sound but strangers to sincerity.
They can move crowds but cannot move Heaven.
They weep on stage but deceive in secret.
They cry "Amen!" in public but curse in private.
They sing of love but live in bitterness.
They speak of holiness but walk in compromise.
The Church today is full of **emotion without devotion,**
noise without depth,
worship without obedience.

> "Not everyone who says to Me, 'Lord, Lord,' shall enter the kingdom of heaven,
>
> but he who does the will of My Father in heaven." — *Matthew 7:21*

God listens beyond the melody; He listens for truth.

He measures worship not by the song of the lips but by the state of the heart.

When Worship Becomes a Performance

When the fear of God disappears, worship becomes performance.
When love fades, service becomes routine.
When the heart is absent, ministry becomes mechanical.

This is what happened to Israel —

they followed *rituals* without relationship.

Their worship was made of *rules taught by men,* not revelations born from intimacy.

They knew how to offer sacrifices, but not how to offer themselves.

They honored the temple but ignored the Presence.

Today, the same spirit remains:

Churches full of noise but void of power.

Altars full of talent but empty of tears.

Leaders who can lead worship but cannot live worship.

We have replaced *purity* with performance, *intimacy* with image, *surrender* with showmanship.

We know how to act Christian, but not how to *be* Christlike.

Truth in the Inner Parts

God told David,

> "You desire truth in the inward parts." — *Psalm 51:6*

This means that God is not looking for actors on His altar.

He does not anoint pretenders — He anoints the pure.

He does not bless those who *say* the right things, but those who *live* them.

He is not seeking perfect people; He is seeking *honest hearts.*

Worship begins where pretending ends.

It begins when we stop performing and start repenting.

It begins when we remove the mask of religion and let His Spirit convict us again.

True worshipers are not known by how they sing, but by how they live.

They may sing softly, but they live loudly for Christ.

They may not be famous, but Heaven knows their name.

Heart Worship — The Only Kind Heaven Receives

Real worship is not about volume — it is about **value.**

It is not about appearance — it is about *alignment.*

It is not about how much you give — it is about how much of yourself you surrender.

God is Spirit, and those who worship Him must worship in **spirit and in truth** (John 4:24).

This means your heart must be engaged, your motives must be pure, your life must reflect the One you adore.

You can fool the congregation, but not the Creator.

You can impress people, but not the Presence.

You can act spiritual, but Heaven knows the difference between performance and purity.

> "The Lord does not look at the things people look at.
>
> People look at the outward appearance, but the Lord looks at the heart." — *1 Samuel 16:7*

A Warning to the Modern Church

God is weary of noise without nearness.

He is tired of lips that speak love but hearts that plan sin.

He is calling His people back to sincerity — back to the altar, back to truth.

Every song that is sung without obedience is just sound.

Every prayer that is prayed without repentance is just words.

Every sermon preached without humility is just performance.

The fire of true worship burns only where there is truth in the heart.

A Call to Return to True Worship

The Spirit of the Lord is saying again:

"Return to Me with all your heart." — *Joel 2:12*

Take off the mask of religion.

Tear down the walls of pride.

Let your tears become your worship and your obedience become your song.

For God is not after perfection — He is after **presence.**
He does not need your voice — He wants your *vulnerability.*
He does not want your performance — He wants your *purity.*
When the heart returns, the fire returns.
When truth returns, power returns.
When obedience returns, revival begins.

Final Reflection

Serving God with your lips will gain you applause from men,
but serving Him with your heart will gain you approval from Heaven.

Religious people act for attention; true worshipers act from affection.

Religious people honor God publicly; true worshipers obey Him privately.

Religious people know about God; true worshipers know *God Himself.*

The Lord is searching for such worshipers today —

those who will not just sing about the cross, but live crucified with Christ;

those who will not just praise with their lips, but serve with their lives;

those whose hearts beat in rhythm with His.

May He find such a worshiper in you.

False Prophets and Fake Miracles

One of the greatest disguises of hypocrisy in our generation is **the robe of false prophecy.**

Not every voice that says, *"Thus says the Lord,"* is speaking for God.
Not every miracle that dazzles the eyes carries the breath of Heaven.
Not every altar that glitters is holy.
Jesus warned clearly,

> "Beware of false prophets who come to you in sheep's clothing,
> but inwardly they are ravenous wolves." — *Matthew 7:15*

They dress like shepherds, but they devour the sheep.
They use the language of Zion but serve the agenda of hell.
They wear the garments of holiness but carry the heart of greed.
They come with smiles, not fangs; with blessings, not warnings.
They speak of destiny, not repentance — because repentance empties their pockets,
but flattery fills their seats.

The Business of Deception

These are not servants — they are salesmen.
They use the name of God to build their own kingdoms.
They perform signs not to glorify Christ, but to glorify themselves.
They sell *holy water, anointing oil,* and *prosperity promises*
while the souls of people remain in chains.
They claim to heal the sick but cannot heal their own pride.
They promise breakthroughs but live in bondage to greed.
They preach about sowing seeds of money, yet never sow seeds of truth.

> "They are shepherds who cannot understand;
> they all look to their own way, every one for his gain." — *Isaiah 56:11*

They cry, *"God told me,"* but it is their ambition that speaks.

They prophesy blessings for those who pay,
and pronounce curses on those who question them.
They build *temples of deception* and call them "houses of miracles."

Miracles That Impress but Do Not Transform

But the devil also performs miracles.
He has **power to impress,** but not **power to save.**
He can create illusions, but not deliverance.
He can move emotions, but not cleanse hearts.
When Moses stood before Pharaoh,
the magicians of Egypt imitated his sign — they also turned their rods into serpents.
But when truth and imitation met, **Moses' rod swallowed theirs.**

"The false will always bow before the true."

God's miracles bring repentance.
Satan's miracles bring pride.
God's power draws people to holiness.
Satan's power draws them to the performer.
The spirit behind the false prophet is the same one that deceived Eve —
it promises power, glory, and gain, but it delivers bondage and death.

The Church of Wolves in Robes

These false prophets are not outside the church — they are inside.
They stand behind pulpits, not altars.
They wear suits and collars, not sheep's wool.
They are celebrated, not discerned.
They attract crowds, not converts.
They speak in tongues but lie in spirit.
They shout "Fire!" but carry no flame of holiness.
They prophesy marriages, visas, money, and fame —
but never preach repentance, humility, or holiness.
Their gospel is not "Deny yourself," but "Indulge yourself."

Their altar calls are not for salvation, but for *transactions.*
They worship the God of gain, not the God of grace.
And the most frightening truth is this:
they believe they are right.
They have deceived themselves, thinking success is proof of approval.
But success without sanctification is satanic imitation.

> "For such are false apostles, deceitful workers, transforming themselves into apostles of Christ.
>
> And no wonder! For Satan himself transforms himself into an angel of light." — *2 Corinthians 11:13–14*

The Spirit of Divination Disguised as Revelation

Many of these false prophets operate not in the Spirit of God but in the **spirit of divination.**

They prophesy by familiar spirits, not by the Holy Spirit.

They see visions that do not come from Heaven but from the realm of darkness.

Their dreams flatter, not correct. Their revelations exalt man, not God.
Like Balaam, they know the voice of God but choose the price of gold.
They have learned to mix light and darkness,
to quote the Word but deny its power,
to preach the cross but never crucify their own flesh.

> "They have seen false visions and lying divinations. They say, 'The Lord says,' when the Lord has not sent them." — *Ezekiel 13:6*

They prophesy peace when God is calling for repentance.
They promise promotion when God is warning of judgment.
They give people comfort when God is crying for consecration.

The Judgment of the False

But the day is coming when every false altar will fall.

Every lying tongue will be silenced.

Every fake miracle will be exposed in the light of truth.
Jesus declared:

> "Many will say to Me in that day, 'Lord, Lord, have we not prophesied in Your name,
>
> cast out demons in Your name, and done many wonders in Your name?'
>
> And then I will declare to them, 'I never knew you; depart from Me, you who work iniquity.'" — *Matthew 7:22–23*

Notice that He did not deny their *miracles* —
He denied their *relationship.*
They performed wonders but never walked in obedience.
They carried His name but not His nature.
They did ministry but never did *His will.*
In the end, their greatest achievement will become their greatest shame.
The same lips that prophesied will tremble before the One they pretended to serve.

The Rise of Discernment in the Last Days

But God is raising a generation with **eyes to discern** and **ears to hear.**
They will not be seduced by charisma but guided by character.
They will not chase prophecy but pursue purity.
They will not fall for miracles but hunger for truth.
The Spirit of God is restoring discernment to His people.
The Word will once again become the measure,
and holiness will once again become the proof of authenticity.

> "Beloved, do not believe every spirit, but test the spirits to see whether they are from God." — *1 John 4:1*

The remnant of the Lord will rise — prophets who will weep more than they shout,
who will call nations to repentance, not riches,

who will speak the truth even when it costs them everything.

Final Reflection

The greatest miracle is not the healing of the sick, but the transformation of the sinner.

The greatest prophecy is not predicting the future, but revealing the heart.

The greatest anointing is not the one that fills stadiums, but the one that fills hearts with conviction.

Beware of voices that entertain but do not enlighten.

Beware of prophets who bless sin instead of breaking it.

Beware of miracles that glorify men more than the Messiah.

Because in the end, every false fire will fade,

but the flame of truth will burn forever.

How the Devil Hides in Religion to Destroy Faith from Within

The devil no longer wages war at the gates of the Church —

he has found a seat *inside* it.

He no longer comes as a roaring lion; he comes as a *robed shepherd.*

He no longer persecutes with swords; he seduces with sermons.

He wears priestly garments.

He sings in choirs.

He quotes Scripture fluently.

He prays loudly in public.

He performs miracles on stage.

But his mission has not changed:

"To steal, to kill, and to destroy." —*John 10:10*

He has not abandoned his plan; he has only changed his disguise.

Satan's New Strategy — Infiltration, Not Opposition

Once upon a time, the enemy attacked the Church openly through persecution.

He burned believers, chained apostles, and shut down gatherings.

But persecution only made the Church stronger —

because pressure purifies.

So he changed his strategy.

If he cannot **beat** the Church, he will **join** it.

If he cannot silence the Word, he will *saturate* it with lies.

If he cannot stop worship, he will *pollute* it with pride.

And now, he has infiltrated choirs, pulpits, and pews.

He whispers into the ears of ministers:

"Don't preach repentance — it will offend people."

"Don't talk about sin — focus on success."

"Preach blessings, preach wealth, keep them comfortable."

And the people clap.
The crowds grow.
The offerings increase.
But the Spirit departs.
What remains is religion without revelation —
sound without substance, gatherings without glory.

The Devil's Favorite Church

The devil is not afraid of *religion* — he helped invent it.

He loves rituals that replace relationship.

He delights in prayers that sound holy but hide hypocrisy.

He celebrates fasting that seeks fame instead of forgiveness.

He attends churches that are filled with activity but empty of the Holy Ghost.

He hides in religion because **religion without the Spirit is a coffin with candles.**

It looks sacred, but it carries death inside.

It speaks of God, but lives without Him.

It honors the Bible but disobeys its Author.

This is why Paul warned:

> "Having a form of godliness, but denying its power." — *2 Timothy 3:5*

The devil does not fear **the form** of godliness — he created it.
He fears **the fire** of holiness — because it exposes him.
He does not tremble at people who quote the Word —
he trembles at those who *live* the Word.
He is not afraid of eloquent preachers —
he fears broken intercessors.
He is not threatened by large churches —
he is terrified of pure hearts.

The Devil's Religion — Form Without Fire

Satan's greatest masterpiece is not witchcraft — it is *empty Christianity.*

He is not as interested in destroying the Church as he is in **corrupting** it.

He would rather see ten thousand lukewarm believers than one burning saint.

He would rather fill churches with singers than with servants.

He would rather have a million worship songs than one true act of obedience.

He replaces **revival** with **routine,**
Spirit with **structure,**
holiness with **hype,**
repentance with **reputation,**
truth with **trend.**

He doesn't need to remove the Bible —
he just needs to make it a decoration instead of a revelation.

He doesn't need to silence prayer —
he just needs to make it formal, cold, and empty.

He doesn't need to stop church attendance —
he just needs to remove conviction.

How the Devil Uses Religion to Kill Faith

1. **He Replaces Conviction with Comfort.**
   People no longer tremble at the Word; they negotiate with it.
   Sermons are designed to entertain, not to expose sin.
   The message of the cross has been traded for the message of convenience.
2. **He Substitutes Truth with Trends.**
   The Gospel that once called men to holiness now calls them to happiness.
   Many now seek what is *popular,* not what is *pure.*
3. **He Turns Shepherds into Celebrities.**
   Ministers once carried towels — now they carry titles.
   They once washed feet — now they demand followers.

The pulpit has become a platform, and the altar a spotlight.

4. **He Divides the Body.**
   While Christ prayed for unity, the devil preaches competition.
   He teaches pastors to compare rather than to care,
   to build empires instead of building disciples.

The Power That Exposes the Enemy

The only thing the devil cannot counterfeit is **the Presence of God.**
He can imitate miracles, mimic tongues, and fake emotions —
but he cannot produce holiness, truth, or genuine transformation.
Where the fire of the Holy Spirit burns, his disguise melts.
Where truth is preached without compromise, his deception collapses.
Where repentance is embraced, his power breaks.
That is why he fears holiness more than anything else.

Because holiness is the atmosphere of Heaven — and hell cannot breathe in it.

> "For the weapons of our warfare are not carnal but mighty through God
> for the pulling down of strongholds." — *2 Corinthians 10:4*

The devil hides in religion, but he cannot hide from *the fire of discernment.*

When the Spirit of Truth is present, falsehood cannot survive.

A Call to the Church

It is time for the Church to wake up —
to recognize that Satan does not come only as a persecutor,
but also as a *partner.*
He comes not just to attack, but to assist — falsely.
He joins hands in prayer circles but poisons hearts with pride.
He stands behind pulpits and whispers compromise into sermons.
He applauds worship that has melody but no meaning.
But God is raising a **remnant Church** —

a people who will not bow to comfort, who will not sell truth for popularity,

who will not trade holiness for hype.

A Church that prays with fire.

A Church that preaches repentance.

A Church that fears God more than losing followers.

A Church that walks in truth even if it walks alone.

Final Reflection

The devil hides in religion because it gives him access to souls who believe they are safe.

He does not mind people calling themselves Christians,

as long as they never become like Christ.

He knows that a religion without transformation is his greatest victory.

So he keeps men busy — singing, clapping, attending, giving —

but never **changing.**

Yet one spark of truth can burn his entire disguise.

One heart on fire can expose a thousand pretenders.

One Church filled with the Holy Spirit can shake every false altar.

Let us therefore guard our hearts, purify our worship, and walk in the fear of God.

For when the Spirit returns to His rightful place,

the devil will have **no place left to hide.**

True Worship Versus Religious Performance

True worship is not noise — it is **surrender.**

True worship is not movement — it is **obedience.**

True worship is not what you do on Sunday — it is **who you are every day.**

> "God is Spirit, and those who worship Him must worship in spirit and in truth." —*John 4:24*

Worship is not a song we sing to God; it is a *life we live before God.*

It is not the volume of your voice, but the posture of your heart.

It is not about impressing people — it is about **pleasing Heaven.**

When Worship Becomes Performance

Worship without truth is **performance.**

Worship without repentance is **entertainment.**

Worship without the Spirit is **manipulation.**

Today, many have confused worship with performance.

They call noise *anointing,* and emotion *encounter.*

But you can sing with the voice of angels and still live like a stranger to God.

You can dance with all your might and still be far from His presence.

You can give all your possessions and still hold back your heart.

> "These people draw near to Me with their mouths and honor Me with their lips,
>
> but their hearts are far from Me." — *Isaiah 29:13*

Performance seeks attention; worship seeks **alignment.**

Performance entertains crowds; worship moves Heaven.

Performance seeks applause; worship seeks intimacy.

Performance ends when the lights go off; worship continues when no one is watching.

The Worship God Rejects

God does not receive every song sung in His name.
He listens not to the melody but to the **motive.**
He hears not the lyrics but the **life** behind them.
You can sing "I surrender all" while holding onto sin.
You can cry "Holy, holy" while gossiping about your neighbor.
You can shout "Hallelujah" while living in rebellion.
God does not measure worship by *how it sounds to men,*
but by *how it smells to Heaven.*

> "Your sacrifices are a stench before Me." — *Amos 5:21–23*

Empty worship is noise in Heaven's ears —
it echoes with rhythm but lacks repentance.
It touches emotions but not eternity.

The Worship God Accepts

But there is a worship that God cannot resist —
a worship that rises not from lips, but from **a broken heart.**

> "The sacrifices of God are a broken spirit;
> a broken and contrite heart, O God, You will not despise." — *Psalm 51:17*

True worship is **humility in action.**
It is when tears replace performance,
when obedience replaces applause,
when repentance replaces rhythm.
God seeks worshipers, not performers.
He is not impressed by sound systems, smoke, or stage lights.
He is moved by purity, humility, and brokenness.
He looks for worshipers who can say,
"I am not here to be seen — I am here to be changed."
"I am not here to sing — I am here to surrender."
"I am not here to lead — I am here to bow."

Worship as a Lifestyle

True worship is not an event — it is a **lifestyle.**

A true worshiper is the same person in private and in public.
He prays when no one is watching.
He forgives when it hurts.
He gives when no one will notice.
He loves when not loved back.
He serves when not celebrated.
He walks in truth, not for applause, but for approval from God alone.

> "Whether you eat or drink, or whatever you do, do all to the glory of God." — *1 Corinthians 10:31*

Worship is not what happens *in* church;
it is what happens *after* church.
It is not confined to a Sunday schedule;
it is expressed in everyday choices —
how you speak, how you forgive, how you obey.
Real worship is revealed in how you treat people,
how you handle pain,
how you respond to correction,
how you live when no one is clapping.

The Spirit and Truth Connection

True worship is born where *Spirit meets truth.*

The Spirit ignites it; truth sustains it.
The Spirit reveals God; truth refines man.
Without Spirit, worship is dead.
Without truth, worship is deceit.
But when Spirit and truth unite, Heaven opens.
That is why Satan fights worship so fiercely —
not because of the music, but because of the **submission** behind it.
He knows that every time a heart bows before God in sincerity,
his throne of pride shakes.

> "Submit yourselves therefore to God. Resist the devil, and he will flee from you." —*James 4:7*

When we truly worship, we dethrone ourselves and enthrone Christ. We trade image for intimacy, performance for purity, stage for surrender.

Final Reflection

The world performs; the Church must worship.

The actor pretends; the worshiper surrenders.
The performer seeks applause; the worshiper seeks the Presence.
You can *act holy* before men,
but you cannot *pretend holy* before God.
True worship begins when the mask falls.
It begins when the music stops and the heart starts to speak.
It begins when you say,
"Lord, not my song, not my will, not my fame — but Yours be glorified."
So let every stage become an altar.
Let every voice become a vessel.
Let every heart burn again for the One who alone is worthy.
For worship is not about *singing before people* —
it is about *bowing before God.*

A Cry from Heaven

The Spirit of God is crying out in this generation:

"Take off the religious mask! Stop pretending to serve Me while serving yourself.

Stop using My name to build your fame.
Stop playing with holy things!"
God is raising a remnant — men and women of truth, not theater;
of repentance, not reputation;
of humility, not hypocrisy.
They will stand for holiness in a world of compromise.
They will live the gospel they preach.
They will walk in the light even when it costs them everything.

Key Scriptures:

- *Isaiah 29:13* — Lips without heart
- *Matthew 7:15–23* — False prophets
- *Luke 12:1* — The leaven of the Pharisees
- *2 Timothy 3:5* — Form without power
- *John 4:24* — Worship in spirit and truth

Chapter 3: The Hypocrisy in Government and Power

The Thrones Built on Lies

Every nation under heaven rises upon promises —
promises of justice, peace, equality, and prosperity.
But most of those promises are written in **ink that never dries** —
words that sound righteous but conceal the poison of deception.
From parliaments to palaces, from congresses to courts,
lies have become the foundation stones of power.
The same spirit that whispered in Eden,
"You shall be like God,"
now whispers in the ears of rulers and kings.
The serpent that once deceived a woman now governs nations through men.

The Language of Hypocrisy

We see leaders who speak of **freedom** while enslaving their people.
They promise reform but enrich themselves.
They talk about **democracy** while silencing dissent.
They parade as servants of the people but live like gods over them.
They raise flags of peace while preparing weapons of destruction.
This is the **hypocrisy of power** —
when leadership becomes theater and governance becomes performance.
When speeches replace substance, and charisma replaces character.
When the microphone replaces morality,
and image becomes more important than integrity.
They smile in public but scheme in private.
They kneel for photos but bow to demons in secret.
They swear by God in ceremonies but consult darkness in decision.
They build monuments to honor truth but destroy those who speak it.

The Corruption of Thrones

Power without righteousness is a curse to the land.
Every throne not founded on truth becomes a seat of deception.

The higher some rise in authority, the farther they fall from humility.
They forget that the One who raises can also remove.

> "He changes times and seasons; He removes kings and sets up kings." — *Daniel 2:21*

When a nation rejects the fear of God,
it invites the rule of liars.
When a ruler loses conscience,
his crown becomes his chain.
Many rulers today no longer lead — they **manipulate.**
They govern not by justice, but by control.
They pass laws not to protect the innocent, but to preserve their power.
They trade truth for votes and righteousness for influence.
They shake hands with men while making covenants with devils.

> "Their throats are open graves;
> their tongues practice deceit." — *Romans 3:13*

They promise the people heaven while preparing hell.
They build systems that serve the elite while crushing the weak.
They wear the garments of servants but live like kings.

The Fall of Moral Leadership

Leadership without morality is nothing but a performance.
When leaders stop fearing God, they start playing god.
They forget that the throne they occupy is temporary,
and the Judge who watches them is eternal.
They deceive the people with visions of progress,
but behind the curtain lies oppression.
They proclaim equality but practice exploitation.
They preach peace while fueling war.
Like Pharaoh, they harden their hearts while God sends warnings.
Like Herod, they love applause more than accountability.
Like Saul, they build altars not for God's glory, but for their own image.

And yet the Word of God remains unshaken:

> "When the righteous are in authority, the people rejoice;
> but when the wicked rule, the people mourn." — *Proverbs 29:2*

The world is mourning because hypocrisy now sits on high places.

Nations groan because justice has been bought and truth has been buried.

The poor cry for bread while the powerful feast on corruption.

The blood of the innocent cries louder than the speeches of politicians.

The Spirit Behind Political Power

Behind many political thrones stands a spiritual power —
an invisible influence that feeds on pride, control, and fear.
These are not just men in suits; they are vessels of spirits.
For the devil has always sought one thing — **dominion.**
He offered it to Jesus in the wilderness, saying:

> "All these kingdoms I will give You, if You bow down and worship me." — *Matthew 4:9*

And while the Son of God refused,
many men since then have accepted that offer.
They have bowed to darkness for thrones, crowns, and applause.
They have sold their souls for elections, traded their integrity for influence.
This is why nations rage and kingdoms fall —
because they are ruled not by servants, but by slaves of pride.
The devil knows he cannot destroy truth,
so he places lies on the throne to rule in its place.

The Cry for Righteous Leadership

God still looks for Davids in a world of Sauls.
He still searches for Daniels who will not bow to Babylon.
He still raises Josephs who can govern with integrity in foreign lands.

He still anoints Esthers who will speak truth before corrupt kings.
The thrones of the world may be built on lies,
but the **Kingdom of God** is built on righteousness.
It cannot be bought, bribed, or bent by man.
Its King reigns in truth, and every false crown will fall before Him.

> "The Lord has established His throne in the heavens,
> and His kingdom rules over all." — *Psalm 103:19*

Final Reflection

The world has crowned liars,
but Heaven is preparing to crown the faithful.
The earth has celebrated hypocrites,
but Heaven will honor the humble.
Every throne built on lies will crumble.
Every empire built on deceit will fall.
Every leader who mocks God will stand before His judgment seat.
Let the nations tremble, for the Judge of all the earth is coming.
Let rulers remember that no man can deceive the One who sees the heart.
And let the righteous take comfort —
for though hypocrisy reigns for a season, **truth reigns forever.**

Leaders Who Use Good Words but Practice Evil

Evil today does not always wear horns —
it wears **suits and smiles.**
It no longer hides in the shadows —
it sits in **parliaments, offices, and boardrooms.**
Its speeches are polished, its language refined, its image controlled.
It quotes Scripture in ceremonies but despises righteousness in decisions.
It talks about "values" while violating them behind closed doors.
It calls itself "servant leadership," but serves only **self-interest.**

The Theater of Power

These leaders promise jobs but create unemployment.
They promise peace but sow division.
They promise justice but sell it to the highest bidder.
They kiss the poor during campaigns but forget them after elections.
They build schools for photos but never for children.
They build roads to their homes but not to the villages they rule.
Their lips drip with honey, but their hands are stained with blood.
They hide behind **laws they never obey** and **systems they never reform.**
They legislate morality in public but live immorality in private.
They quote God on television but consult demons for strategy.
They fund churches for image while destroying truth for profit.

> "They speak peace with their neighbors,
> but mischief is in their hearts." — *Psalm 28:3*

This is the **language of hypocrisy** —
the ability to say everything right while doing everything wrong.
The ability to appear righteous while practicing rebellion.
The ability to wear compassion on the lips and corruption in the heart.

The Gospel of the Greedy

In such nations, corruption is not a mistake — **it is a culture.**

It is baptized in the name of politics and sanctified by propaganda.

The system feeds on lies and thrives on fear.

Those who speak truth are silenced;

those who flatter are promoted.

Righteous men are mocked as "extremists."

Honest leaders are called "naïve."

Those who refuse to bow to bribery are branded as enemies of progress.

This is how evil hides in plain sight —

not as darkness, but as **light that lies.**

> "Woe to those who call evil good and good evil,
> who put darkness for light and light for darkness." — *Isaiah 5:20*

Governments that once protected life now profit from its destruction.

Courts that once defended justice now defend the unjust.

Leaders who once took oaths before God now treat His name as decoration.

The Hypocrisy of the Platform

Politics has become a pulpit of pretense.

Every speech begins with hope and ends with betrayal.

Every promise sounds divine but delivers decay.

They wear microphones as crowns,

and cameras as halos.

They are not servants — they are actors.

They are not governing — they are performing.

They practice deception as policy and call it diplomacy.

They master the art of lying so eloquently that even the righteous begin to doubt truth.

They swear to protect the people but protect their power instead.

The nations applaud them for their speeches,

but Heaven weeps for their souls.

> "The Lord detests lying lips,
> but He delights in people who are trustworthy." — *Proverbs 12:22*

The Curse of Corrupt Leadership

Where hypocrisy rules, the land groans.
When leaders deceive, the people despair.
When truth is silenced, corruption multiplies.
When power becomes an idol, justice becomes a slave.
Corrupt leadership is not only a political problem —
it is a **spiritual epidemic.**
For leadership without truth invites demonic rule.

> "When the righteous are in authority, the people rejoice;
> but when the wicked rule, the people mourn." — *Proverbs 29:2*

The mourning of the poor is the music of heaven's courtroom.
Their tears rise as testimony against those who exploit them.
And though the wicked boast in their thrones,
God still sits as Judge above them all.

> "He who sits in the heavens laughs;
> the Lord holds them in derision." — *Psalm 2:4*

A Prophetic Warning to the Powerful

O leaders of the earth —
your titles will not defend you before the Throne of God.
Your power will perish; your secrets will be exposed.
The palaces you built on deceit will become your prison.
The hands that signed corruption will tremble in His judgment.
For the Lord says,

> "Your rulers are rebels, partners with thieves;
> they all love bribes and chase after gifts.

> They do not defend the fatherless,
> and the widow's case does not come before them." — *Isaiah 1:23*

The higher men rise in hypocrisy,
the deeper they will fall in judgment.
The louder they speak lies,
the stronger the truth will echo against them.

The Hope of the Righteous

Yet God always preserves a remnant —
men and women who refuse to be bought or bribed,
who lead not for profit but for purpose,
who fear God more than losing position.
He still raises Josephs in Pharaoh's palace,
Daniels in Babylon's courts,
and Esthers in wicked kingdoms.
Through them, righteousness still has a voice.
The thrones of deceit will one day bow before the King of Truth.
The crowns of corruption will melt in the fire of His coming.
And every hidden work of darkness will be judged by His light.

Final Reflection

Leaders who use good words but practice evil
build nations on sand and call it strength.
But every empire built on lies is already collapsing.
Truth may be crucified,
but it will always resurrect.
And when it does,
the fake will fall,
the proud will perish,
and the righteous will reign with the King of kings.
For evil can wear a suit,
but it cannot escape the gaze of God.

Corruption, Manipulation, and Political Theater

Politics has become the **new religion of the world**,

and corruption has become its **form of worship.**

Its temples are parliaments, its priests are politicians,

and its offerings are made not of bulls or goats, but of **conscience and truth.**

They have built altars of deception and burned the incense of manipulation.

Their ceremonies are televised. Their rituals are elections.

They raise their hands not in surrender to God, but in **oaths to power.**

They speak of *"unity,"* but only unite to **steal.**

They speak of *"peace,"* but their peace is built on **oppression.**

They speak of *"development,"* but their progress is measured by **personal gain.**

They speak of *"justice,"* but it is justice for sale to the highest bidder.

The Gospel of Deception

This is the **gospel of politics** —

a message that promises salvation through systems,

but delivers bondage through deceit.

They manipulate the media to control minds.

They use promises as traps and poverty as a weapon.

They invent crises to appear as saviors.

They create enemies to unite their followers.

They destroy the righteous to preserve their reign.

> "They make lies their refuge and under falsehood they hide themselves." — *Isaiah 28:15*

Every speech is a sermon,

every slogan a song of false hope,

every handshake a hidden transaction.

They have perfected the art of public holiness and private corruption — smiling before cameras while stabbing nations in silence.

The Theater of Power

It is all **theater** — well-written, well-staged, well-acted.

Every election is a play. Every press conference is a performance.

The actors change, but the script remains the same.

The world watches.

The people clap.

The votes are cast.

And the same actors return — only with new costumes, new slogans, new lies.

But Heaven is not entertained.

Heaven does not clap.

Heaven grieves.

For God sees beyond the speeches and the smiles.

He sees the hidden deals, the stolen wealth, the silenced truth, the suppressed poor.

He sees the hands that take bribes and the hearts that love lies.

> "Woe to those who make unjust laws,
> to those who issue oppressive decrees." — *Isaiah 10:1*

The Spirit Behind Corruption

Behind the curtain of politics lies a spirit —

the same one that tempted Eve, the same one that offered Jesus the kingdoms of the world.

It whispers to rulers: *"Bow to me, and I will give you power."*

And many have bowed.

They have sold their souls for votes, their conscience for crowns, their people for profit.

This spirit feeds on pride, sustained by deception,

and thrives wherever truth is silenced.

It disguises itself as wisdom but breathes destruction.

It promises influence but delivers emptiness.

> "For what will it profit a man if he gains the whole world, and loses his soul?" — *Mark 8:36*

The Oppression of the People

The fruit of political hypocrisy is **oppression.**

The poor are crushed under policies they never wrote.
Children starve while leaders feast.
Workers labor while rulers steal.
Justice is delayed, truth is distorted, and corruption is normalized.
When the righteous cry for help, they are ignored.
When the poor plead for fairness, they are taxed instead of helped.
When prophets speak, they are persecuted or mocked.
The powerful build monuments in their own honor
and call them "national progress,"
while the forgotten lie buried under poverty,
their cries rising like incense before the throne of Heaven.

> "The cry of the harvesters has reached the ears of the Lord Almighty." —*James 5:4*

The Judgment of Heaven

But the Judge of all the earth sees and remembers.

He weighs the hearts of rulers and measures the motives of kings.
He hears the cries of nations and records every act of injustice.
The palaces of corruption will tremble.
The thrones of deceit will collapse.
The crowns of liars will melt before His glory.

> "For the Lord of hosts will have a day of reckoning
> against everyone who is proud and lofty." — *Isaiah 2:12*

The world may forget, but Heaven keeps receipts.
And the God of truth will soon stand to judge the gods of lies.

A Prophetic Call to the Nations

Let every leader remember:

The throne you sit on is borrowed.
The power you hold is temporary.
The people you rule belong to God.
And the judgment you escape on earth awaits you in eternity.
Let every citizen awaken:
Do not worship your politicians.
Do not trade truth for tribalism.
Do not call loyalty what God calls idolatry.
Stand for righteousness even if you stand alone.

> "Righteousness exalts a nation,
> but sin is a reproach to any people." — *Proverbs 14:34*

Final Reflection

Politics may deceive the earth,
but it cannot deceive Heaven.
Corruption may sit on the throne,
but truth still reigns above it.
The theater of man will end,
but the Kingdom of God will never close its stage.
The actors of power will bow before the Author of eternity.
The Judge will rise, and the play will be over.

And every lie ever spoken in the name of leadership will echo as a witness against them.

Let the world know:

The King is coming, and His government will not be built on deceit — but on truth, justice, and righteousness forever.

> "Of the increase of His government and peace there shall be no end...
> to establish it with justice and with righteousness forever." — *Isaiah 9:7*

How the Spirit of Hypocrisy Rules Nations

The spirit of hypocrisy is no longer confined to individuals — it has become a **principality**, a **ruling power** that governs nations. It wears crowns, signs treaties, builds monuments, and writes laws. It hides behind culture, politics, religion, and diplomacy. It builds **systems that appear fair but are founded on deceit.** It raises **leaders who speak of God but despise His truth.** It sponsors **policies that promise peace but deliver oppression.**

This is not mere politics — this is **spiritual warfare at the level of nations.**

It is the unseen government of darkness masquerading as light.

It is the whisper behind the thrones of the world saying:

"You are wise enough, strong enough, and divine enough to rule without God."

The Ancient Pattern of Hypocrisy in Power

Every generation has witnessed this spirit in operation:

- **Pharaoh** enslaved Israel while claiming divine power, saying,

  "Who is the Lord, that I should obey His voice?" (Exodus 5:2).

  He ruled through fear and built monuments to his own name —

  yet God humbled him in one night by the power of truth.

- **Nebuchadnezzar** erected a golden statue and commanded nations to bow,

  glorifying his image instead of the Almighty.

  Pride turned his throne into madness until he confessed,

  "Those who walk in pride He is able to humble." (Daniel 4:37).

• **Herod** pretended to worship the Christ-child but secretly plotted His death.

Hypocrisy always disguises hatred as honor.

It smiles at truth while sharpening its sword behind the scenes.

From ancient empires to modern governments,
the pattern is the same — pride, power, pretense.
Men rise to the thrones of the earth claiming to represent light,
yet serve the kingdom of darkness through deception.

"The kings of the earth set themselves,
and the rulers take counsel together,
against the Lord and against His Anointed." — *Psalm 2:2*

The Machinery of National Hypocrisy

This ruling spirit of hypocrisy builds nations on false foundations:

- **In culture,** it redefines morality to fit human pleasure.
- **In education,** it removes God to enthrone human pride.
- **In law,** it protects sin and punishes righteousness.
- **In media,** it hides truth behind entertainment and propaganda.
- **In religion,** it replaces faith with performance.

It blinds leaders with greed and fills their hearts with pride.

It teaches them to **worship their own image** — their success, their title, their nation.

It makes men believe they are gods while they are dust.
They bow not before the cross, but before their own reflection.
They declare their independence from Heaven and call it progress.
They call rebellion "freedom," and moral decay "modernization."
They pass laws that bless sin and curse truth.

"They exchanged the truth of God for a lie,

and worshiped and served created things rather than the Creator."
— *Romans 1:25*

The Reign of False Glory

When hypocrisy rules, righteousness becomes unpopular.
Truth becomes offensive.
Lies become patriotic.
And silence becomes survival.
Leaders no longer serve the people — they perform for them.
Politics becomes a **competition for thrones**, not a **compassion for souls.**
Governments become theaters of pride instead of instruments of justice.
The microphone becomes the crown, and applause becomes the reward.
The people, like actors in the same play, repeat the same script —
trusting, voting, applauding, and forgetting —
while injustice hides behind beautiful speeches.

"Their mouths are full of lies;
their right hand is a right hand of falsehood." — *Psalm 144:8*

When Nations Lose the Fear of God

When a nation loses the fear of God,
it gains the favor of demons.
When truth is mocked, darkness reigns.
When righteousness is silenced, corruption multiplies.
The spirit of hypocrisy rules not by force, but by **seduction.**
It does not destroy instantly; it deceives gradually.
It builds its empire one compromise at a time —
until the entire nation becomes numb to evil.
People begin to celebrate sin, normalize corruption, and mock holiness.
Churches become silent for fear of losing popularity.
Prophets are replaced by influencers.
Justice becomes a product for sale.
And the land groans under the weight of its deceit.

"Justice is turned back,
and righteousness stands far away;
for truth has stumbled in the streets." — *Isaiah 59:14*

The Collapse of False Kingdoms

Yet every kingdom built on lies will one day collapse.
No throne that rejects truth will stand forever.
Empires rise with pride but fall with deception.
The Tower of Babel still falls in every generation.
The spirit of hypocrisy may sit in high places,
but the King of Kings sits higher still.
He laughs at their schemes, confuses their tongues,
and overturns their plans in due time.

"The Lord brings the counsel of the nations to nothing;
He frustrates the plans of the peoples." — *Psalm 33:10*

A Call to the Nations

The time has come for nations to remove their masks.
For governments to remember that power is a loan, not a possession.
For leaders to return to humility before God.
Let righteousness return to the courts.
Let truth return to the classrooms.
Let justice return to the palaces.
Let the fear of God return to the hearts of kings.
For only when truth rules will peace dwell.
Only when repentance comes will revival begin.
Only when men bow to Heaven will the earth be healed.

"Blessed is the nation whose God is the Lord." — *Psalm 33:12*

Final Reflection

The spirit of hypocrisy has ruled for generations,
but its time is short.

The King of Glory is rising to reclaim His throne.
And when He comes, no lie will stand,
no deceit will hide,
no false system will survive.
Every crown will fall before His cross.
Every kingdom will bow to His name.
And the nations that once mocked truth
will tremble before the Truth Himself —
Jesus Christ, the Righteous Judge.

The Biblical Example of King Saul — Appearance Without Obedience

King Saul stands as one of the clearest portraits of **political hypocrisy** in Scripture.

He looked like a king — tall, strong, handsome, and chosen by the people.

He began with humility but ended in pride.

He wore the crown but lost the character.

He sat on the throne but lost the presence of God.

At first, Saul was a man of promise.

He hid among the baggage when called to leadership — a sign of modesty.

But later, he hid his sin behind excuses — a sign of hypocrisy.

The same man who once waited for God later acted without Him.

The Test of True Leadership

When God commanded Saul to destroy Amalek, it was a **test of obedience**, not a test of strength.

God wanted to see if Saul would fear **Him** or **the people.**

But Saul failed.

He spared what God told him to destroy.

He preserved the things that looked good in his eyes but were cursed in God's.

He disobeyed God — and then **staged obedience** to impress Samuel.

> "I have performed the commandment of the Lord," Saul declared proudly.
>
> But the prophet replied,
>
> "What then is this bleating of sheep in my ears and the lowing of oxen which I hear?" — *1 Samuel 15:13–14*

Saul sinned — but worse, he **pretended he hadn't.**
He sinned — but instead of repentance, he chose **reputation.**
He disobeyed God, but wanted to look spiritual.
That is the essence of hypocrisy: **appearance without obedience.**

The Trap of Image

Saul's downfall was not ignorance — it was **image.**
He cared more about **how people saw him** than how God saw him.
He confessed,

> "I have sinned, for I feared the people and obeyed their voice." — *1 Samuel 15:24*

His throne was built on popularity, not purity.
He wanted the applause of men more than the approval of Heaven.
He feared losing the crowd more than losing the crown of righteousness.
This is the **root of political and spiritual hypocrisy** —
when leaders shape truth to protect their image,
when obedience becomes optional but appearance becomes everything.

The Danger of Partial Obedience

Saul obeyed God halfway, and half obedience is still full disobedience.
He killed what was easy to kill but spared what benefited him.
He sacrificed to God what cost him nothing —
forgetting that God rejects offerings born from rebellion.

> "To obey is better than sacrifice, and to heed than the fat of rams." — *1 Samuel 15:22*

God was not impressed by Saul's ceremonies.
He was looking for **submission**, not spectacle.
The smell of burnt offerings could not cover the stench of disobedience.

The Fall of the Pretender

Saul lost his throne not because of a **public scandal**,

but because of a **private rebellion.**

It wasn't the noise of his sin that removed him — it was the silence of his repentance.

He still wore the crown,

still led the army,

still sat on the throne,

but God had already left him.

That is the most tragic state a leader can reach —

when you still have the position but not the Presence.

When people still call you "king," but Heaven has already chosen another.

The Lesson of Saul's Fall

God does not measure leadership by appearance.

He measures it by **obedience.**

He does not judge by charisma,

but by character.

He does not anoint the gifted,

but the submitted.

David, the shepherd boy, replaced Saul not because he was perfect,

but because he was **pure in heart.**

Where Saul built altars for himself, David built altars for God.

Where Saul blamed others, David repented before God.

> "The Lord has sought a man after His own heart." — *1 Samuel 13:14*

Final Reflection

The story of Saul warns every generation:

God can anoint you today and reject you tomorrow if you trade obedience for appearance.

He can raise you up in glory and bring you down in shame if you value reputation over repentance.

Every leader, every pastor, every ruler must remember —

God does not judge by what you do in front of the crowd,
but by what you do when no one sees.
You may keep your title,
but if you lose His trust,
your crown means nothing.

"For the Lord sees not as man sees;
man looks on the outward appearance,
but the Lord looks on the heart." — *1 Samuel 16:7*

God's Judgment on Unjust Systems

Throughout history, the God of justice has overthrown every system built on deceit.

He has tolerated rebellion for a season, but **never forever.**

His patience is mercy, but His silence is not approval.

Every empire that mocked righteousness eventually met its ruin.

Every nation that exalted lies above truth faced divine exposure.

Every ruler who hardened his heart against Heaven became an example of what pride produces.

The Pattern of Divine Judgment

From Genesis to Revelation, God's justice follows a pattern —

He **warns**, He **waits**, and then He **acts.**

- **Egypt** trusted in oppression and enslaved God's people.

But the Lord turned its rivers into blood, and its armies drowned in the sea.

Pharaoh's crown sank beneath the waves, proving that no king can stand against truth.

- **Babylon** glorified itself as the "queen of kingdoms,"

but in one night, its walls of pride were breached,

and its golden empire fell under the weight of its own arrogance.

The handwriting appeared on the wall — "Mene, Mene, Tekel, Upharsin" —

and judgment came before the morning.

- **Rome** exalted its power and persecuted the saints,

but its fires of pleasure became fires of destruction.

It burned from within — not because of weak enemies,

but because sin consumed its foundation.

"The nation and kingdom which will not serve You shall perish."
— *Isaiah 60:12*

Every throne built on lies is destined to collapse under the truth it rejected.

Every government that removes God from its law removes stability from its foundation.

The Justice of Heaven

"For the Lord is a God of justice;
blessed are all those who wait for Him." — *Isaiah 30:18*

God is patient, but He is not blind.
He watches every transaction, every bribe, every secret meeting.
He records every injustice, every manipulation, every broken promise.
He allows evil to grow only until it fills its cup —
and when that cup overflows, **He moves suddenly.**
He exposes, He shakes, and He replaces.
He turns kings into captives and captives into kings.
He tears down proud thrones and builds up humble hearts.
The shaking of nations is not random — it is **the voice of justice.**
When sin matures, judgment ripens.
When truth is buried, God resurrects it in fire.

When Men Oppress, God Intervenes

When men use power to **oppress,**
God raises **prophets** to confront them.
When rulers use lies to **govern,**
God raises **truth** to overthrow them.

When systems exploit the poor,
God shakes economies and dethrones the greedy.
When churches compromise with politics,
God sends revival through the remnant that refuses to bow.

> "He brings down rulers from their thrones
> but lifts up the humble." — *Luke 1:52*

He dethroned Saul and raised David.
He humbled Nebuchadnezzar and exalted Daniel.
He silenced Pharaoh and delivered Israel.
He turned the cross — the greatest injustice —
into the greatest revelation of divine justice.

The Fire of Righteous Judgment

God's judgment is not only **punitive** — it is **purifying.**

He judges not to destroy truth, but to defend it.

He tears down the structures of deception so that righteousness can reign.

When God rises, no nation can hide behind its flag.

No ruler can bribe His justice.

No power can resist His decree.

He weighs every government on the scales of His holiness.

And when He finds them wanting, He replaces them with those who fear His name.

> "For the kingdom is the Lord's,
> and He rules over the nations." — *Psalm 22:28*

The rise and fall of empires are not determined by history books —
they are decided by the hand of God.
Babylon may boast, but Heaven keeps the record.
Egypt may enslave, but Heaven writes the ending.
Rome may reign, but Heaven remembers the martyrs' tears.

The Cry of the Oppressed

Every tear shed by the innocent is a **petition in Heaven's court.**

Every voice silenced on earth is a **witness before God's throne.**

Every unjust system that crushes the poor and mocks the righteous
is gathering wrath against itself.

The poor may not have lawyers, but they have **God.**

The orphans may not have defenders, but they have **a Father in Heaven.**

The oppressed may not have armies, but they have **angels on assignment.**

> "For He will not forget the cry of the humble." — *Psalm 9:12*

The longer evil rules, the more sudden its fall will be.
For the God who watches in silence is preparing His sentence.

Every Generation Will See His Justice

The story of history is the story of **God's sovereignty.**

He still dethrones the proud and lifts the humble.
He still exposes secret corruption and honors quiet faithfulness.
He still rewards obedience and punishes rebellion.
No throne is too high for His hand to reach.
No empire too vast for His breath to scatter.
No leader too powerful for His justice to humble.
The kingdoms of this world may appear strong,
but they are temporary scaffolds compared to His eternal throne.

> "The Lord reigns; let the nations tremble." — *Psalm 99:1*

Final Reflection

The God who judged Pharaoh, Babylon, and Rome
will judge every modern empire that defies His truth.
He will expose the lies of governments,
the greed of corporations,
and the corruption of religious systems.

The Lord will arise to defend the widow, the orphan, and the oppressed.
He will replace deception with discernment,
darkness with light,
and pride with humility.
For His justice is not delayed — it is **precise.**
It moves not by man's calendar but by Heaven's command.
Let every nation tremble and every leader repent.
For the Judge of all the earth still reigns,
and His verdict is eternal:
"The proud shall be brought low,
but the humble shall inherit the earth."

A Call to Righteous Leadership

True leadership is not about position but submission —
not about image but integrity.

The greatest leader is not the one who rules over many but the one who serves faithfully before God.

God is calling for leaders with clean hearts and clear hands.
Leaders who fear Him more than the press.
Leaders who love truth more than titles.
Leaders who will lead with transparency, humility, and compassion.
A nation led by hypocrites is a nation under judgment.
But a nation led by righteous men is a nation under grace.

> "Righteousness exalts a nation,
> but sin is a reproach to any people." — *Proverbs 14:34*

Key Scriptures:

- *Proverbs 29:2* — When the wicked rule, the people mourn
- *Psalm 28:3* — They speak peace, but mischief is in their hearts
- *Isaiah 10:1* — Woe to those who make unjust laws
- *1 Samuel 15* — Saul's disobedience and downfall
- *Proverbs 14:34* — Righteousness exalts a nation
- *Psalm 2:2* — Rulers take counsel against the Lord

Part II – The Masks of Society

Chapter 4: The Mask in the Church

The House That Forgot Its Owner

The Church was meant to be **the house of truth** —
a place where light exposes darkness,
where holiness confronts sin,
where repentance opens the heavens,
and where the power of God transforms broken lives.
But today, many churches have become **stages**, not sanctuaries.
The altar has turned into a platform.
The worship has become a show.
And the pulpit, once the voice of Heaven, now echoes the opinions of men.
We have built **cathedrals without conviction**,
ministries without message,
and congregations without consecration.
We have filled buildings with people but emptied hearts of purity.
The Church has become **the house that forgot its Owner.**
It still carries His name but not His nature.
It still sings His songs but not from His Spirit.
It still preaches His Word but not in His will.

The Exchange of Glory for Image

Once, the Church was a flame — now it has become a form.
Once, it raised disciples — now it gathers fans.
Once, it preached repentance — now it promotes comfort.
Once, it sought the Kingdom — now it chases crowds.
We have replaced **presence** with **performance**,
purity with **popularity**,
truth with **trend**,
submission with **strategy.**
The altar that should burn with repentance now burns with competition.
The pulpit that should carry the voice of God now repeats the slogans of men.
The Spirit who once convicted hearts now grieves in silence —

pushed aside by pride, greed, and entertainment.

> "My house shall be called a house of prayer for all nations,
> but you have made it a den of thieves." — *Mark 11:17*

The Tragedy of Spiritual Acting

Many who enter God's house have learned **how to act holy — not how to be holy.**

They lift their hands in worship, but their hearts remain unbowed.
They cry in prayer but refuse to repent.
They shout "Glory!" in public but live in secret sin.
They speak in tongues but gossip in two languages.
They know how to **shout**, but not how to **submit.**
They know how to **sing**, but not how to **serve.**
They know how to **look anointed**, but not how to **live crucified.**
They can preach about forgiveness yet cannot forgive.
They can quote Scripture yet cannot obey it.
They can prophesy over others yet cannot overcome their own pride.
This is the tragedy of our generation:
We have learned the **language of Zion** but lost the **life of Christ.**
We have built ministries that impress men but no longer move Heaven.

The Church That Entertains the Flesh

The Church that was meant to crucify the flesh now entertains it.

We organize events that glorify talent but not truth.
We celebrate gifts more than godliness.
We honor charisma more than character.

We promote leaders who can attract crowds, not those who can attract God.

Many altars burn with strange fire —
fire of ambition, competition, and pride.
We invite God to visit, but we do not give Him room to dwell.
We seek miracles, but not **the Master.**

We want blessings without brokenness, crowns without crosses, and revival without repentance.

> "Having a form of godliness but denying its power." — *2 Timothy 3:5*

The Owner Is Knocking Again

The Owner of the house has not forgotten His Church —
but He stands at the door and knocks.

> "Behold, I stand at the door and knock;
> if anyone hears My voice and opens the door,
> I will come in to him and dine with him." — *Revelation 3:20*

He is knocking on the doors of pulpits that have closed Him out.

He is knocking on worship teams that sing about Him but do not know Him.

He is knocking on hearts that serve His name but not His nature.
He is calling His house back to order,
back to prayer,
back to purity,
back to power.
For the true Church is not the one with the best building,
but the one with the cleanest heart.
The true Church is not the one with the loudest praise,
but the one with the deepest repentance.

The Mask of the Modern Church

This is the mask of the modern Church —

a generation that **knows how to look spiritual without being surrendered.**

We have exchanged the Holy Ghost for human glory.
We have turned the Gospel into a product, and the cross into a brand.
We wear the uniform of Christianity but lack the authority of Christ.
But the Lord is removing the mask.

He is purifying His Bride.

He is separating wheat from weeds, truth from imitation, fire from smoke.

> "For the time has come for judgment to begin at the house of God." — *1 Peter 4:17*

The Church that forgot its Owner will soon remember Him —
because He will return not as a guest, but as a Judge.

Final Reflection

The house of God was never meant to entertain — it was meant to **transform.**

It was not built for applause, but for altar fire.

It was not built for comfort, but for conviction.

It was not built for the show, but for the **Shekinah.**

Let the Church rise again —

not as a brand, but as a bride.

Not as a stage, but as a sanctuary.

Not as an organization, but as an organism — alive with the Spirit of God.

For the Church belongs not to men,

not to denominations,

not to systems —

but to **Christ alone, the rightful Owner.**

Christians Who Act Holy on Sunday but Live Worldly Lives During the Week

On Sunday morning, churches are full.

Men wear suits, women wear dresses, children carry Bibles.

Voices rise in harmony, hands stretch toward Heaven, and tears flow down faces.

But by Monday morning — the holiness disappears.

The same tongues that praised God on Sunday
gossip, curse, and lie on Monday.
The same lips that cried "Lord, have Your way"
now speak words of pride, lust, and deceit.
The same believers who shouted "Hallelujah!"
walk back into compromise as if the altar never happened.
They cry in church but sin in secret.
They sing "I surrender all" but surrender nothing.
They appear holy for two hours a week,
then live like the world for the other six days.
This is not Christianity — **it is acting.**
It is religion without relationship,
emotion without transformation,
and worship without obedience.

> "These people honor Me with their lips,
> but their hearts are far from Me." — *Matthew 15:8*

The Spirit of Sunday Religion

Many today have reduced faith to **a Sunday event.**

They treat worship like a schedule, not a surrender.
They visit God once a week as if He were a hobby,
not a King who demands their whole life.
They think holiness is what you wear to church,
not how you walk in the world.
They think Christianity is about appearance,

not repentance.

They think church attendance equals salvation,

but forget that Judas attended every meeting — and still betrayed Jesus.

True Christianity is not a weekend performance; it is a **daily crucifixion.**

You cannot serve God on Sunday and serve sin on Monday.

You cannot praise Jesus with your mouth and please Satan with your lifestyle.

You cannot wear the cross as jewelry but refuse to carry it in reality.

> "No one can serve two masters... You cannot serve God and mammon." — *Matthew 6:24*

The Religion of Masks

The devil loves **Sunday Christians** —

because they look holy enough to fool others,

but empty enough to pose no threat to Hell.

He is not afraid of people who attend church;

he is afraid of people who **become** the church.

He does not tremble at your worship songs;

he trembles when you **live** what you sing.

Many believers wear a mask of holiness:

they smile during worship but harbor bitterness inside.

They raise their hands but refuse to raise their standards.

They dance in the Spirit but live in the flesh.

They speak in tongues but gossip in English.

This is why the modern church has power in sound but not in spirit.

The songs are louder, but the hearts are colder.

The crowds are larger, but the fruit is smaller.

We have learned how to **act Christian** without being **Christlike.**

> "Having a form of godliness but denying its power." — *2 Timothy 3:5*

The Power of Everyday Holiness

The devil does not fear a Sunday Christian —
he fears a believer who walks in holiness all week.
He fears the one who prays when no one sees.
He fears the one who obeys when no one claps.
He fears the one who chooses purity when temptation whispers.
He fears the one who forgives quietly, loves deeply, and gives secretly.
You see, holiness is not proven in public — it is proven in private.
Faith is not measured by what you do when others are watching,
but by who you are when no one is.
The real Christian is the same person in the dark as in the light,
the same in secret as on stage,
the same at work as in worship.
True Christianity is consistency — not convenience.
It is obedience when it hurts, purity when it's hard,
and humility when no one praises you for it.

"Be holy, for I am holy." — *1 Peter 1:16*

Members or Disciples

The Church today is full of **members,**
but God is looking for **disciples.**
Members attend — disciples abide.
Members sing — disciples serve.
Members listen — disciples obey.
Members follow crowds — disciples follow Christ.
Disciples walk in truth when no one is watching.
They love righteousness more than reputation.
They fear God more than losing friends.
They choose integrity over popularity.
They would rather be right with God and wrong with the world
than right with the world and wrong with God.

"If anyone would come after Me, let him deny himself,

take up his cross daily, and follow Me." — *Luke 9:23*

The Call to Authentic Christianity

God is not looking for perfect people —
He is looking for **honest hearts.**
He would rather have a broken sinner who repents
than a polished hypocrite who pretends.
It's time for believers to stop visiting the cross
and start carrying it.
To stop playing church
and start being the Church.
To stop quoting verses
and start living them.
The world does not need more sermons —
it needs more examples.
It needs Christians who will **walk the Word,**
not just **talk the Word.**

"Let your light so shine before men,
that they may see your good works
and glorify your Father in heaven." — *Matthew 5:16*

Final Reflection

Heaven is not impressed by Sunday attendance.
Hell is not intimidated by Sunday noise.
But both Heaven and Hell recognize one thing:
a believer who lives every day in truth.
For the kingdom of God is not in words,
but in **power** — the power of a changed life.
Let every Christian take off the mask,
live the same life in private as in public,
and carry holiness beyond Sunday morning.
Because the true test of your faith
is not how you worship in the crowd —

but how you **walk when the service ends.**

Choirs Singing with Bitterness, Pastors Preaching for Money, Members Pretending to Love

The saddest thing in this generation is not that the **world** is corrupt, but that **corruption has entered the sanctuary.**

The disease of hypocrisy that once plagued politics has now infected the pulpit.

The spirit that destroyed kingdoms has now climbed the altar.

In many churches today:

The choirs **sing about heaven** while secretly **hating one another.**

Pastors **preach about love** while competing for followers.

Members **greet each other with smiles** but carry jealousy in their hearts.

The house of God has become a house divided —

bitterness has replaced brotherhood,

greed has replaced grace,

and *popularity has replaced purity.*

The Choir Without Unity

The choir that once brought down the glory now performs for applause.

Voices blend in harmony while hearts burn with envy.

They sing of Zion but live like Babylon.

Their melodies rise to the ceiling, but never reach Heaven.

Worship without forgiveness is **noise**, not **praise.**

You cannot lift holy hands that are stained with hatred.

You cannot sing of the blood while gossiping about your brother.

You cannot harmonize in public while dividing in private.

> "If you bring your gift to the altar and there remember that your brother has something against you,
>
> leave your gift there before the altar, go your way, first be reconciled to your brother." — *Matthew 5:23–24*

The songs of bitterness do not move angels; they grieve the Spirit.
God listens not to the melody but to the motive.
He measures not the sound of your voice but the sincerity of your heart.

The Pulpit for Sale

Many pastors today no longer preach to **save souls,**
but to **fill seats.**

They preach what people want to hear, not what Heaven wants to say.

The gospel has become a business, and the pulpit has become a platform for self-promotion.

They no longer carry the cross; they carry contracts.

They no longer preach Christ; they preach convenience.

They no longer prepare sermons through prayer; they download them for profit.

> "You received freely; give freely." — *Matthew 10:8*

But they sell **holy oil**, **miracle water**, and **prosperity packages**
as if the Holy Spirit were a product for sale.

They make merchandise of the name of Jesus.

The same temple Jesus once cleansed has been rebuilt — with microphones and banners instead of money changers.

And the Lord still walks among the churches,
turning over tables of greed, saying,

> "My house shall be called a house of prayer,
> but you have made it a den of thieves." — *Matthew 21:13*

The Members Who Pretend to Love

The congregation mirrors the pulpit.
As the leader goes, so goes the flock.
Members have learned to perform the same hypocrisy they see.
They smile on Sunday but slander on Monday.
They hug in fellowship but harbor envy in silence.
They pretend unity but secretly compete.

They appear kind but celebrate others' downfall.
Love has become a word, not a way.
Forgiveness has become a verse, not a virtue.
Holiness has become tradition, not transformation.

> "By this all will know that you are My disciples, if you have love for one another." —*John 13:35*

The world no longer believes the Church's message because it cannot see the Church's love.

When the pews are full but the hearts are empty, Heaven weeps.

When the Church Becomes a Marketplace

God never called us to **perform**; He called us to **transform.**
He never asked for **showmanship** but for **sincerity.**
He never wanted **applause** but **obedience.**
When the church becomes a marketplace, the **presence of God departs.**
When the pulpit becomes a stage, the **cross becomes decoration.**
When worship becomes business, **Ichabod** is written over the door:

> "The glory has departed." — *1 Samuel 4:21*

And though the lights still shine and the music still plays,
the Spirit has already left the building.
Men still clap, but Heaven is silent.
Souls still gather, but angels no longer rejoice.

The Fire That Purifies the House

But the Lord is raising a **remnant Church** —
a people who will not sell His name for gain,
who will not trade holiness for hype,
who will not perform before men but will weep before God.
He is cleansing His temple again.
He is calling the choir to repentance, the preacher to purity,
and the congregation to compassion.

He is restoring the altar of truth,
reigniting the fire of holiness,
and rebuilding a Church that loves more than it performs.

"Who may ascend the hill of the Lord?
He who has clean hands and a pure heart." — *Psalm 24:3–4*

The music will be pure again.
The message will be holy again.
The love will be real again.
And the glory will return — not to the building, but to the hearts of the redeemed.

Final Reflection

The time has come for the Church to sing without bitterness,
to preach without greed,
to serve without pretense.
For when love returns, power returns.
When holiness reigns, Heaven responds.
And when Christ becomes the center again,
the glory that once departed will descend once more.
Let the Church rise — not as a business, but as a **bride.**
Not as an industry, but as an **altar.**
Not as an entertainment hall, but as a **house of God.**

How Witchcraft, Sorcery, and Demonic Manipulation Hide in Churches Today

The greatest deception of this generation is not found in the streets, the clubs, or the shrines — **it is sitting comfortably inside the Church.**

Witchcraft no longer wears black robes or dances around fires.

It now wears white collars, holds microphones, and preaches from pulpits.

Sorcery has rebranded itself as "prophecy."

Demonic manipulation now calls itself "anointing."

The very altars meant for deliverance have become stages for deception.

Satan has not left the Church — he has joined it.

He knows that the easiest way to destroy the flock is to wear the shepherd's clothes.

> "For such men are false apostles, deceitful workers, transforming themselves into apostles of Christ.
>
> And no wonder, for Satan himself transforms himself into an angel of light."
>
> — *2 Corinthians 11:13–14*

The Disguise of Light

Today, witchcraft has changed its form.

It no longer hides in the dark; it thrives under the spotlight.

Demons no longer hide in caves; they hide behind crosses.

The devil no longer whispers from the shadows; he preaches with charisma, quoting Scripture to seduce the ignorant.

False prophets and magicians have infiltrated the pulpit.

They perform miracles, but the source is not the Holy Spirit — it is darkness disguised as light.

They call down "fire," but it is strange fire, not the fire of the Holy Ghost.

They prophesy with accuracy, but their insight comes from familiar spirits that spy on souls.

They claim to heal, but they transfer bondage through touch and "deliverance" rituals.

They mix the Word of God with occultism —

using **candles, oils, salt, rings, incense, and colored water** as if the blood of Jesus were insufficient.

They teach believers to depend on objects instead of obedience, and on rituals instead of repentance.

This is not Christianity — it is **Christianized witchcraft.**

The Fruits of Hidden Witchcraft

Witchcraft in the church is not only in the pulpit — it is in the pews.

It manifests in manipulation, pride, and sexual immorality.

It is seen when leaders control minds instead of leading hearts.

It is felt when fear replaces faith, and loyalty to man replaces obedience to God.

Every time a parent sleeps with their child,
a brother with his sister,
a man with another man,
or a woman with another woman —
it is the spirit of witchcraft at work, corrupting what God made pure.

Every act of **sexual perversion, abortion, adultery, and prostitution** is a covenant with demons of darkness.

Satan uses these sins as doors to capture souls and enslave generations.

Many families today live under hidden curses because of ancestral altars and secret sins never confessed.

These demonic powers operate through lust, control, and rebellion — the three pillars of witchcraft.

The Spirit of Simon Still Lives

In Acts 8, Simon the sorcerer followed Philip and tried to buy the Holy Spirit.

That same spirit still operates today — people who seek **power without purity**, gifts without godliness, fame without faithfulness.

They want the stage but not the cross.

They desire applause, not holiness.

And many follow them because they perform wonders, not realizing that not every wonder is from Heaven.

> "Many will say to Me on that day, 'Lord, Lord, did we not prophesy in Your name and in Your name drive out demons and perform many miracles?'

> Then I will tell them plainly, 'I never knew you. Depart from Me, you workers of iniquity.'"
>
> — *Matthew 7:22–23*

The Devil's Strategy: To Corrupt Worship

Satan's goal is not to destroy churches — it is to **corrupt them from within.**

He knows that once the altar is polluted, everything that flows from it becomes unclean.

That is why today we see churches that are full of crowds but empty of conviction,

loud in worship but silent in repentance,

rich in money but poor in truth.

The devil no longer attacks the altar — **he stands upon it.**

He no longer fights the choir — **he leads it.**

He no longer tempts from outside — **he teaches from within.**

He uses music, emotions, and false visions to replace revelation and obedience.

And the people, hungry for blessings but not for holiness, follow him blindly.

They seek miracles but not the Miracle Worker.

They seek prophecy but not repentance.

They seek power but not purity.

The Call for Discernment

The time has come for the Church to wake up.

Not everything spiritual is holy, and not every miracle is divine.

Discernment is not suspicion — it is spiritual awareness born from intimacy with God.

The Holy Spirit reveals truth, while demons imitate it.

Without discernment, even the elect can be deceived (Matthew 24:24).

The Church must return to the simplicity of the Gospel —

the Cross, the Blood, the Word, and the Spirit of Truth.

When these four foundations are restored, witchcraft loses its power, and the altar of deception is replaced by the altar of holiness.

The Need for Discernment and Spiritual Fire

We are living in an **age of spiritual confusion**, where deception wears the robe of revelation and rebellion hides behind religion.

It is an age where people **call evil good and good evil**,
where popularity has replaced purity,
and emotional excitement has replaced the presence of the Holy Spirit.
Today, not every preacher with a microphone carries God's message,
not every miracle comes from Heaven,
and not every revival is born of the Spirit.

Crowds can be deceived, lights can be bright, and voices can sound anointed — but the true test of the Spirit is **truth and holiness**, not applause or emotion.

> "Do not believe every spirit, but test the spirits to see whether they are from God." — *1 John 4:1*

The Holy Spirit cannot be fooled by numbers or titles.
He does not measure a ministry by its attendance, but by its **obedience**.
He does not measure a church by its building, but by its **holiness**.
He does not measure a believer by their gifts, but by their **fruit**.

What Is Discernment?

Discernment is not suspicion — it is **spiritual sight**.

It is the ability to see beyond what the eyes can see,
to recognize when God is speaking and when the devil is pretending.
It is the fire that separates gold from garbage,
truth from lies,
and light from darkness.

Without discernment, the Church will continue to call **demons "prophets"** and **false fire "revival."**

Without discernment, believers will continue to follow personalities instead of the presence of God.

And without discernment, the altar will continue to host both the Holy Spirit and unclean spirits at the same time.

The Need for Fire

The Church doesn't just need emotion — it needs **fire**.

Not the strange fire of manipulation and showmanship,

but the holy fire of the Spirit that **burns hypocrisy**, **exposes hidden sin**, and **purifies worship**.

We need **fire that consumes pride**,

fire that breaks false altars,

fire that melts hard hearts,

and **fire that revives true holiness** in the hearts of God's people.

Because when the **Spirit's fire returns to the altar**,

truth will return to the pulpit.

When truth returns to the pulpit,

repentance will return to the people.

And when repentance returns to the people,

revival will return to the world.

This is the cry of Heaven today —

that the Church would no longer be a stage for entertainers,

but an altar for intercessors.

That we would stop admiring the false shine of men and start seeking the true glory of God.

That believers would rise, not with empty words, but with **holy fire**,

discernment sharp as a sword,

and hearts fully surrendered to the Spirit of Truth.

> "Our God is a consuming fire." — *Hebrews 12:29*

A Cry from Heaven to the Church

The Spirit of the Lord is crying — not in anger, but in grief.

He weeps over His Church that has lost her first love.

He mourns over pulpits that have become stages, over altars that have become platforms, over ministers who have traded purity for popularity.

> "He who has an ear, let him hear what the Spirit says to the churches." — *Revelation 2:7*

The cry from Heaven is clear and piercing:

> "**Church, take off your mask!**
> Stop pretending to be holy while your heart is far from Me!
> Stop lifting hands in worship while living in secret sin!
> Stop calling what is unclean 'anointing,' and what is worldly 'wisdom!'
> Return to Me before the light fades from your lampstand!"

This is not a call of condemnation — it is a call of mercy.

God is not seeking perfect people; He is seeking **repentant hearts**.

He is calling His Bride to return — to wash her garments, to purify her altar, and to love Him again with undivided devotion.

Return to Your First Love

The Church that once prayed now entertains.

The Church that once fasted now feasts.

The Church that once preached repentance now preaches prosperity.

The Church that once sought the fire of God now chases the favor of men.

But Heaven is calling:

"Return to your first love.
Return to tears of intercession.
Return to brokenness before My presence.
Return to holiness, where My glory once rested."

> "Remember therefore from where you have fallen; repent and do the first works." — *Revelation 2:5*

The Remnant Rising

Though compromise fills many altars, **God is raising a remnant.**

Men and women who love Him more than money,

who serve Him more than systems,

who carry **fire**, not fashion.

They will not be famous, but they will be faithful.

They will not seek crowds, but they will carry the **cloud of His presence**.

They are the ones who have refused to bow to the idols of pride, entertainment, and false doctrine.

Their hearts burn for truth, and their lives are marked by purity.

They are **warriors of light** in an age of deception —

watchmen on the walls who will not be silent until the Church is restored to holiness.

True Worship Restored

These are the true worshipers that Jesus spoke of:

> "The hour is coming, and now is, when the true worshipers will worship the Father in spirit and in truth." —*John 4:23*

True worship is not in songs but in surrender.

It is not in rhythm but in repentance.

It is not in sound but in spirit.

Heaven is not moved by noise — it is moved by truth.

The Church that Heaven desires is not glamorous — it is glorious.

Not popular — but powerful.

Not rich in money — but rich in mercy.

Not known by men — but known by God.

This is Heaven's cry:

Return, Church! The Bridegroom is coming. Trim your lamp, purify your heart, and let your flame burn bright again.

"Awake, you who sleep, arise from the dead, and Christ will give you light." — *Ephesians 5:14*

Final Warning

The Spirit of God is speaking clearly in this generation:

"Repent, for the Kingdom of Heaven is at hand."

The time for comfort is over. The time for compromise has ended.

Now is the hour of decision — for both believers and churches.

A church that refuses to repent will be judged.

A church that entertains sin will lose her lampstand.

A church that fears men more than God will soon fall.

The Lord will not share His glory with a polluted altar.

He will not dwell where pride replaces prayer and where performance replaces purity.

"No one can serve two masters." — Matthew 6:24

Many churches today have chosen comfort over conviction, prosperity over purity, and applause over anointing.

They have exchanged the presence of God for the praise of men.

But Heaven is watching, and the Spirit is warning —

***Ichabod** has already been written over many altars: "The glory has departed." — 1 Samuel 4:21*

The Church That Endures

Yet, in the midst of corruption, God is preserving a remnant.

*A **holy church** that will not bend to the world.*

*A **pure Bride** preparing for the return of her King.*

A people whose garments are washed in the blood of the Lamb,
whose lamps are filled with oil,
and whose hearts are burning with truth and holiness.

For Christ is not coming back for a rich church,
not for a famous church,
not for a politically correct church —

*but for a **holy church**,*
"without spot or wrinkle or any such thing." — Ephesians 5:27

Let the Fire Fall Again

Let the mask fall.
Let the stage crumble.
Let the fear of God return.
Let the fire of Heaven consume every false altar and every hidden sin.
The hour has come for the Bride to awaken from her sleep.
The King is at the door.
The trumpet of judgment is about to sound.
Only those who walk in truth will stand in the day of His appearing.

> *"For Satan himself masquerades as an angel of light." — 2 Corinthians 11:14*

> *"Beloved, do not believe every spirit, but test the spirits, whether they are of God." — 1 John 4:1*

> *"The true worshipers will worship the Father in spirit and in truth." — John 4:23*

The Call

Church, return to your first love.
Leaders, purify your altars.
Believers, guard your hearts.
The King is not delaying — He is preparing.
And when He comes, may He find you faithful, awake, and burning with holy fire.
For the cry from Heaven is echoing through the earth:

> ***"Behold, the Bridegroom is coming; go out to meet Him!"** — Matthew 25:6*

Chapter 5: Hypocrisy in Families and Relationships

When Love Becomes a Mask and Trust Becomes a Trap

The greatest tragedy in the world today is not found in broken governments or corrupt systems — it is found in broken homes.
Families that smile in public but bleed in private.
Couples that pray together on Sunday but curse each other on Monday.
Parents who preach morality to their children but live in secret sin.
Children who honor their parents in words but dishonor them in deeds.

This is the hypocrisy that has invaded the sacred foundation of family, the very institution designed by God to reflect His image of unity, truth, and love.

"These people honor Me with their lips, but their hearts are far from Me." — *Matthew 15:8*

We live in an age where appearances matter more than integrity,
where people wear masks of affection but hide hearts of betrayal.
Many marriages are partnerships of convenience, not covenants of faithfulness.
Many friendships are built on self-interest, not sincerity.
And even in Christian homes, false peace replaces real repentance.

Behind the smiles are secrets.
Behind the prayers are pretenses.
Behind the promises are manipulations.

This hypocrisy is not just emotional — it is spiritual warfare.
Because Satan knows that if he can corrupt the family, he can weaken the Church;
and if he can weaken the Church, he can deceive nations.

In many homes today, love has become a performance. Spouses deceive each other, children rebel against their parents, and parents neglect the spiritual upbringing of their children — all while pretending that everything is fine. Social media shows "perfect" families, but behind the screens are tears, abuse, adultery, and division.

God did not design family to be a show — He designed it to be a sanctuary.
A place of truth, healing, humility, and holiness.
But when lies, pride, and hidden sin enter, the family becomes a battlefield.

The Spirit of the Lord is calling families back to authenticity — to remove the mask, confront the truth, and rebuild relationships on the solid foundation of Christ.
Because you cannot heal what you continue to hide,
and you cannot have unity without honesty.

This chapter will expose the spiritual roots of hypocrisy in families and relationships —
how manipulation, lust, greed, and pride destroy what God intended for love and truth to build.
It will also show the path to restoration — where forgiveness replaces bitterness, truth replaces deception, and the home becomes once again the altar of God's presence.

The Broken Foundations of Love

Before there was a church, a temple, or a throne — there was a **family**.

It was God's first creation, His first covenant, His first reflection of heaven on earth.

The family was meant to be a **sanctuary of love**, a dwelling of truth, peace, and divine order.

In its harmony, God saw His image; in its unity, He revealed His nature.

"It is not good for man to be alone." — *Genesis 2:18*

But today, many families have lost their foundation.

The home that should be a **holy altar** has become a **stage for performance**.

Love has been replaced by lust.

Truth has been replaced by manipulation.

Commitment has been replaced by convenience.

And faithfulness has been replaced by selfish ambition.

People marry for appearance, not for purpose.

They choose partners for pleasure, not for covenant.

They seek wealth, status, and beauty — but neglect character, holiness, and truth.

Many call it *love*, but in heaven's eyes, it is **idolatry disguised as affection.**

We are living in a generation that **speaks love but lives lies** —
a generation that posts affection online but hides betrayal offline;
that takes wedding vows with lips but breaks them with lust;
that shares smiles in public but fights in secret.

The dining table, once a place of fellowship, has become a courtroom of accusation.

The marriage bed, once a place of unity, has become a battlefield of guilt and shame.

Children grow up seeing hypocrisy more than holiness —
hearing prayers from parents whose hearts are filled with unforgiveness.

This is the **spirit of hypocrisy** — a silent destroyer working in the very foundation of homes.

It teaches people to *pretend peace while living in conflict,*
to *wear rings but not carry responsibility,*

to *say "I love you" while secretly planning betrayal.*
And yet, God's design for family has never changed.
Love was never meant to be a feeling — it was meant to be a **covenant.**
A divine commitment that reflects the heart of Christ —
selfless, sacrificial, and steadfast through every storm.

> "Unless the Lord builds the house, they labor in vain who build it." — *Psalm 127:1*

When God is removed from the center, the home collapses,
for He alone is the **foundation that holds love together.**
It is time for families to return to truth,
for husbands and wives to rebuild their homes on repentance and forgiveness,
for parents to lead with humility and prayer,
for children to honor and walk in obedience.
Because a nation is only as strong as its families —
and a family is only as pure as its love.

Love Without Truth — The Root of Family Hypocrisy

Love without truth is not love — it is manipulation dressed as compassion.
It looks gentle but hides deception; it speaks sweetly but wounds deeply.
True love does not hide sin — it heals it.
True love does not tolerate evil — it confronts it.
True love does not flatter — it disciplines.
True love does not seek self — it seeks God.

> "Love does not delight in evil but rejoices with the truth." — *1 Corinthians 13:6*

In many homes today, love has lost its purity because it has lost its truth.
Parents excuse disobedience in their children and call it "understanding."
Spouses tolerate immorality and call it "forgiveness."
Siblings betray one another and call it "weakness of the flesh."
People live in lies but keep smiling to protect reputation.

This is not love — it is **hypocrisy in disguise.**

And hypocrisy in the home is more dangerous than witchcraft in the village because it destroys the foundation of trust.

Where there is no truth, there can be no healing.

Where there is no repentance, there can be no restoration.

Where there is no light, darkness rules even in the name of love.

Satan's greatest strategy in families is to **replace truth with emotion**.

He makes people believe that peace means silence,

that love means tolerance of sin,

and that forgiveness means ignoring wrongdoing.

But God's Word teaches the opposite:

- Love corrects, even when it hurts.
- Love rebukes, even when it risks rejection.
- Love exposes, because it refuses to let darkness stay hidden.

Many couples and families today are bound not because demons are strong, but because truth is weak.

They pray together but live in lies.

They ask God to bless them but refuse to confess.

They call each other "beloved" but secretly despise one another in the heart.

The spirit of deception has made many homes **holy on Sunday and hellish on Monday.**

They build altars of appearance but destroy the altar of honesty.

They love in word but not in truth — and that is why their peace fades and their unity collapses.

If love is not built on truth, it becomes idolatry.

If marriage is not built on righteousness, it becomes a prison.

If parenting is not built on God's Word, it becomes manipulation.

True love says, *"I will tell you the truth even if it hurts, because your soul is more important than your comfort."*

That kind of love builds heaven on earth.

> "You shall know the truth, and the truth shall make you free." — *John 8:32*

Until families return to truth, they will remain bound in beautiful lies — smiling in public while dying in private.

But when truth enters, light shines, peace returns, and love becomes what God designed it to be — **a reflection of His own heart.**

Pretending to Love While Harboring Hatred

Love is the language of Heaven — hypocrisy is the accent of hell.

To say *"I love you"* while secretly envying, competing, or despising someone

is to speak the devil's language with holy words.

It is to put sugar on poison and call it peace.

Love is supposed to heal, but when it is mixed with deceit, it wounds.

It is the mask most people wear when they want to look kind but refuse to be clean.

And nowhere is this mask more visible than in families, churches, and relationships.

The Divided Heart at Home

Many husbands and wives **live together physically but are separated spiritually.**

They walk in the same house but dwell in different worlds.

They smile at each other in public but speak daggers in private.

They post pictures of unity on social media,

but sleep under the same roof with bitterness between them like a wall.

Their home has everything — except peace.

They speak politely before guests but exchange cold silence when the door closes.

They say "I forgive you" but keep records of every wrong.

They call each other "dear" but think "enemy" in their hearts.

This is not marriage — this is acting.

And God cannot bless a union that performs love but withholds truth.

> "Love must be without hypocrisy.
> Hate what is evil; cling to what is good." — *Romans 12:9*

True love does not pretend to forgive — it forgives.

It does not cover hatred with hugs — it heals through humility.

It does not manipulate emotion — it manifests transformation.

The Legacy of Hypocrisy

Children grow up watching what we think they cannot see.

They see parents act kind in church but cruel at home.

They hear *"I love you"* but feel rejection in the atmosphere.

They watch apologies spoken with lips but canceled by behavior.

They learn to lie not from lessons, but from **example.**

They imitate what they witness: a home that praises God publicly but dishonors Him privately.

And soon the same hypocrisy becomes their inheritance.

When a generation grows up seeing fake love,
they begin to believe real love does not exist.
They enter relationships built on pretense,
repeat the cycle of deception,
and call survival "love."

But God is not mocked — whatever is sown in pretense will reap in pain.

Love Without Truth Is a Mask

Love without truth is **a mask.**

Love without forgiveness is **manipulation.**

Love without sincerity is **poison.**

Many say *"I love you"* to gain control, not to give care.

They flatter with their mouths but plot in their minds.

They comfort you with words but compete with you in secret.

They hold your hand in public but hope for your failure in private.

This is not love — it is **camouflage.**

The same spirit that kissed Jesus to betray Him still walks among men.

> "Judas, do you betray the Son of Man with a kiss?" — *Luke 22:48*

Love that hides hatred is not divine — it is demonic.

For Satan also disguises himself as an angel of light.

So do his children — smiling in your face while stabbing your peace.

The Power of True Love

True love is not emotion; it is **decision.**
It is not the warmth of a moment but the weight of a choice.
It is the will to act truthfully before God and man.
It is the courage to forgive when revenge feels right.
It is the humility to bless the one who hurt you.
It is the strength to speak truth even when it costs you.
It is the maturity to choose peace over pride.
True love does not wear masks — it wears mercy.
It does not fake kindness — it faces conflict with honesty.
It does not hide behind silence — it speaks life through grace.

> "Love your enemies, bless those who curse you,
>
> do good to those who hate you, and pray for those who spitefully use you." — *Matthew 5:44*

That is not weakness — that is power.
Because hatred imprisons the soul,
but love sets it free.

The Call to Unmasked Love

If love is the language of Heaven,
then honesty is its tone.
God is calling His people to remove the mask —
to love with clean hearts and pure motives.
You cannot claim to love God while despising your brother.
You cannot sing "I love You, Lord"
while refusing to reconcile with your neighbor.
You cannot say "God bless you"
while secretly hoping they fail.

> "If anyone says, 'I love God,' and hates his brother, he is a liar." — *1 John 4:20*

Love is not proved in what you say; it is revealed in what you do.
It is seen when you choose grace over gossip,
mercy over malice,
and truth over titles.

Final Reflection

Pretending to love is easy —

but loving truly costs your pride, your comfort, and sometimes your tears.

Hypocrisy hides — love heals.
Hatred divides — love restores.
Bitterness enslaves — love delivers.
If your words say "I love you," but your heart says "I resent you,"
you have not yet known the love of Christ.
Let the Church, the home, and every heart return to this:

Love without hypocrisy, truth without fear, and forgiveness without condition.

For when love is pure,
God Himself dwells there —
because **God is love.**

> "He who abides in love abides in God, and God in him." — *1 John 4:16*

Marriages Built on Lies and Appearances

Many marriages today are not built on the **rock of truth**,
but on the **sand of pretense.**
They look stable on social media but crumble in silence at home.
They shine in photos but bleed in private.
They call it love, but it is lust dressed in religion.
Couples fall in love with **appearance**, not with **character.**
They marry for beauty, not for purpose.
They marry for status, not for submission.
They marry for comfort, not for covenant.
They wear the **ring** but not the **responsibility.**
They say "for better or worse,"
but secretly mean "for better only."
They hide behind smiles while their hearts are breaking.
They attend church together but never pray together.
They show unity before people but live in quiet war behind closed doors.

The Hypocrisy of the Holy Couple

Some husbands act spiritual in public but are unfaithful in secret.
They preach forgiveness but hold grudges.
They raise hands in worship but raise voices at home.
They speak of love in church but speak of control in private.
Some wives act humble before others but manipulate behind the scenes.
They cry in worship but curse in anger.
They submit in appearance but rebel in spirit.
They pretend patience but live in silent punishment.
And together, they wear the **mask of holiness**
while harboring the disease of hypocrisy.

"A house divided against itself cannot stand." — *Mark 3:25*

When the Altar Becomes a Stage

Marriage is a **covenant**, not a performance.

It was meant to reflect Christ and the Church —
a bond of truth, loyalty, and love that endures storms.
But when couples replace truth with performance,
their altar becomes a **stage**.
They start living to impress others instead of pleasing God.
Their conversations become rehearsed.
Their affection becomes an act.
Their marriage becomes a show that fools the audience but not Heaven.
When the altar becomes a stage,
the cross becomes a **prop** — something you wear, not something you bear.
And when lies enter a marriage,
the presence of God quietly departs.

The Hidden Cracks Beneath the Surface

Many homes today collapse not because of storms,
but because of **secrets.**
Storms reveal the truth; secrets destroy it.
A marriage built on deception is like a wall painted beautifully but cracked inside.
You can fake affection,
but you cannot fake peace.
You can post photos,
but you cannot post truth.
You can lie to people,
but you cannot lie to God.

> "Unless the Lord builds the house,
> they labor in vain who build it." — *Psalm 127:1*

When Christ is not the foundation,
the home becomes a battlefield of egos instead of a sanctuary of love.

The Disguises of Marriage

Some marriages are built not on covenant but **convenience.**
Some on **lust**, not **love.**
Some on **status**, not **sacrifice.**
Some on **fear**, not **faith.**
They appear holy but are hollow inside.
They wear crosses but carry curses.
They celebrate anniversaries but not intimacy.
They share a bed but not a burden.
And when the mask finally falls,
they blame each other for what they both ignored —
the absence of God in their foundation.

The Consequences of Pretense

When truth leaves a home, peace follows it out the door.
When prayer is absent, pride takes its place.
When forgiveness dies, bitterness begins to breed.
Soon, the marriage becomes a warzone.
Communication turns into competition.
Love turns into obligation.
Covenant turns into contract.
And what God joined together,
man's ego begins to tear apart.

> "For where envy and strife exist, there is confusion and every evil work." —*James 3:16*

You cannot build a lasting relationship on what you fake.
Only what is true can endure.
A house built on deceit may stand tall for a while,
but one day, the rain of reality will fall,
and the floods of truth will expose the foundation.

The Path to Restoration

But God is merciful.
He can rebuild what deception has destroyed.
He can heal what pride has broken.
He can restore what lies have buried.
A marriage can be revived —
but not through pretending, only through **repenting.**
It begins when both hearts bow before the Lord and say,
"Forgive us for faking peace. Teach us to walk in truth."
When honesty returns, harmony follows.
When repentance flows, love revives.
When Christ becomes the center again,
the home becomes an altar of His glory.

> "Love rejoices in the truth." — *1 Corinthians 13:6*

Final Reflection

Marriage is not a performance for people;
it is a covenant before God.
Do not let appearance replace authenticity.
Do not let pride replace prayer.
Do not let lies replace love.
If you want your marriage to last,
build it on what is **real** — not what looks right.
For every home built on truth will stand,
but every home built on pretense will eventually fall.

> "The rain descended, the floods came, and the winds blew,
> and beat upon that house; and it did not fall,
> for it was founded upon the Rock." — *Matthew 7:25*

Let every husband, every wife, and every home return to that Rock —
Christ Jesus, the foundation that never fails.

Parents Who Destroy Their Children Through Double Life

Children do not become who you tell them to be —
they become who you **show them** to be.
You can preach a thousand sermons at home,
but they will remember the one you **live.**
You can speak of faith, but if they never see you walk in it,
your words become noise to their hearts.

> "Children learn more from what they see than from what they hear."

You cannot teach them truth while living a lie.
You cannot preach holiness while walking in hypocrisy.
You cannot demand obedience while you yourself rebel against God.
Many parents destroy their children **unknowingly** —
not by poverty, but by **double life.**
They act righteous in church but act wicked at home.
They carry Bibles in public but carry bitterness in private.
They quote Scripture to their children but live contrary to it.
They discipline their children for sins they themselves commit in secret.

The Hypocrisy of the Home

When a father lies, he teaches his son that truth is optional.

When a mother gossips, she teaches her daughter that love can coexist with slander.

When parents pretend to love each other but fight behind closed doors,
the children grow up confused — and confusion breeds rebellion.

Many parents speak of forgiveness but practice revenge.

They pray with their children before bed but curse their enemies in the morning.

They tell their sons to trust God but live in constant fear.

They tell their daughters to be humble but model pride.

And the children grow up not rejecting **faith**,
but rejecting **falsehood**.
They are not rebelling against God — they are running from hypocrisy.
They cannot reconcile what they were told with what they have seen.

> "These people honor Me with their lips, but their hearts are far from Me." — *Matthew 15:8*

When the Home Becomes a Battlefield

Worse still, many families are no longer homes —
they are **battlefields.**
Sibling against sibling, brother against brother,
parent against child, husband against wife.
Jealousy, manipulation, and competition have replaced love.
Family gatherings become performances of unity,
while the real war continues in silence.
They pray together but plot against one another.
They pretend to support but secretly sabotage.
They act united in funerals but divided in life.
They share blood but not blessing.
The home that should be a **sanctuary of peace**
has become a **courtroom of rivalry.**
Children grow up learning that love is temporary,
forgiveness is fake, and loyalty is dangerous.

> "A man's enemies will be the members of his own household." — *Matthew 10:36*

The Spiritual Consequences

When hypocrisy rules a home,
the **presence of God departs.**
Because God will not dwell where truth is absent.
Children raised in such homes grow up spiritually wounded.
Some rebel against God because they saw His name abused.

Some refuse to marry because they never saw love modeled.
Some stop praying because prayer became a performance in their house.
They are not lost because the world deceived them —
they are lost because the church at home betrayed them.
Parents forget:
You are the first pastor your child will ever know.
Your home is their first church.
Your words are their first Bible.
Your example is their first sermon.
If you live in hypocrisy,
you disciple your children in deceit.

The Family God Designed

God never designed families to be prisons of jealousy and rivalry.
He designed them to be **altars of truth, forgiveness, and love.**
The family was meant to be a picture of Heaven —
a place where the father leads in righteousness,
the mother nurtures in grace,
and the children grow in faith and unity.
The home should be a training ground for holiness,
not a theater for hypocrisy.
It should echo with prayer, not arguments.
It should radiate forgiveness, not bitterness.
It should host the Holy Spirit, not hidden hatred.

> "How good and pleasant it is when brothers dwell together in unity." — *Psalm 133:1*

The Cost of Parental Pretense

Every lie parents live teaches their children that truth is flexible.
Every fight ignored becomes a seed of division in their hearts.
Every unresolved wound becomes a generational curse.
When a father cheats, his son may justify it tomorrow.
When a mother manipulates, her daughter may repeat it in her marriage.

When parents fake holiness, their children lose faith in all holiness.
The enemy does not need to attack the Church from outside
when he already lives comfortably in families that wear masks.

The Call to Repentance and Restoration

But God is merciful — and **it is not too late**.
He can heal the broken home and restore the lost generation.
It begins when parents stop pretending.
When fathers confess instead of cover.
When mothers forgive instead of accuse.
When families gather, not to argue, but to pray.
Repentance opens the door that hypocrisy closed.
Truth invites the Holy Spirit back where He was grieved.
And when truth reigns, peace returns.

> "If we confess our sins, He is faithful and just to forgive us and to cleanse us from all unrighteousness." — *1 John 1:9*

Final Reflection

A double life produces double pain.
A fake home produces real wounds.
But a truthful home invites real healing.
Parents, if you want your children to know God — **live like Him.**
Let them see you love when you're hurt.
Let them see you pray when you're weak.
Let them see you humble when you're wrong.
Because the greatest sermon your children will ever hear
is not the one you preach —
it's the one you **live.**
Let the home return to truth.
Let the family altar burn again.
Let the Spirit of God find a dwelling where hypocrisy once lived.
Then your children will not just carry your name —
they will carry **your legacy of truth.**

Sibling Against Sibling — When Family Becomes a Battlefield of Hypocrisy

The family was meant to be a garden of love,
but for many, it has become a battlefield of envy, rivalry, and betrayal.
The blood that should bind now bleeds with bitterness.
The home that should unite now divides.
Jealousy has entered where joy once lived,
competition where compassion once dwelt,
and hypocrisy has built a throne where humility should reign.

The Ancient Pattern of Family Betrayal

From the beginning of time, the spirit of division has sought to destroy families.

Cain rose against Abel — not because Abel wronged him,
but because Abel's righteousness exposed his hypocrisy.
Joseph's brothers sold him — not to survive, but because envy blinded their love.
Absalom betrayed David — not because David hated him,
but because pride turned a son into a usurper.
The same spirit still walks among us.
It whispers in families, saying:
"Compare yourself to your brother."
"Compete with your sister."
"Covet what they have."
And when those whispers are entertained,
families that once prayed together begin to plot against each other.

> "A man's enemies will be the members of his own household." — *Matthew 10:36*

The Hypocrisy of Family Unity

Many families pretend to be united when they are secretly divided.

They smile together in photos but glare at each other in silence.
They celebrate birthdays together but curse one another in private.
They gather for funerals but scatter in life.
They say, "We are one blood," but their hearts have dried of mercy.
Brothers sabotage each other's progress out of envy.
Sisters gossip about each other to feel superior.
Uncles manipulate inheritance.
Parents take sides, breeding bitterness in the next generation.

They call each other "family," but in truth they are competitors wearing the same last name.

Their love is conditional — as long as interests align.
Their loyalty is temporary — as long as benefits last.
This is the hypocrisy that kills the family altar —
when people pretend to care but secretly compete,
when they speak blessings but plan betrayal.

The Curse of Jealousy

Jealousy is the root of most family destruction.

It poisons the heart, blinds the mind, and corrupts relationships.
It makes a man rejoice in his brother's failure
and mourn at his success.
It turns blessings into burdens, and relationships into rivalries.
The devil uses jealousy as his favorite weapon in the home.
He used it to make Cain kill Abel,
to make Joseph's brothers sell him,
to make Miriam speak against Moses.
And today, that same spirit whispers in families:
"Why him? Why her? Why not you?"
But love rejoices when others are lifted.
True family celebrates another's success as their own.

> "For where envy and strife exist, there is confusion and every evil work." —*James 3:16*

The Hypocrisy of Inheritance

One of the greatest tests of truth in a family is money — especially inheritance.

How many families have been torn apart after a funeral?

How many brothers no longer speak because of property?

How many sisters no longer visit because of greed?

They once prayed together when the father was alive,
but when he died, the mask came off.

They fight not for love, but for land.

They fight not for unity, but for possessions.

They honor the dead in words but dishonor him in actions.

They forget that the same soil that holds their father's body will one day hold theirs.

And the wealth they fight for will be inheritted by strangers when they are gone.

> "For what shall it profit a man if he gains the whole world,
> and loses his own soul?" — *Mark 8:36*

When Parents Favor and Families Fracture

Favoritism is another seed of hypocrisy.

When parents love one child more than another,
they create wounds that last generations.

Isaac loved Esau, Rebekah loved Jacob — and deception entered their tent.

Jacob loved Joseph more than his brothers — and hatred filled their hearts.

Parents who favor one child feed the serpent of jealousy.

And children who live in comparison grow with broken identity.

Favor breeds competition, and competition breeds rebellion.

God is a Father who loves without partiality.

He blesses each child uniquely, not equally — for His gifts are different but divine.

Parents must learn to reflect His heart, not their preferences.

The Path to Family Healing

There can be no peace where there is pretense.
There can be no healing where there is hatred.
There can be no unity where there is unforgiveness.
Family healing begins when truth replaces pretense.
When we stop pretending and start repenting.
When brothers stop competing and start confessing.
When sisters stop gossiping and start praying.
When parents humble themselves and lead with love again.
True family is not built on blood alone —
it is built on truth, humility, and forgiveness.

> "If it is possible, as much as depends on you,
> live peaceably with all men." — *Romans 12:18*

Final Reflection

A family that prays together but plots against each other
is not a family — it is a performance.
But a family that forgives, confesses, and humbles itself before God
becomes a fortress no devil can penetrate.
Let the home return to truth.
Let brothers embrace again.
Let sisters rejoice again.
Let parents lead again.
Let love reign again.
For when love reigns, hypocrisy dies.
And when truth returns, Heaven visits the home.

> "Behold, how good and how pleasant it is
> for brothers to dwell together in unity." — *Psalm 133:1*

How Hypocrisy Kills Trust and Peace at Home

Every home stands on two sacred pillars: **truth** and **trust**.

Truth is the foundation; trust is the roof.

When truth collapses, the roof falls — and when the roof falls, peace cannot survive.

A house built on lies may look beautiful, but it cannot stand the storm.

Every secret becomes a crack in its walls,

and every pretense becomes a leak that slowly destroys its strength.

When Truth Dies, Peace Follows

When a husband lies to his wife, he kills her security.

She no longer feels safe, not because the house is small,

but because the truth has left its walls.

When a wife deceives her husband, she destroys his confidence.

He no longer trusts her love — he questions her loyalty.

When children hide from their parents,

the connection that once made the home warm becomes cold.

The laughter disappears, replaced by suspicion and silence.

A family without honesty becomes a house of strangers.

Everyone speaks, but no one listens.

Everyone smiles, but no one feels seen.

Everyone lives together, but no one belongs.

> "The work of righteousness will be peace,
>
> and the effect of righteousness will be quietness and assurance forever." — *Isaiah 32:17*

When families lose righteousness, they lose peace.

When they lose peace, they lose joy.

And when joy is gone, love dries up — and relationships become mechanical.

The Masked Atmosphere

Hypocrisy changes the atmosphere of a home.

It replaces warmth with suspicion, intimacy with distance, peace with pressure.

Everyone starts performing.

The husband acts strong while secretly wounded.

The wife acts calm while quietly resentful.

The children act happy while deeply confused.

The home turns into a theater of survival —
where people wear smiles to hide pain,
say "I'm fine" when they are breaking,
and act united while silently divided.

A hypocritical home is not peaceful — it is **pretending**.

The laughter becomes noise, the hugs become hollow,
and the prayers become powerless.

God cannot dwell in an atmosphere of lies.

The Holy Spirit is the Spirit of Truth — where there is deception, He departs.

The Invisible War

A family that lives in lies becomes its own enemy.

They stop fighting the devil and start fighting each other.

They start defending their image instead of healing their hearts.

They become more concerned with *looking godly* than *being godly*.

Everyone walks on eggshells.

Every conversation is careful.

Every silence is heavy.

Every word is weighed, not for truth, but for image.

That is not peace — that is **pressure**.

And where pressure replaces prayer, the family breaks.

The Spiritual Root of Broken Trust

Hypocrisy does not begin in the mouth; it begins in the heart.

It is born when we start fearing people more than we fear God.

When we want approval more than transformation.

When we prefer reputation over repentance.

That spirit moves from one heart to another until the whole home is infected.

It turns honest people into actors,

and loving homes into cold hotels where no one stays by heart.

You cannot have **divine peace** in a home that hides the truth.

Peace is the fruit of righteousness — not the reward of pretending.

> "The Lord detests lying lips, but He delights in people who are truthful." — *Proverbs 12:22*

The Path to Restoration

Peace does not return through pretending everything is fine.

It returns through confession, humility, and forgiveness.

It starts when a husband says, "I was wrong."

When a wife says, "I forgive you."

When children say, "We want to start again."

Confession breaks the walls that hypocrisy built.

Truth invites the Holy Spirit back into the home.

Forgiveness cleanses the wounds that lies created.

When families start walking in truth again,

peace becomes their portion,

joy becomes their song,

and God's presence becomes their protection.

Final Reflection

You cannot fake peace.

You can decorate your home with crosses,

but if Christ is not the center, the cross becomes decoration, not salvation.

Truth is costly, but lies are deadly.

One exposes you; the other destroys you.

If you want peace to reign in your home,

choose truth, no matter how painful.
Because only truth heals,
only truth unites,
and only truth invites the Prince of Peace to dwell within.

"Blessed are the pure in heart, for they shall see God." — *Matthew 5:8*

Rebuilding Truth on the Family Altar

But there is **hope** — even for broken homes and divided hearts.

No family is too wounded for the healing power of God.

No marriage is too cold for His fire to reignite.

No child is too far gone that truth cannot find them again.

God can rebuild any family that is willing to remove the mask and return to the truth.

He does not rebuild with appearances; He rebuilds with repentance.

He does not start with the walls; He starts with the hearts.

> "Unless the Lord builds the house, they labor in vain who build it." — *Psalm 127:1*

The True Altar Is the Heart

The altar of the family is not the dining table or the couch — **it is the heart.**

If the hearts are healed, the home will heal.

If truth returns, trust will return.

If prayer returns, peace will return.

A home without truth is a building without foundation.

A home without prayer is a body without breath.

But a home where truth and prayer dwell together
becomes a **living sanctuary** — a place where Heaven and earth meet.

> "If we walk in the light as He is in the light,
> we have fellowship with one another." — *1 John 1:7*

Where Hypocrisy Dies and Truth Is Reborn

The family altar is the place where **hypocrisy dies** and **truth is reborn.**

It is where masks fall and mercy rises.

It is where secrets lose their power,
where pride bows to humility,
and where bitterness melts under the flame of forgiveness.

At the family altar,

husbands stop pretending and start leading,
wives stop complaining and start praying,
children stop rebelling and start listening.
It is the place where every wound finds healing,
and every lie loses authority.
When a family kneels together, the devil loses his seat.

From Performance to Prayer

Families must learn to **pray together again**, not perform together.
Prayer is not a show — it is a surrender.
You do not impress God by how you speak;
you move Him by how you repent.
They must learn to **confess sins**, not hide them.
To **speak truth in love**, not gossip in bitterness.
To **restore honor**, not demand perfection.
Because prayer without repentance is noise,
and worship without truth is hypocrisy.
When families pray honestly, Heaven listens attentively.
When families walk in light, darkness loses its grip.
And when truth reigns, love becomes easy.

The Restoration of Roles

Every home has divine order:
Fathers must lead in truth.
Mothers must nurture in truth.
Children must grow in truth.
A father who walks in righteousness becomes a shelter for his family.
A mother who lives in purity becomes a well of wisdom for her children.
And children raised in honesty become the generation that restores the land.
Truth must not only be spoken — it must be **lived.**
Because what parents live, children will inherit.

"Train up a child in the way he should go,

and when he is old he will not depart from it." — *Proverbs 22:6*

The Fire of the Family Altar

When truth burns again on the family altar,
the presence of God fills the home.
Forgiveness replaces pride.
Understanding replaces suspicion.
Peace replaces performance.
The Word of God becomes the family's foundation,
and love becomes its language.
In that home, anger cannot dwell long,
bitterness cannot find room,
and hypocrisy cannot survive.
Because where there is truth, there is light.
Where there is light, there is life.
And where there is life, **there is God.**

Final Reflection

The healing of nations begins with the healing of families.
And the healing of families begins with the return of truth.
If the father kneels, the family will stand.
If the family prays, the house will shine.
If the house walks in truth, Heaven will dwell within.
Let every family rebuild its altar —
not of stone, but of sincerity;
not of ritual, but of repentance;
not of habit, but of holiness.
Then the home will once again become what God designed it to be:
a reflection of **Heaven on earth**,
a dwelling place for **truth, peace, and love** —
where Christ Himself reigns as the unseen Head of the house.

"As for me and my house, we will serve the Lord." —*Joshua 24:15*

A Prayer for Families

Lord, heal our homes.

Burn away the masks we have worn for too long.
Forgive us for pretending to love while hiding hatred.
Cleanse our marriages from lies and pride.
Deliver our families from jealousy and division.
Restore the altar of truth and worship in every house.
Let Your peace reign again,
and let our homes become places where Your presence dwells.

> "Unless the Lord builds the house, those who build it labor in vain." — *Psalm 127:1*

Key Scriptures:

- *Romans 12:9* — Let love be without hypocrisy
- *Mark 3:25* — A house divided cannot stand
- *Matthew 10:36* — Enemies in your own household
- *Isaiah 32:17* — The work of righteousness is peace
- *1 John 1:7* — Walk in the light, have fellowship
- *Psalm 127:1* — Unless the Lord builds the house

Chapter 6: The Mask of Hypocrisy in Friendship

**Friendship was meant to be a gift from God —
a reflection of His love, loyalty, and faithfulness.
But in this generation, true friendship has become rare.
Many call you "brother" or "sister,"
but their hearts are far from yours.
They smile to your face but plot behind your back.
They walk with you in peace but wait for the day of your fall.**

**We are living in an age where friendship has become a tool, not a covenant.
People no longer love; they use.**

**They draw close not because of who you are,
but because of what you can give.
And when your usefulness ends, so does their loyalty.**

**This is the mask of hypocrisy in friendship —
where words are sweet but intentions are sour,
where hands embrace but hearts compete,
where promises are spoken but never meant.**

The Bible says,

**"Faithful are the wounds of a friend,
but deceitful are the kisses of an enemy." — *Proverbs 27:6***

**Today, many people are surrounded by "friends"
who kiss like Judas —
friends who praise you in public but poison you in private,
friends who clap for you while secretly hoping you fail,
friends who listen to your pain but share it with others for entertainment.**

**True friendship has become a performance,
a relationship of convenience instead of covenant,
a playground for hypocrisy instead of a foundation for love.**

But the Word of God still calls us back to truth:

**"A friend loves at all times,
and a brother is born for adversity." — *Proverbs 17:17***

**Real friendship is not built on gain but on grace.
It does not change with circumstances.
It stands firm when the crowd leaves.
It speaks truth when silence would be easier.
It protects, not pretends.
It prays, not plots.
It lifts, not laughs when you fall.**

This chapter will unveil the deception that hides behind smiles,
the pain caused by betrayal,
and the beauty of loyal friendship rooted in Christ.

For in a world full of false companions,
God is raising a remnant of true friends —
friends who love from a pure heart,
walk in light,
and mirror the faithfulness of Jesus,
the Friend who never betrays.

The Disguise of Loyalty

Once, **friendship was sacred** — a covenant of hearts joined by truth, sealed by loyalty, and strengthened by love.

In the beginning, friendship reflected the very nature of God Himself.

Jonathan loved David "as his own soul" (*1 Samuel 18:1*),

and Jesus called His disciples "friends," saying,

> "Greater love has no one than this, than to lay down one's life for his friends." —*John 15:13*

True friendship was not built on benefit, but on **sacrifice.**

It was not measured by what you could receive, but by what you were willing to give.

It stood firm in times of trouble, and it rejoiced in the truth even when truth hurt.

But in our generation, that sacred bond has been **corrupted.**

The spirit of hypocrisy has entered the realm of friendship,

turning love into leverage and loyalty into a disguise.

Many no longer love — **they use.**

Many no longer protect — **they expose.**

Many no longer walk together in light — **they conspire together in darkness.**

The word *"friend"* has lost its meaning because it has lost its truth.

The Masked Friend

Behind many smiles are swords.

Behind many handshakes are hidden daggers.

Behind many sweet words are deadly motives.

What used to be genuine connection has become calculated manipulation.

People call you "friend" not because they value you,

but because they can benefit from you.

They show loyalty when you are strong,

but disappear when you are weak.
They sing your praises in public,
but whisper your flaws in private.
They walk beside you, not out of love, but out of convenience.
Such loyalty is not love — it is **strategy.**
It is the same loyalty Judas showed when he followed Jesus with a kiss.

"Judas, do you betray the Son of Man with a kiss?" — *Luke 22:48*

The kiss was not affection — it was a signal of betrayal.
And today, many people still kiss to betray,
using the appearance of friendship to deliver others into the hands of pain.

When Friendship Becomes a Transaction

Friendship has become a **marketplace** where loyalty is traded for advantage.
Many stay close as long as they profit.
Many support you as long as you shine.
But when you stumble, they sell your story for sympathy.
When you fall, they share your failure like gossip, not grief.
Their loyalty lasts only as long as the benefits do.
Their love is conditional,
their words rehearsed,
their hearts divided.
This is not friendship — it is **performance.**
And God is exposing these counterfeit loyalties,
for He is tired of masks being worn in His name.

The Pain of Betrayal

The deepest wounds are not inflicted by enemies,
but by friends who turned into strangers.
David cried,

"It was not an enemy who reproached me; then I could have borne it.

> But it was you, a man my equal, my companion, my acquaintance.
>
> We took sweet counsel together and walked to the house of God in the throng." — *Psalm 55:12–14*

Betrayal from an enemy is attack.
Betrayal from a friend is heartbreak.
It shatters trust, wounds identity, and poisons peace.
It makes you question every smile, every word, every gesture.
And that is exactly what Satan wants —
to destroy divine connections by turning loyalty into deceit.

True Loyalty Is Born in Truth

Loyalty that hides lies is not loyalty — it is deception.
Loyalty that covers sin is not love — it is compromise.
True loyalty is not silence in evil,
but courage in truth.
A true friend does not flatter — he **warns.**
He does not gossip — he **guards.**
He does not compete — he **compliments.**
He does not leave when you are broken — he **kneels beside you in prayer.**

> "A friend loves at all times, and a brother is born for adversity." — *Proverbs 17:17*

Godly friendship is a reflection of divine loyalty —
the kind that does not change with seasons or circumstances.
It stands in the storm.
It speaks truth even when it hurts.
It prays when others mock.
It believes when others doubt.

Final Reflection

The world is full of **false friends,**

but Heaven still calls for **faithful ones.**
True friendship is not found in those who admire you,
but in those who correct you in love.
Not in those who clap for your success,
but in those who help you when you fall.
Not in those who talk about you,
but in those who talk to God for you.
Let every believer examine their circle:
Are your friends partners in truth or actors in disguise?
Do they lift you toward God, or lead you into sin?
Do they love you for who you are, or for what you have?
It is time to remove the masks of fake loyalty
and restore the beauty of **true friendship** —
friendship rooted in honesty, humility, and holiness.
Because in a world full of Judas kisses,
God is still looking for Jonathans —
friends who will love beyond benefit,
stand beyond convenience,
and remain loyal beyond this life.

When Friendship Becomes a Trap

The greatest pain in life does not come from your enemies —
it comes from your **friends**.
Enemies attack you from a distance,
but friends wound you from within.
Enemies fight your position,
but friends betray your trust.
David cried out,

> "If an enemy were insulting me, I could endure it;
> if a foe were rising against me, I could hide.
> But it is you, a man like myself,
> my companion, my close friend." — *Psalm 55:12–13*

Betrayal is not born in the mouths of enemies —
it grows in the hearts of those you once embraced.
It is not the knife that hurts the most,
but the hands that held it — hands you once held in prayer,
hands that clapped for you, hands you thought were clean.

The Pain of Betrayal

Betrayal hurts deeper because it comes **after trust.**
It is the wound that only those closest to you can inflict.
You shared your heart, your struggles, your victories —
and they used them as weapons.
You prayed with them,
but later discovered they were praying *against* you.
We live in a world where:

- The one you lifted up can later step on you.
- The one you defended can later accuse you.
- The one you helped rise can later rejoice at your fall.
- The one you called "friend" can later call you "enemy."

The tragedy of this generation is not the **lack of friendship**,
but the **abundance of fake ones**.
People no longer look for hearts to love — they look for ladders to climb.
They draw close, not out of care, but out of curiosity.
They celebrate you publicly but compete with you privately.
They pretend to listen, but only to collect information —
not to help you heal, but to use it against you later.

> "Even my close friend, someone I trusted,
> one who shared my bread, has turned against me." — *Psalm 41:9*

The Spirit of Betrayal

The same spirit that entered Judas still walks today.
It hides in smiles.
It speaks in kindness.
It serves beside you while secretly planning your fall.
Judas was not a stranger — he was a disciple.
He walked with Jesus, ate with Him, listened to Him,
and yet he sold Him for thirty pieces of silver.
He did not attack from outside — he kissed from inside.
That is how the spirit of betrayal operates:
It pretends loyalty to gain access.
It studies your weaknesses to exploit them.
It acts close enough to wound you where you are most vulnerable.

The Trap of False Friendship

Friendship becomes a **trap** when loyalty is fake and intentions are hidden.
It becomes a snare for your soul —
a place where you are disarmed by trust and destroyed by deceit.
Many have been ruined not by strangers,
but by those they called *"brother," "sister," "best friend."*
It is easy to guard yourself from an enemy,
but almost impossible to guard yourself from hypocrisy.
Fake friends are like shadows —

they follow you in light but disappear in darkness.
They are like actors — loyal in scenes, faithless behind the curtain.
They say "I'm with you" until standing with you costs them something.
They offer comfort in words but bring chaos in deeds.
This is the **mask of hypocrisy in friendship** —
to stand beside someone with your lips,
but to stand against them in your heart.
To say "I love you" while secretly envying them.
To call them "family" while plotting their fall.
To pretend to support while waiting for their collapse.

The Subtle Poison of Jealousy

At the root of false friendship lies **jealousy** —
a poison that disguises itself as care.
Jealousy makes people smile at your success
but secretly grieve when you prosper.
It turns admiration into rivalry and closeness into competition.
Cain was not far from Abel — he was his brother.
But jealousy turned brotherhood into bloodshed.
And even today, jealousy still kills silently —
not always with weapons, but with words, gossip, and withdrawal.
A jealous friend is more dangerous than a declared enemy
because they fight you while pretending to celebrate you.
They sabotage while smiling.
They destroy while disguising.

The Call for Discernment

Not every hand that helps you is holy.
Not every listener is loyal.
Not every smile means support.
Discernment is the only shield against the deception of false friendship.
Jesus knew Judas' heart and still called him "friend" —
not because He was blind,
but because His purpose was greater than the betrayal.

You must also learn to walk in **love with wisdom**,
to forgive without being foolish,
and to trust God more than men.

> "Be wise as serpents and harmless as doves." — *Matthew 10:16*

Final Reflection

Friendship without truth becomes a trap.
Loyalty without love becomes manipulation.
And connection without discernment becomes destruction.
Guard your heart.
Do not let betrayal make you bitter — let it make you wiser.
Do not stop loving — just love with light.
Do not stop trusting — just trust with discernment.
The wounds of betrayal may break your heart,
but they also open your eyes.
They teach you to depend less on people and more on God.
For He alone is the **Friend who never deceives, never abandons, never betrays.**

> "There is a friend who sticks closer than a brother." — *Proverbs 18:24*

The Friend Who Betrayed the Son of God

Even **Jesus**, the perfect and sinless Son of God,
was not spared the pain of **false friendship**.
He walked among twelve men whom He called, taught, and loved.
He shared His heart with them, washed their feet,
ate with them, prayed for them, and trusted them with the mysteries of the Kingdom.
Yet among those twelve was one who wore a **mask** — **Judas Iscariot**.
He looked like a disciple,
spoke like a disciple,
worked miracles like a disciple,
but his heart was not with the Master.
He followed Jesus, not for truth, but for **treasure**.
He listened to Jesus' words, but his soul listened to **Satan's whispers**.

"He walked with the Master but never knew His heart."

The Kiss of Deception

When Judas came to the garden that night,
he did not come with open confession — he came with a **kiss**.
The very symbol of affection became a **signal of betrayal.**

"Now His betrayer had given them a sign, saying,
'Whomever I kiss, He is the one; seize Him.'" — *Matthew 26:48*

He kissed Jesus — not as a gesture of love,
but as a **weapon of deception.**
And even in that moment of treachery,
Jesus, full of mercy, looked at him and said,

"Friend, why have you come?" — *Matthew 26:50*

That is how deep **hypocrisy** can go —
even the word *"friend"* can be used by a **traitor.**

Even the holy act of love can be turned into a tool of destruction.
Judas used the intimacy of friendship to deliver his Savior into the hands of sinners.
He sold the Son of God for **thirty pieces of silver** —
the price of a slave.
He betrayed eternal glory for temporary gain.

The Spirit of Judas Still Lives

Every generation has its **Judas**.
He walks beside you not to bless you, but to betray you.
He praises you in public but plots against you in private.
He calls you *"brother"* or *"sister"* while secretly competing with you.
He stays close, not to help you rise, but to watch you fall.
The spirit of Judas hides behind smiles,
camouflages itself with compliments,
and pretends loyalty while carrying the seeds of betrayal.
But Judas is not always outside the church —
sometimes, he sits in the choir, preaches from the pulpit,
or works beside you in ministry.
He knows the language of prayer but not the **life of truth**.
He knows the ways of religion but not the **ways of repentance.**

When Betrayal Becomes Prophecy

Yet, the betrayal of Judas did not destroy Jesus — **it revealed Him.**
What looked like the victory of deceit was the doorway to destiny.
Judas thought he was ending the mission,
but God was using his betrayal to **fulfill redemption.**

> "For the Son of Man goes as it has been determined." — *Luke 22:22*

Every false friend in your life has a divine expiration date.
Their betrayal cannot stop your purpose —
it only **pushes you closer** to it.

Their deception cannot cancel your anointing —
it only **purifies** it.
Their departure does not diminish you —
it **defines** you.
The cross was not the end of Jesus; it was His elevation.
And sometimes, God allows betrayal so that you can rise where loyalty could never take you.

Lessons from Judas

- **Not everyone who walks with you is for you.**
Some walk with you for what they can gain, not for what they can give.
- **Betrayal exposes hearts that flattery hides.**
When people show you who they truly are, believe them.
- **Don't curse your Judas — thank God for him.**
For his betrayal becomes your graduation.
It moves you from comfort to calling, from friendship to fulfillment.
- **Jesus still called Judas "friend."**
Not because Judas was loyal, but because Jesus was love.
Even betrayal could not change His nature.
He remained pure even when others were polluted.

Final Reflection

You may have your own Judas —
someone who walked with you but wounded you,
someone who smiled at you but sold you,
someone who claimed to love you but lied about you.
Do not let betrayal make you bitter; let it make you **better.**
Do not let pain make you close your heart; let it make you guard it with wisdom.
Do not fear betrayal — it cannot destroy your destiny.
It only **reveals** what God is protecting you from.
For every Judas that betrays,

there is a Peter who will repent,
and a John who will remain.
And above all, there is **Jesus** —
the Friend who will never betray,
never abandon, and never deceive.

"There is a friend who sticks closer than a brother." — *Proverbs 18:24*

The Spirit of Jealousy Among Friends

Many friendships today are **poisoned by jealousy** —

a silent killer that smiles to your face but stabs your joy in secret.

Jealousy is love contaminated, admiration corrupted, and loyalty infected.

It is the disease that turns friends into competitors,

partners into rivals, and brothers into enemies.

Instead of rejoicing in your success, some secretly wish for your failure.

Instead of praying for your growth, they plot against your peace.

They smile at your blessings but **celebrate your mistakes.**

They say "I'm happy for you," but their heart burns with envy.

Their lips speak encouragement while their spirit whispers resentment.

This is the same **ancient spirit** that entered **Cain** —

the spirit that cannot stand to see another **favored, blessed, or chosen.**

The Ancient Root of Jealousy

Jealousy did not begin in the world; it began in the heart of Lucifer.

He was once surrounded by light, beauty, and glory,

but instead of worshiping God, he wanted to **be God.**

And that same spirit was passed down to Cain,

who killed his own brother because he could not celebrate him.

> "And the Lord respected Abel and his offering,
> but He did not respect Cain and his offering.
> And Cain was very angry, and his countenance fell." — *Genesis 4:4–5*

Jealousy is the refusal to rejoice when God blesses another.

It is the anger of pride when Heaven smiles on someone else.

It is the unwillingness to accept that God can favor others without forgetting you.

When jealousy enters a heart, love leaves it.

It blinds you from seeing your own blessings

because you are too busy counting someone else's.

Joseph's Brothers — Love Turned Into Envy

When Joseph shared his dream, he saw **brothers**;
but his brothers saw **competition**.
He spoke with excitement; they listened with bitterness.
He was inspired by Heaven; they were influenced by hell.

> "Now Joseph had a dream, and he told it to his brothers; and they hated him even more." — *Genesis 37:5*

That is how the devil destroys friendships —
by turning **admiration into envy** and **love into rivalry**.
He whispers lies:
"Why not you?"
"Why them?"
"Why are they succeeding while you struggle?"
Soon, the friend who once celebrated you begins to criticize you.
The one who used to pray for you begins to compete with you.
The one who once held your hand now holds resentment in their heart.
Jealousy is the beginning of betrayal — it makes people trade love for comparison.

The Subtle Signs of Jealous Friends

Not all jealousy is loud — some of it is silent, polite, and well-dressed.
It hides behind smiles and compliments.
It disguises itself as advice but is rooted in resentment.
Be careful of friends who:

- Always want your **secrets**, but never share theirs.
- **Clap** when you are weak, but go **silent** when you are strong.
- **Comfort** you in sorrow, but **compete** with you in success.
- **Praise** you in public, but **criticize** you in private.
- **Borrow** your ideas, but **erase** your name from them.

Such people are not inspired by you — they are intimidated by you.

They do not want to be like you; they want to replace you.

They will walk with you only until your light begins to shine brighter than theirs.

> "Wrath is cruel and anger a torrent,
> but who is able to stand before jealousy?" — *Proverbs 27:4*

The Spiritual Cost of Jealousy

Jealousy kills not only friendships — it kills destinies.

It makes people lose focus on their calling
because they are busy chasing someone else's blessing.
Jealousy blinds you from gratitude,
steals your peace,
and turns your heart into a grave of bitterness.
That is why many gifted people remain small —
they waste their energy competing instead of growing.
They compare themselves instead of completing one another.

But true success in the Kingdom is not competition — it is **collaboration.**

When one rises, all are lifted.

The Purity of True Friendship

True friendship is never jealous — it celebrates your **elevation** and protects your **reputation.**

A real friend does not compete with you; they **cover** you.
They do not gossip about you; they **guard** you.
They do not envy your blessing; they **thank God** for it.
They do not imitate your calling; they **honor** it.

> "Rejoice with those who rejoice, and weep with those who weep."
> — *Romans 12:15*

Love and jealousy cannot live in the same heart.
Where love reigns, jealousy dies.

Where truth reigns, hypocrisy flees.
If you have a friend who celebrates your victory as their own, you have found a **treasure in a world of envy.**

Final Reflection

Jealousy is proof that the heart has lost sight of God's goodness.
It says, "What about me?" instead of "Thank You, Lord."
It focuses on others' blessings and forgets your own.
Ask God to deliver you — not from enemies,
but from friends who secretly envy what He is doing in your life.
And even more, ask Him to cleanse your own heart
from every root of jealousy and comparison.
Because true friendship is born not in competition,
but in **contentment** — the joy of seeing others rise without fear of falling behind.
May God raise a generation of **pure-hearted friends**
who love without envy, support without competition,
and remain loyal even when your light outshines theirs.

"Love does not envy." — *1 Corinthians 13:4*

Cibline Against Cibline: The Spirit of Betrayal Among Close Friends

Many friendships today resemble **Cain and Abel** more than **David and Jonathan**.

Brother against brother, sister against sister —
cibline against cibline, friend against friend —
destroying one another for **personal interest**.
What was once sacred trust has become selfish transaction.
What was once loyalty has turned into manipulation.
We now live in a world where those you helped to rise
use the same ladder to climb above you and then push you down.
Those you defended before others
are now the ones spreading your weaknesses behind closed doors.

"People you once trusted now use your words against you.
They borrow your trust, then spend it to buy your downfall."

They share your secrets not to **heal** you but to **humiliate** you.
They manipulate emotions to appear loyal
while quietly planting seeds of division behind your back.
They cry with you in public but laugh at you in private.
They hold your hand in the crowd but hold envy in their hearts.

The Spirit Behind Betrayal

This is not friendship — this is **witchcraft disguised as loyalty.**

For witchcraft is not only found in charms and spells;
it is found in **manipulation, deceit, and control**.
It is when someone pretends to love you in order to destroy you.
It is when emotional closeness becomes a spiritual weapon.
False friends are modern-day sorcerers —
they don't need potions; they use information.
They don't cast spells with words of enchantment;
they curse through gossip, flattery, and betrayal.

> "The words of a whisperer are like tasty morsels;
> they go down into the inmost parts of the body." — *Proverbs 18:8*

Their gossip is not mere talk — it is **spiritual poison.**

It spreads confusion, kills unity, and opens the door for demons of division.

The Hypocrisy of Emotional Friendship

These kinds of friends know how to **act** but not how to **love.**

They will comfort you in your tears but secretly rejoice that you're broken.

They will defend you before people but accuse you before others.

They will tell you, "I'm here for you,"
but their presence is the reason for your pain.
They love to be needed, but they hate to see you grow beyond them.
They love to hear your secrets, but they never reveal their own.
They love your vulnerability because it gives them control.
That is **the witchcraft of emotional hypocrisy** —
using love as a leash and loyalty as a lie.

True Friendship vs. False Friendship

True friendship builds; false friendship destroys.

True friendship corrects; false friendship deceives.

True friendship covers faults in love; false friendship exposes them in gossip.

A true friend does not use your weakness as a weapon.
He speaks truth even when it hurts,
and prays for you when everyone else walks away.
He will tell you the truth privately before defending you publicly.
He will bleed with you in your battle and celebrate you in your victory.

> "Faithful are the wounds of a friend,
> but the kisses of an enemy are deceitful." — *Proverbs 27:6*

Better one **honest friend** who tells you the truth,

than a hundred **hypocrites** who tell you what you want to hear.

The Cain and Abel Spirit in Modern Friendships

The spirit that made Cain kill Abel has not died — it has evolved.
It hides in false friendships.
It smiles in your face while sharpening the knife of envy.
It calls you "family" but secretly competes with your favor.
Cain could not celebrate Abel's offering; he envied it.
And so, instead of learning from his brother, he murdered him.
That same spirit today destroys ministries, teams, and homes.
Instead of learning from another's success,
many would rather **kill the source** of their conviction.

The Healing Truth

If you have ever been betrayed by a friend, do not lose heart.
Even Jesus had a Judas.
But remember — Judas could not stop His mission;
he only revealed His cross.
Likewise, betrayal cannot kill your destiny;
it only **refines** your discernment.
Every false friend you lose is a door God closes for your protection.
Learn from the wound, but don't live in it.
Forgive, but don't forget wisdom.
Pray for your betrayers, but guard your heart with discernment.

> "Keep your heart with all diligence,
> for out of it spring the issues of life." — *Proverbs 4:23*

Final Reflection

We are living in a generation of **performers**, not partners.
Many can share laughter but not loyalty.
Many can share secrets but not struggles.
Many can speak "brotherhood" while harboring jealousy.
But God is purifying friendships in this season.

He is removing counterfeits to reveal the authentic.
He is separating those who use you from those who are sent to you.
Let your circle be small, but let it be **real**.
Let your friendships be built not on emotions,
but on truth, prayer, and purpose.
Because in the end, one faithful friend in Christ
is worth more than a thousand flattering hypocrites.

"A friend loves at all times,
and a brother is born for adversity." — *Proverbs 17:17*

The Pain That Purifies

Betrayal hurts — but it also **purifies.**

It is one of the sharpest tools in God's refining fire.

It cuts deep, but it cleanses.

It wounds the heart, but it opens the eyes.

It breaks the illusion of false loyalty so that truth can finally breathe again.

God allows **false friends to leave** so that **true ones can remain.**

He allows deception to surface so that discernment can grow.

He allows the kiss of Judas to expose the faithfulness of John.

Because every **Judas** reveals who your **Peter** is.

Every betrayal uncovers who is truly standing by your side — and who was only standing in your shadow.

Betrayal as Heaven's Teacher

Every betrayal carries a lesson from Heaven.

It teaches you to depend on **God** more than on people.

It removes the idols of human affection and resets your focus on divine connection.

For as long as you trust people more than the Lord,

He will allow their words to fail you so that you may trust His Word instead.

When David was betrayed, he did not run to **revenge** — he ran to **God.**

He poured out his pain before the Lord and found peace in His presence.

He said,

> "It is good for me that I have been afflicted,
> that I may learn Your statutes." — *Psalm 119:71*

David understood that betrayal is not always a punishment — sometimes it is **promotion.**

God used betrayal to move him from the field to the throne.

If Saul had not hunted him, David might have never discovered his destiny.

Sometimes the pain of betrayal is the only sermon that can teach you discernment.

Sometimes God lets people betray you not to destroy you,

but to **deliver you** from depending on them.

Because some connections must break before your calling can bloom.

The Tears That Grow Wisdom

The **tears of betrayal** are not wasted — they water the soil of wisdom.

They cleanse your vision and deepen your prayer life.

You stop talking carelessly because you learn that not every ear is safe.

You stop sharing every dream because you realize not every heart is clean.

You stop chasing company because you discover the beauty of God's companionship.

Betrayal forces you to pray harder, listen longer, and trust slower.

It transforms your pain into perception, your wounds into watchfulness.

It does not make you bitter — it makes you **better** if you let God heal you.

The Blessing Hidden in Separation

Do not curse those who left you — **thank God they revealed themselves.**

Their exit was your **deliverance**.

Their betrayal was your **blessing in disguise**.

Because some people must leave for God's peace to enter.

Some friendships must die for your purpose to live.

Some "losses" are Heaven's way of pruning your circle to protect your destiny.

"They went out from us, but they were not of us." — *1 John 2:19*

It is better to walk alone with truth than to march with a crowd of lies.

Better to have solitude with peace than popularity with poison.

Better to cry in God's presence than to laugh in the company of deceivers.

The Refining Fire of Pain

Betrayal is a **refining fire.**

It burns the counterfeit from around you and the pride from within you.

It teaches you to see people as human, not as gods.

It purifies your love from dependency and replaces it with discernment.

What fire does to gold, betrayal does to the soul —

it removes impurities until only the authentic remains.

So do not despise the pain that purifies.

God is not punishing you; He is **perfecting** you.

He is teaching you to love wisely, to walk carefully, and to trust Him completely.

Final Reflection

If betrayal has visited your life,

do not let it harden your heart — let it **holy** your heart.

Do not let it drive you away from people — let it draw you closer to God.

You would rather **lose a friend** than lose your **peace.**

You would rather be **alone in truth** than surrounded by **liars in love.**

You would rather be **betrayed by man** than **abandoned by God.**

For every false friend that left,

God is preparing true ones who will love you in spirit and in truth.

He is replacing manipulation with ministry, and hypocrisy with holiness.

Let the pain purify you.

Let the tears teach you.

Let the betrayal build you.

Because when you come out of this fire,

you will not only be free — you will be **faithful, wiser, and unshakable.**

"After you have suffered a little while,

the God of all grace... will Himself restore, confirm, strengthen, and establish you." — *1 Peter 5:10*

The Need for Discernment and Spirit-Led Friendship

Not every friend is **sent by God** — some are **sent by the enemy.**
Not everyone who smiles at you is safe for you.
Not everyone who walks beside you walks with the same spirit.
Some are sent to **build**, others are sent to **break**.
Some come to **help your destiny**, others come to **harvest your secrets**.
That is why **discernment** is not optional; it is **spiritual survival**.
Discernment is not suspicion — it is **spiritual vision**.
Suspicion sees faces; discernment sees **spirits**.
Suspicion judges by words; discernment listens to **motives**.
The Holy Spirit reveals hearts that human wisdom cannot expose.
Before you open your heart to anyone,
ask the **Holy Ghost** to reveal their spirit.
He knows the truth behind the tone,
the heart behind the handshake,
and the intention behind the invitation.

"The Spirit searches all things,
yes, the deep things of God." — *1 Corinthians 2:10*

The Fruits Reveal the Root

True friends are not known by their **words**,
but by their **fruits**.

"You will know them by their fruits." — *Matthew 7:16*

Anyone can speak well, quote Scripture, and act kind for a season.
But time will always expose what spirit they carry.
A friend who gossips about others will one day gossip about you.
A friend who loves attention will compete for your spotlight.
A friend who lies to others will eventually lie to your face.
Do not measure friendship by charm — measure it by **character**.

Words can deceive; fruits cannot.
Look at what grows around a person's life:
Are their words producing peace or division?
Are their actions drawing you nearer to God or closer to sin?
Do they lift your faith or drain your fire?

The Purpose of Spirit-Led Friendship

A **Spirit-led friendship** is one that pushes you **closer to God**, not farther from Him.

A real friend prays with you, not preys on you.
They see your calling and protect it.
They see your weakness and cover it in love, not expose it in gossip.
They correct you in truth, not condemn you in pride.
If someone leads you into gossip, sin, jealousy, or pride —
that is not a friend, but a **trap**.
If someone discourages your prayer life,
despises your growth, or disrespects your calling,
they are not sent by God — they are an **agent of distraction**.

> "Do not be deceived: evil company corrupts good habits." — *1 Corinthians 15:33*

True friendship **strengthens your purpose**;
false friendship **weakens your soul**.
True friends remind you who you are in Christ;
false ones make you forget Him altogether.

The Spiritual Test of Friendship

Every friendship must pass the test of the Spirit.

You cannot discern with emotion what must be judged by revelation.
Ask the Holy Spirit:

- "Lord, is this connection covenant or convenience?"
- "Is this person assigned to my destiny or attached to my weakness?"

- "Are they a helper or a hindrance?

And when the Spirit reveals, obey.
Because keeping the wrong friend after God has exposed them
is the same as **inviting betrayal knowingly**.
Some friendships must end for your anointing to begin.
The closer you move toward your purpose,
the fewer people can walk with you —
not because you hate them,
but because your **calling requires clarity**.

The Gift of Divine Companionship

When you walk with God, He will surround you with the right people.
He will send **Jonathans** who protect you,
Elizabeths who confirm you,
and **Marys** who carry His presence beside you.
Spirit-led friends sharpen you, not shame you.
They do not feed your ego; they **fuel your fire**.
They do not compete with your grace; they **complement it**.
They see your flaws and still choose to love you in truth.

> "As iron sharpens iron, so a man sharpens the countenance of his friend." — *Proverbs 27:17*

Such friends are rare — they are Heaven's gift.
They don't just walk with you; they **walk you closer to Jesus**.

Final Reflection

In a world full of masks and manipulation,
pray for **Spirit-led friendships**.
Ask God to surround you with people who love truth more than comfort,
who love your soul more than your success,
and who love Christ more than your company.
Because when friendship is Spirit-led, it becomes sacred —

it becomes a channel of grace, not a tool of gossip;
a covenant of growth, not a contract of gain.
Let discernment guard your heart.
Let the Holy Spirit choose your circle.
And let your friendships glorify the One who called you.

"He who walks with the wise will become wise." — *Proverbs 13:20*l.

Rebuilding Trust and True Friendship

Though the world today is overflowing with **fake friends and masked loyalty**, God still sends **real ones** —

those who love purely, stand faithfully, and walk truthfully beside you.

He sent **Jonathan** to David when the king's jealousy sought his life.

He sent **Ruth** to Naomi when everyone else turned away.

He sent **Barnabas** to Paul when the apostles doubted his conversion.

These were not friends of convenience — they were friends of **covenant**.

They stood when others fled, believed when others doubted, and encouraged when others mocked.

Such friendships are rare, but they still exist —

not built on social media likes, shared interests, or personal gain,

but on **truth, love**, and **divine purpose**.

Becoming the Friend You Desire

To rebuild true friendship, we must first rebuild **truth within ourselves**.

We cannot attract what we are not.

If you want a loyal friend, be a loyal person.

If you want truth, walk in truth.

If you want love, love without hypocrisy.

> "Let love be without hypocrisy.
> Abhor what is evil; cling to what is good." — *Romans 12:9*

We must become the kind of friend we want to have.

Speak honestly, even when it's uncomfortable.

Love sincerely, even when it's not returned.

Forgive quickly, even when it hurts.

You cannot build lasting friendship on bitterness or pride.

You cannot walk in unity while hiding resentment.

When we walk in the light of truth, our relationships are purified from the shadows of deception.

Light exposes pretense and heals wounds that secrecy protects.

> "If we walk in the light as He is in the light,
> we have fellowship with one another." — *1 John 1:7*

The Foundation of True Friendship

True friendship is not about **frequency of communication** but about **purity of connection.**

It is not about how often you talk, but how deeply you care.

It is not about how much you get, but how much you give.

You can speak to someone every day and still not be close,

and you can speak rarely but remain deeply connected in spirit.

What binds friends together is not time — it is **truth.**

A friend who stands in your storm is worth more than a thousand who stand in your sunshine.

A friend who prays for you in secret is more valuable than one who praises you in public.

A friend who corrects you with love is greater than one who flatters you with lies.

> "A friend loves at all times,
> and a brother is born for adversity." — *Proverbs 17:17*

Let God Be the Center

All human friendship collapses when God is not at the center.

Without Him, relationships become **idols** or **illusions.**

When God is absent, betrayal is near;

when the Spirit is silent, confusion reigns.

True friendship is not just emotional — it is **spiritual.**

It is two hearts walking toward the same cross.

It is a bond sealed by faith, not by flesh.

Let God be the foundation of your friendships.

Pray together.

Seek truth together.

Forgive each other.

When Christ becomes the center, hypocrisy loses its power.

When both hearts are anchored in Him, even betrayal cannot destroy the bond.

> "Two are better than one, because they have a good reward for their labor.
> For if they fall, one will lift up his companion." — *Ecclesiastes 4:9–10*

Final Reflection

We live in a generation where **trust is broken** and **loyalty is rare**,
but God is still in the business of **restoring friendship**.

He can heal the wounds of betrayal and raise up relationships rooted in truth.

He can bring divine connections — people who sharpen your faith,
speak truth with love, and walk beside you through fire.

So do not give up on friendship.

Pray for it.

Live for it.

Be it.

For when friendship is born in God, it will last beyond this life —
because every friendship built on truth is a reflection of **Heaven's own love**.

> "By this all will know that you are My disciples,
> if you have love for one another." —*John 13:35*

A Prayer for True Friendship

Lord, deliver me from false friends and hypocritical hearts.

Expose the Judas that walks beside me and strengthen the Jonathans who stand with me.

Give me discernment to see beyond smiles and titles.

Teach me to love truthfully, to forgive quickly, and to guard my heart wisely.

Make me a friend after Your heart — loyal, pure, and faithful until the end.

> "He who walks with the wise will become wise,
> but the companion of fools will suffer harm." — *Proverbs 13:20*

Key Scriptures:

- *Psalm 55:12–13* — Betrayed by a close friend
- *Matthew 26:50* — Judas betrays Jesus with a kiss
- *Proverbs 27:6* — Faithful are the wounds of a friend
- *Proverbs 17:17* — A friend loves at all times
- *Matthew 7:16* — You will know them by their fruits
- *Proverbs 13:20* — Companion of fools suffers harm

Chapter 7: The Mask of Deception in the Workplace

When Ambition Replaces Integrity

**The workplace — once meant to be a place of service, diligence, and excellence — has become one of the greatest stages for hypocrisy and deception.
Behind the smiles of teamwork often hide motives of competition, jealousy, and self-promotion.
Many no longer work to serve with honesty; they work to be seen, praised, and promoted.
They wear the mask of diligence, but beneath it lies the hunger for status.
They act humble before their bosses but despise those beneath them.
They pretend loyalty, but in secret, they gossip, manipulate, and scheme for position.**

This is the mask of deception in the workplace — where people use kindness as strategy, not as character; where integrity is sacrificed on the altar of ambition; and where

success is measured not by faithfulness but by visibility.

In many offices and organizations today, truth has been replaced by politics.
People learn how to perform humility, not how to live it.
They praise publicly but plot privately.
They call others "team," but compete for every opportunity to rise.
They pretend to care for the company's mission, but in reality, their mission is themselves.

"A double-minded man is unstable in all his ways." —*James 1:8*

This spirit of double-mindedness rules modern workplaces.
It makes people wear two faces — one for management, another for their coworkers.
It rewards deception and punishes integrity.
It calls compromise "wisdom" and deceit "strategy."

But God sees beyond the résumé, beyond the politeness, beyond the performance.
He weighs hearts, not handshakes.
He measures motives, not meetings.
And He is still calling His children to shine in truth even in corrupt systems.

A true believer must not just work hard — he must work honestly.
He must not just show skill — he must show spirit-led integrity.
Because the light of Christ shines brightest where the shadows of deception grow darkest.

"Whatever you do, do it heartily, as to the Lord and not to men." — *Colossians 3:23*

In this chapter, we will expose how the spirit of hypocrisy operates in the workplace, how ambition corrupts the heart, how false loyalty destroys unity, and how believers can rebuild a culture of truth, excellence, and honor in the presence of God.

The Marketplace of Masks

The workplace — once a sacred ground of **service, teamwork, and honest labor** — has now become a **theater of performance.**

What used to be a place to build vision and character has turned into a stage where people act for survival and applause.

Today, **professionalism has replaced purity**, and **ambition has replaced authenticity**.

People wear **professional smiles** but hide **personal agendas**.
They speak the language of respect but harbor hearts full of rivalry.
They appear loyal until a better opportunity arises,
then quickly change sides like actors switching roles in a play.
We live in a generation where many work not out of **love**, but **ambition.**
They are driven not by **calling**, but by **competition.**
They strive not for **excellence**, but for **exposure.**
The workplace has become a **marketplace of masks** —
a place where manipulation is called management,
flattery is mistaken for teamwork,
and deceit is labeled as professionalism.
In this environment:

- **Managers manipulate** to maintain control.
- **Employees flatter** to gain promotion.
- **Colleagues pretend to support** while secretly sabotaging.

This is the **hypocrisy of the modern career world** —
where appearance is valued more than honesty,
and effort is celebrated more than motive.
People now polish their résumés more than their character.
They attend ethics seminars but ignore moral truth.
They speak about integrity in meetings yet betray it in decisions.

"The Lord detests differing weights,
but honest scales delight Him." — *Proverbs 11:1*

God's standard has not changed.
He still weighs the heart, not the performance.
He still honors truth over talent, and faithfulness over fame.
The **marketplace of masks** may reward deception for a time,
but Heaven never applauds hypocrisy.
For the eyes of the Lord run to and fro throughout the earth,
seeking not the most gifted worker, but the most genuine one —
those who work as unto Him, not unto men.

> "Whatever you do, work at it with all your heart,
> as working for the Lord, not for human masters." — *Colossians 3:23*

People Who Pretend to Be Good for Promotion

In many nations — especially in places of high opportunity like **America** — the **spirit of competition** has quietly replaced the **spirit of community**.

What used to be teamwork has turned into silent warfare.

What once was service has become self-promotion.

People appear kind, but their kindness is calculated.

They appear humble, but their humility is rehearsed.

They appear helpful, but their help hides hunger for recognition.

This is the new face of workplace deception — **strategic goodness.**

People no longer do what is right because it is righteous;
they do it because it looks profitable.

They smile at you because they need your recommendation.

They assist you because they want to be noticed.

They act loyal because they want to rise above you.

Their goodness is not born of love — it is born of **ambition.**

Their service is not from sincerity — it is **strategy.**

They speak kindly when supervisors are near but complain when backs are turned.

They act honest when being watched but careless when unseen.

> "The eyes of the Lord are in every place,
> keeping watch on the evil and the good." — *Proverbs 15:3*

A System That Rewards Deception

The danger in this generation is that this **deception is often rewarded.**

Supervisors promote those who **perform** well outwardly,
not realizing that inwardly, they are proud, deceitful, and manipulative.

The system honors **results**, not **righteousness.**

It crowns **cleverness**, not **character.**

It celebrates **image**, not **integrity.**

In such systems, honesty becomes a disadvantage,
and pretense becomes a profession.

But Heaven does not evaluate as men do.
God's promotion does not depend on politics or performance — it depends on **purity of heart**.

> "Do not be deceived: God is not mocked.
> Whatever a man sows, that shall he also reap." — *Galatians 6:7*

You may fool your boss, your coworkers, and even your church,
but you cannot fool the **God who watches the motives of your heart**.
He sees through every résumé, every smile, and every "God bless you."
He knows who you are when the lights go off and the crowd disappears.

True Promotion Comes from God

Promotion built on pretense is only temporary.

It rises fast but collapses faster.

You can manipulate your way up the ladder,
but when God shakes it, your foundation will crumble.

True promotion is not earned by pretending; it is granted by **faithfulness.**

Joseph did not flatter Pharaoh — he **feared God**.

Daniel did not bow to men — he **stood in integrity**.

Esther did not scheme for the crown — she **submitted to purpose**.

Every true elevation in the Kingdom begins with humility before God, not hypocrisy before men.

> "For not from the east, nor from the west,
> nor from the desert comes exaltation,
> but it is God who judges;
> He brings one down, He exalts another." — *Psalm 75:6–7*

So, work with integrity even when unnoticed.
Serve with truth even when unrewarded.
For when Heaven promotes you, **no man can demote you**.

The Spirit of Deception in Career Culture

The **spirit of deception** has mastered the modern workplace.

It moves silently through meetings, boardrooms, and offices —
not with horns or flames, but with **smiles and strategy**.
It whispers,

> "Pretend to care. Pretend to listen. Pretend to agree — just make sure you win."

It trains people to perform instead of serve,
to please men instead of honor God,
to seek advancement at any cost, even at the expense of truth.
This spirit has made **many slaves of image and prisoners of pretense**.
They no longer measure success by obedience, but by **visibility**.

They no longer pursue excellence for **God's glory**, but for **human applause**.

They no longer serve from **calling**, but from **competition**.
They no longer labor from **the heart**, but from **ambition**.
The workplace that once celebrated diligence now rewards deception.
It teaches, "Say what they want to hear. Do what benefits you.
Keep your smile, hide your truth, and climb higher."
But the truth is: **every ladder built on lies eventually breaks.**

When Truth Becomes Dangerous

In such an environment, **honesty becomes dangerous** and **truth becomes offensive.**

Those who speak up for righteousness are labeled "difficult."
Those who refuse to play the game are mocked as "naïve."
Integrity is treated as weakness, and compromise is called wisdom.
But God still looks for Daniels in Babylon —
men and women who will stand for truth even if it costs their position.

He is looking for Josephs who will serve faithfully in prison before ever sitting in Pharaoh's palace.

He is searching for Esthers who will risk reputation for righteousness.

"Better is a poor man who walks in his integrity
than one who is perverse in his ways, though he be rich." — *Proverbs 28:6*

The world says, *"Protect your image."*
Heaven says, *"Protect your integrity."*
The world says, *"Do what it takes to rise."*
Heaven says, *"Humble yourself, and I will lift you up."*

False Success vs. True Promotion

The tragedy of deception is that it often looks like success.

You can lie your way into a position, but you cannot lie your way into peace.

You can manipulate people to open doors, but you cannot force God to keep them open.

Promotion that comes from manipulation is corruption,
and **success that comes from deceit is failure in Heaven's eyes**.

"For promotion comes neither from the east, nor from the west, nor from the south.

But God is the judge: He puts down one and exalts another." — *Psalm 75:6–7*

True promotion is not achieved — it is **entrusted**.
It is not earned through cunning — it is given through character.
It is not taken by deceit — it is received through obedience.
If **God does not promote you**,
then the world's promotion will **destroy you**.
But if God lifts you, no one can pull you down.
For what is built by men can fall by men,
but what is built by God stands forever.

Final Reflection

The spirit of deception in career culture is not just about lying —
it's about **living without truth**.
It's about pretending to serve while secretly striving.
It's about chasing titles instead of transformation.
But the Lord is calling His children to **be different** —
to be light in dark workplaces,
to be truth in deceptive systems,
to work not for eye-service, but for the glory of Christ.

> "Whatever you do, do it heartily, as to the Lord and not to men."
> — *Colossians 3:23*

Integrity may cost you recognition on earth,
but it will earn you **eternal reward in Heaven**.
Let the world chase applause — you chase **approval from God**.
For in the end, only truth will stand when the masks fall.

Competition Without Character

Workplaces today are **full of competition but empty of character.**

What once was meant to be a space of teamwork and shared purpose has turned into a battlefield of pride, comparison, and selfish ambition.

People no longer serve to contribute — they strive to **outshine**.

They no longer work to build others — they work to **beat** them.

Colleagues compete for **recognition instead of cooperation.**

They fight for **titles** but neglect **teamwork.**

They chase **numbers** but lose **compassion.**

They celebrate **achievements** but hide **exhaustion.**

They praise **hustle** but despise **humility.**

They post **motivational quotes** online but **mistreat people** offline.

This is the deception of modern success —
a **culture that looks driven but is spiritually dead.**

It rewards those who run fast, not those who run right.

It crowns those who perform, not those who persevere.

It glorifies achievement while ignoring the condition of the heart.

People **run fast but in the wrong direction.**

They climb the ladder of success
only to discover at the top that it was **leaning on the wrong wall.**

They rise in rank but fall in righteousness.

They gain influence but lose innocence.

They expand careers but shrink in character.

> "What will it profit a man if he gains the whole world
> and loses his own soul?" — *Mark 8:36*

What kind of victory is it if your job pays well but your conscience is bankrupt?

What kind of promotion is it if your title grows but your peace dies?

What kind of success is it if your light fades while your name shines?

If your job **costs your peace, your integrity, and your walk with God,**
it is not success — **it is slavery.**

Slavery to image, to money, to status, to self.
For the Lord did not call His children to chase crowns of gold,
but to carry crowns of glory.

True Greatness in God's Eyes

True greatness is not measured by position but by **purity**.
Not by how high you climb, but by how **low you kneel**.
Not by how much you gain, but by how much you give.
In Heaven's economy, character is currency.
Integrity is influence.
Faithfulness is fame.
And humility is the highest honor.

> "Humble yourselves before the Lord, and He will lift you up." — *James 4:10*

Let your ambition be **to please God**, not people.
Let your competition be **against your old self**, not your coworkers.
Let your drive be to finish your work with faith and truth.
For when the world applauds performance,
Heaven rewards **purity**.
When the world celebrates winners,
God crowns **the faithful.**

How Hypocrisy Kills Trust in the Workplace

A workplace without **truth** becomes a **toxic battlefield** dressed in professionalism.

Behind polite greetings and polished presentations often lies **a culture of pretense and distrust**.

People walk on eggshells, not because they lack skill, but because they lack **sincerity** around them.

When people **pretend to be kind but gossip behind your back**, **trust dies**.

When **leaders preach teamwork but exploit employees**, **loyalty vanishes**.

When **colleagues compete secretly**, **peace disappears**.

This is how **hypocrisy kills organizations** — not from external threats, but from **internal rot**.

It is not incompetence that destroys most teams; it is **dishonesty**.

The Culture of Pretending

In many offices, the atmosphere looks calm, but beneath the surface there is poison.

People **smile in meetings but hate each other in their hearts.**

They **praise ideas publicly but plot privately.**

They **share plans to appear collaborative** but later **steal credit** for themselves.

They **pretend unity for the report**, while **wishing secretly for others to fail**.

This is not teamwork — it is **theater**.

And the longer people act, the more exhausted they become.

Because performing goodness is harder than living it.

> "The integrity of the upright guides them,
> but the unfaithful are destroyed by their duplicity." — *Proverbs 11:3*

The Death of Trust

Every act of hypocrisy is a **blow to trust**.

Trust dies not when people make mistakes, but when they **lie about them**.

Trust dies not when goals are missed, but when **truth is manipulated** to hide failure.

Trust dies when words no longer match actions, and when promises become propaganda.

Once trust dies, fear takes over.

Employees fear speaking up.

Leaders fear losing control.

Colleagues fear sharing ideas.

Everyone becomes defensive, suspicious, and self-protective.

The result is **stress, burnout, anxiety, and frustration** —
because in a dishonest culture, everyone must perform to survive.

There is no peace in pretending.

There is no strength in secrecy.

And there is no unity where truth has been replaced by flattery.

The Spiritual Cost of Deception

When deceit becomes culture, God withdraws His favor.

Because **God does not dwell where lies lead.**

He blesses truth, not performance.

He delights in sincerity, not image management.

> "Lying lips are an abomination to the Lord,
> but those who deal truthfully are His delight." — *Proverbs 12:22*

A workplace that honors deceit may look prosperous for a while,
but its foundation is already crumbling.

Because any system built on hypocrisy will eventually collapse —
whether it is a **company**, a **church**, or a **nation**.

God designed work to be an act of **worship**, not manipulation.

Every task, every meeting, every decision is meant to reflect His truth and integrity.

But when people lie to impress men, they lose the blessing of Heaven.

Restoring Trust Through Truth

To rebuild a healthy workplace, we must first rebuild **truth**.

Leaders must model transparency.

Colleagues must choose honesty over flattery.

Teams must value integrity more than image.

Trust cannot be bought, forced, or faked — it must be **earned through truth**.

And no company, no ministry, no team can prosper
when deception becomes the language of its culture.
True strength is not found in the size of the organization,
but in the **sincerity of its people**.
For when truth returns, trust revives —
and where trust lives, God blesses.

> "Through love and faithfulness sin is atoned for;
> through the fear of the Lord evil is avoided." — *Proverbs 16:6*

Working for God, Not for Men: The Call to Integrity in Hidden Places

The true test of character is not how you act when people are watching,
but how you live when ***no one sees.***
Integrity is not proven in public applause —
it is proven in ***private obedience.***
Many work hard to impress supervisors, managers, and leaders.
They shine brightly in meetings but grow lazy in secret.
They act respectful when the boss is near but complain when he leaves.
They look faithful on reports but dishonest in reality.
This is not excellence — this is ***eye-service.***
The Bible warns against such hypocrisy:

> *"Servants, obey in all things your masters according to the flesh,*
> *not with eye-service, as men-pleasers,*
> *but in sincerity of heart, fearing God." — Colossians 3:22*

When you truly belong to God, your work becomes ***worship.***
Every task — from the smallest duty to the highest role —
is an opportunity to honor Him with excellence and honesty.
For the believer, the workplace is not just a job; it is a ***spiritual altar.***
Your diligence speaks louder than your words,
and your honesty preaches a sermon louder than your mouth ever could.

The Hidden Power of Faithful Work

God sees every moment of unseen labor.
He watches when you stay late to finish with integrity.
He records when you choose truth over comfort,
and when you keep your word even when it costs you.
He notes every time you refuse to lie for promotion,
and every time you choose righteousness over reward.
Heaven's promotion begins in hidden places.
Before David ever wore the crown, he was faithful in the fields.

Before Joseph ruled Egypt, he was trustworthy in prison.
Before Daniel influenced kings, he was consistent in prayer.
The path to divine elevation is paved with secret faithfulness.

> *"His master said to him, 'Well done, good and faithful servant;*
> *you have been faithful over a few things,*
> *I will make you ruler over many things.'" — Matthew 25:21*

Integrity in Corrupt Systems

Working in a corrupt environment is one of the greatest spiritual tests.
It's easy to compromise when everyone else is doing it.
It's easy to cut corners when dishonesty looks profitable.
But integrity is choosing righteousness even when it costs you reputation,
and trusting that ***God's reward is greater than man's recognition****.*
When others cheat, you tell the truth.
When others flatter, you stay humble.
When others play politics, you walk in peace.
You may not rise as fast, but you will rise ***securely****.*

> *"The integrity of the upright will guide them,*
> *but the perversity of the unfaithful will destroy them." — Proverbs 11:3*

Integrity may slow your promotion on earth,
but it will speed up your favor in Heaven.
You may be overlooked by men,
but you are being noticed by God.

The Reward of Hidden Righteousness

Every honest act is a seed in God's field.
You may not see the harvest immediately,
but it is growing in Heaven's time.
God promotes not just the skilled, but the sincere.
He lifts not just the talented, but the trustworthy.

*He honors not just the excellent, but the **ethical**.*
If you remain faithful when others fall,
God will use you as a light in the darkness of your workplace.
*He will make you an example of what it means to serve with both **competence and conscience**.*

> *"And whatever you do, do it heartily, as to the Lord and not to men,*
>
> *knowing that from the Lord you will receive the reward of the inheritance." — Colossians 3:23–24*

Final Reflection

*The world teaches us to work **for men**; the Kingdom calls us to work **for God**.*
*The world promotes based on talent; Heaven promotes based on **truth**.*
The world crowns the visible; God rewards the faithful.
So, in every task, big or small,
remember who your true Employer is.
You are not just an employee of a company — you are an ambassador of Heaven.
Your real performance review happens not in the boardroom,
but before the throne of God.
Work with integrity, speak with honesty, live with humility.
*For even when the world forgets, **Heaven remembers**.*

> *"Therefore, my beloved brethren, be steadfast, immovable,*
> *always abounding in the work of the Lord,*
> *knowing that your labor in the Lord is not in vain." — 1 Corinthians 15:58*

When Work Becomes Idolatry — The Danger of Worshiping Success Instead of God

*Work was created by God to be a **blessing**, not a **burden** — a sacred act of service and stewardship.*

In Eden, Adam worked in fellowship with God; his labor was worship.
*But when sin entered the world, man began to work **without God**,*
*and labor became **idolatry** instead of intimacy.*
*Today, many no longer serve through their work; they **bow** to it.*
Their jobs have become their gods.
Their offices have become their temples.
Their schedules have become their altars.
Their achievements have become their sacrifices.
They say with their lips, "God is first,"
*but with their lives, **career comes first**.*
They no longer ask, "What pleases God?" but "What advances me?"
They no longer seek the Kingdom, but promotions, pay raises, and positions.
*Their worth is no longer found in **who they are**, but in **what they do**.*

"You cannot serve God and mammon." — Matthew 6:24

The Subtle Idol Called Success

The idol of modern times is not carved in stone — it is written on contracts.

It hides behind good intentions, but it steals devotion from God.

People justify their obsession with words like "ambition," "progress," or "vision,"

but in reality, they are no longer driven by purpose — they are driven by pride.

They sacrifice prayer time for overtime.
They trade devotion for deadlines.
They replace family dinners with endless meetings.
They miss church for conferences and justify it as "networking."

They have time for clients but no time for Christ.
*They worship the god of **achievement**,*
*the god of **status**,*
*and the god of **security**,*
yet none of these gods can save them when life falls apart.

"Their idols are silver and gold,
the work of human hands.
They have mouths but do not speak,
eyes but do not see." — Psalm 115:4–5

The Lie of Endless Achievement

The spirit of idolatry tells you, "If you just work harder, you'll finally be fulfilled."
But it never tells you that your heart will still be empty.
It says, "Just one more promotion, one more project, one more success,"
but once you get there, it whispers again, "You need more."
*This is the deception of **career idolatry** —*
it feeds your ego while starving your soul.
It applauds your success while erasing your peace.
You may rise in rank, but you fall in rest.
You may gain the world's approval, but lose Heaven's presence.

"What will it profit a man if he gains the whole world
and loses his own soul?" — Mark 8:36

Success without God is failure in disguise.
Because the farther you climb without Him,
the harder your fall will be when the foundation cracks.

Balancing Work and Worship

*God is not against work; He is against **worshiping work**.*
He wants you to labor diligently, but with Him — not apart from Him.
He desires excellence, but not at the cost of your intimacy.
*He blesses effort, but not when effort replaces **obedience**.*
The Bible says,

> *"Seek first the Kingdom of God and His righteousness,*
> *and all these things shall be added to you." — Matthew 6:33*

When God comes first, everything else finds its place.
When your identity is rooted in Him, success will not corrupt you.
When your ambition is surrendered to Him, promotion will not blind you.
Let your job be an assignment, not your addiction.
Let your success be testimony, not temptation.
*Work hard, but **worship harder**.*
Pursue excellence, but never at the expense of eternity.

Restoring God to His Rightful Place

*To be free from the idol of work, you must **return to the altar of rest**.*
*Rest is not laziness — it is **trust**.*
It is the confession that God, not you, sustains your success.
It is the humility to say, "I am not my job. I am His child."
When you learn to rest, you prove your faith.
When you step away from work to worship, you show who your real Master is.
And when you give your career back to God, He gives your soul back to peace.

> *"Unless the Lord builds the house,*
> *those who build it labor in vain." — Psalm 127:1*

Work hard, but don't let work harden your heart.
Pursue success, but never let success possess you.
*Earn your bread, but never lose your **breath of prayer**.*
For a career without Christ is a crown without glory —
it looks bright for a moment but fades into dust.
*Let your greatest ambition be to **hear Him say**,*

> *"Well done, good and faithful servant." — Matthew 25:23*

That is the only promotion that lasts forever.

The Cost of Compromise — When Ethics Are Sacrificed for Success

Every generation faces a choice: ***to stand for truth or to bow to gain.***

In today's world, many have chosen gain.

They sacrifice integrity for income, holiness for hierarchy, and conscience for convenience.

They justify small lies to protect big positions.

They call dishonesty "strategy" and corruption "opportunity."

This is not wisdom — it is ***spiritual suicide*** *disguised as success.*

A man or woman who compromises their values for advancement
may rise quickly in the eyes of men,
but they fall silently in the eyes of God.

They gain promotions on earth but lose ***promotion in Heaven.***

> *"Better is the poor who walks in his integrity*
> *than one who is perverse in his ways, though he be rich." — Proverbs 28:6*

When you sell your soul for success,
you are not moving forward — you are ***trading eternity for a paycheck.***
For what you compromise to gain, you will eventually lose to regret.

Small Lies, Great Loss

Compromise rarely begins as rebellion — it begins as ***a small excuse.***

A little dishonesty in a report.

A silent approval of injustice.

A false compliment to win favor.

A manipulated number to meet a quota.

But each small compromise builds a pattern of corruption.

Soon, what once grieved your spirit becomes normal to your flesh.

Sin begins in inches but ends in miles.

And by the time you realize it, your heart has grown numb to conviction.

> *"Whoever is dishonest with very little will also be dishonest with much." — Luke 16:10*

A lie may help you today, but it will haunt you tomorrow.
It may build your image, but it will break your peace.
*You may hide it from your boss, but you cannot hide it from your **Judge**.*

The Fear That Feeds Compromise

Why do people compromise? Because they are afraid.
Afraid of losing their jobs.
Afraid of being rejected.
Afraid of being left behind.
But every time fear leads, faith leaves.
When fear becomes your master, deception becomes your method.
You start choosing survival over sanctification, comfort over conviction.
*But remember — **God is your provider, not your paycheck.***

> *"The Lord will perfect that which concerns me." — Psalm 138:8*

If God opened the door, no lie can keep it open.
If God gave the opportunity, no manipulation can improve it.
When you compromise for success, you declare that God is not enough.
But when you stand for righteousness, even in loss,
*you declare that **He alone is your source**.*

The Reward of Integrity

Integrity may cost you temporary opportunities,
*but it will guarantee you **eternal rewards**.*
When you stand for truth, you may lose a position,
but you gain Heaven's attention.
When you refuse to lie, cheat, or flatter,
God Himself becomes your promoter.

> *"For the Lord God is a sun and shield;*
> *the Lord bestows favor and honor.*

No good thing does He withhold
from those who walk uprightly." — Psalm 84:11

Righteousness may look slow, but it never loses.
The world promotes the clever, but God promotes the clean.
He may test your heart through delay,
but He will always reward your faith through destiny.
Joseph refused compromise in Potiphar's house,
and that integrity became the foundation of his influence in Pharaoh's palace.
Daniel refused to defile himself with the king's food,
and that purity opened the door to divine revelation.
When you honor God in private, He honors you in public.

Standing When Others Bow

We are living in a generation that calls compromise "wisdom"
and conviction "fanaticism."
But when everyone bows to the golden image of success,
God is looking for ***Shadrachs, Meshachs, and Abednegos*** *—*
those who will say, "Even if we lose everything, we will not bow."
If standing for truth costs you your job, remember:
you may lose a salary, but you will gain ***spiritual authority****.*
You may lose favor with men, but you will find ***favor with God****.*
And that favor is eternal.

"We must obey God rather than men." — Acts 5:29

Compromise is expensive — it costs your soul.
Integrity may cost you money, time, or recognition,
but compromise costs you ***peace, presence, and purpose****.*
The path of the righteous is narrow,
but it leads to honor that no man can manipulate.
Stand firm in truth, even when it's unpopular.
Do what's right, even when it's unrewarded.
Because when the world's applause fades,

only God's approval will matter.

> *"The righteous who walks in his integrity—*
> *blessed are his children after him!" — Proverbs 20:7*

The Christian Worker: Light in the System

God did not place His children in workplaces to **blend in with the crowd** — He placed them there to **shine as light**.

The workplace is not just a field of labor; it is a **field of testimony**.

Every task, every meeting, every assignment is an opportunity to reveal the character of Christ in a world drowning in compromise.

> "You are the light of the world.
> A city that is set on a hill cannot be hidden." — *Matthew 5:14*

As believers, we are called to work not for **eyes**, but for **eternity**.
Not for the applause of men, but for the approval of God.
Not to build careers that fade, but to build character that lasts.

> "Whatever you do, work at it with all your heart,
> as working for the Lord, not for men." — *Colossians 3:23*

The Mark of a True Christian Worker

A true Christian worker carries the fragrance of Heaven into the system of the world.

He does not just **speak of Christ** — he **shows Christ** through his conduct.

His light is not loud, but it is lasting.

- He is **honest**, even when honesty costs him promotion.
- He is **faithful**, even when no one is watching.
- He **shows up early**, not to impress his boss, but to **honor his God.**
- He **speaks truth**, even when truth risks his popularity.

- He **respects others**, not because of their position, but because he **fears God**.

Integrity is his uniform.
Excellence is his witness.
And humility is his secret strength.

Faithfulness Over Fame

You cannot represent Christ and live in **hypocrisy**.

You cannot preach **integrity on Sunday** and cheat the system on Monday.

You cannot pray for promotion while walking in **manipulation**.

You cannot say "God is my provider" while lying to protect your paycheck.

God does not promote **the clever** — He promotes **the clean**.

He does not bless **the strategic deceivers**, but **the sincere servants**.

He raises those who walk in truth when everyone else cuts corners.

He honors those who choose faithfulness over fame.

> "For the Lord detests the perverse but takes the upright into His confidence." — *Proverbs 3:32*

Every honest believer in a corrupt system becomes a **weapon of righteousness**.

Your consistency becomes conviction to the careless.

Your integrity becomes intercession for the impure.

Your example becomes a sermon louder than words.

The Mission of the Marketplace Believer

God's vision is not just to fill churches — it is to fill **the marketplace** with His presence.

He sends His children into schools, hospitals, offices, governments, and companies

to establish His Kingdom through **character and truth**.

You may never preach from a pulpit, but your desk can be an altar.

Your excellence can be a testimony.
Your patience can be a sermon.
Your humility can be a message of grace.
When others cheat to rise, you stay pure and trust God to lift you.
When others gossip, you guard your tongue.
When others compromise, you stand firm.

That is how **light overcomes darkness** — not through argument, but through example.

> "Let your light so shine before men,
> that they may see your good works
> and glorify your Father in heaven." — *Matthew 5:16*

The Christian worker is not called to survive the system,
but to **sanctify** it — to bring holiness where hypocrisy reigns.
You are God's ambassador in your workplace.
Your honesty is your ministry.
Your diligence is your worship.
Your excellence is your evangelism.
So do not lose your light trying to fit into darkness.
Do not trade your calling for comfort.
Work with joy, lead with humility, and serve with integrity.
For in the end, the Lord Himself will say:

> "Well done, good and faithful servant.
> You have been faithful over a few things;
> I will make you ruler over many things." — *Matthew 25:23*

Working With the Fear of God

The only true antidote to **workplace hypocrisy** is the **fear of God.**

Not fear as in terror, but **holy reverence** — the awareness that God sees, hears, and judges everything we do.

When the fear of God governs your heart, integrity becomes natural, even when it's costly.

You no longer work for approval; you work for accountability.

You no longer chase recognition; you seek righteousness.

> "The fear of the Lord is the beginning of wisdom." — *Proverbs 9:10*

When you fear God, you work with truth even when no one is watching.

You refuse to lie even when deceit could advance your career.

You treat others with respect even when they mistreat you.

You stay faithful in small things because you know **Heaven is watching**.

You do what is right not because it is rewarded, but because it is **righteous**.

Examples of God-Fearing Workers

Joseph feared God in every circumstance.

In Potiphar's house, he worked with diligence.

In the prison, he served with humility.

In Pharaoh's palace, he led with wisdom.

At every level, Joseph's excellence flowed from **reverence**, not ambition.

He didn't manipulate men to rise — he **honored God**, and God lifted him.

> "The Lord was with Joseph, and he was a prosperous man." — *Genesis 39:2*

Daniel also walked in the fear of God while living in a corrupt system.

He refused to eat the king's food, refused to bow to idols, and refused to lie to gain favor.

He remained truthful in Babylon — and God lifted him above every deceiver.

His integrity made him a light in a dark empire.

Even his enemies could not find fault in his conduct.

> "They could find no corruption in him, because he was trustworthy." — *Daniel 6:4*

Both Joseph and Daniel were surrounded by hypocrites, but they never became one.

They didn't need to blend in to belong; their purity became their promotion.

Their fear of God was greater than their fear of man.

True Success Defined

True success is not climbing higher than others; it is **standing pure before God**.

It is not about the size of your salary but the **state of your soul**.

It is not measured by your title, but by your **truthfulness**.

It is not how far you go, but how **faithfully you walk**.

> "Better is a little with righteousness
> than great revenues without right." — *Proverbs 16:8*

When you walk in the fear of God:

- He becomes your Boss even when you have a boss.
- His eyes replace your supervisor's approval.
- His Word becomes your company policy.
- His Spirit becomes your HR department — guiding, correcting, and convicting you.

The Blessing of the God-Fearing Worker

A worker who fears God cannot be bought by money or moved by manipulation.

He is firm but humble, diligent but dependent, bold but broken before the Lord.

And because of that, **God can trust him** with greater responsibility.

The world may overlook you, but Heaven takes notice.

While others hustle for promotion, God Himself opens doors for you.

While others fake loyalty to be noticed, God surrounds you with favor.

For the eyes of the Lord search throughout the earth,
seeking those whose hearts are loyal to Him.

> "Them that honor Me I will honor." — *1 Samuel 2:30*

The fear of God transforms work from **labor** to **worship**.
It turns your daily routine into divine service.
It keeps your heart clean when systems are corrupt.
It makes you honest when deceit is easy.
If you fear God, you will never need to fear losing your job —
for the same God who opened one door can open another.
Your career is not your security; your character is.
And when you walk in reverence, **He will raise you in due time**.

> "By humility and the fear of the Lord
> are riches, honor, and life." — *Proverbs 22:4*

The Reward of the Righteous Worker — God's Favor in the Field

Heaven does not measure success the way the world does.
While men promote based on performance,
God promotes based on purity.
While the world crowns talent,
God crowns truth.
And while the system rewards results,
Heaven rewards righteousness.
When you work with integrity, you may not always rise quickly,
*but you will **rise securely**.*
*You may be overlooked by men, but you are **seen by God**.*
*You may not receive a trophy, but you will receive a **testimony**.*
Because the same God who watched Joseph in the prison
was the One who lifted him to the palace.

"For the Lord takes pleasure in His people;
He will beautify the humble with salvation." — Psalm 149:4

Divine Favor Over Human Approval

The favor of God cannot be faked, bought, or forced.
It is not earned through charm or manipulation;
*it is granted through **obedience and humility**.*
When you walk uprightly before Him,
God Himself becomes your promoter.
He opens doors that no man can close.
He raises you when others try to bring you down.
He surrounds you with grace even in hostile environments.

"For You, O Lord, will bless the righteous;
with favor You will surround him as with a shield." — Psalm 5:12

When others depend on politics, you depend on Providence.

When others trust their network, you trust His name.
You do not have to chase recognition;
the hand of God will find you where faithfulness keeps you.

God Remembers the Faithful

The world forgets easily, but God ***remembers every act of righteousness.***
Every extra hour you worked honestly.
Every temptation you resisted.
Every truth you spoke when silence was easier.
Every seed of service you planted without applause.
Heaven keeps records more accurate than any HR department.
Your reward may not come today,
but it is ***on the way*** *— written in Heaven's calendar.*

> *"God is not unjust to forget your work and labor of love*
> *which you have shown toward His name." — Hebrews 6:10*

When others are promoted through deceit,
your promotion is delayed only to make it ***divine.***
When God lifts you, no one can undo it,
for your foundation is built not on flattery, but on ***faithfulness.***

Prosperity With Purpose

The blessing of the righteous worker is not just ***prosperity,***
but ***purpose.***
God blesses the hands that honor Him,
but He also uses them to bless others.
He prospers you not to inflate your pride,
but to extend His Kingdom.
He gives you favor not to make you famous,
but to make you fruitful.

> *"The blessing of the Lord makes rich,*
> *and He adds no sorrow with it." — Proverbs 10:22*

When your promotion comes from God, it carries peace with it.
No anxiety, no pretense, no fear of exposure — just grace.
You work freely because your success does not depend on scheming,
but on ***His sustaining power****.*

Your Work Becomes Your Witness

When unbelievers see your honesty, your humility, and your excellence,
they begin to ask, "What makes you different?"
That difference is Christ in you — the ***light of truth*** *in a world of deception.*
Your work becomes your witness,
and your attitude becomes your altar.
When others lie, you tell the truth.
When others complain, you give thanks.
When others panic, you pray.
This is how your life preaches louder than your words.

> *"Let your light so shine before men,*
> *that they may see your good works*
> *and glorify your Father in heaven." — Matthew 5:16*

The reward of the righteous worker is not just in ***earthly promotion,***
but in ***eternal recognition****.*
One day, your real performance review will not come from a boss,
but from the ***King of Kings****.*
He will look at your life — your diligence, your integrity, your faith —
and say the words that no earthly title can match:

> *"Well done, good and faithful servant." — Matthew 25:21*

That is the ultimate promotion —
not a corner office, not a pay raise, not a title,
but the smile of God upon your life.
So keep working with truth.
Keep serving with humility.
Keep shining with purity.

For even when the world forgets, ***Heaven remembers.***
And when God rewards, His reward lasts forever.

A Call to Integrity and Truth

If you are a worker, manager, or leader, ask yourself:

Do I work for truth or for titles?
Do I serve people or use them?
Do I act honest only when someone is watching?
God is calling His children to be different —
to shine in the midst of hypocrisy,
to build trust in places of deceit,
to serve with humility in a culture of pride.
Let the workplace see in you the light of Christ,
the peace of the Spirit, and the honesty of Heaven.

Because one day, every workplace, every system, and every title will pass away —
but what you did in truth will follow you forever.

> "Well done, good and faithful servant... enter into the joy of your Lord." — *Matthew 25:23*

Key Scriptures:

- *Galatians 6:7* — God is not mocked; you reap what you sow
- *Psalm 75:6–7* — Promotion comes from God
- *Mark 8:36* — What profits a man to gain the world but lose his soul
- *Proverbs 12:22* — Lying lips are an abomination to the Lord
- *Colossians 3:23* — Work as for the Lord, not men
- *Proverbs 16:8* — Better a little with righteousness than great gain without justice

- *Matthew 25:23* — Well done, good and faithful servant

Chapter 8: The Mask of Hypocrisy in Love

When Emotion Pretends to Be Devotion

Love — the most sacred gift from God — has become one of the most abused and counterfeited words in our generation.
What was meant to reflect God's covenant has been reduced to temporary convenience.
What was meant to build has become a tool to manipulate.
What was designed to heal now often wounds.

We live in a time when many wear the mask of love but not the heart of it.
People say *"I love you"* not because they mean it, but because they need something.
They promise forever but prepare for departure.
They give compliments not out of affection, but out of agenda.
They hold hands in public but hide betrayal in private.

This is the tragedy of modern love — emotion without integrity, affection without truth.
Relationships today are often built on appearance, attraction, and advantage rather than on covenant, character, and Christ.
Men and women act holy before marriage but reveal corruption after it.
They speak sweetly before commitment but change bitterly afterward.
They act spiritual to win hearts but live carnal once they have them.

"Having a form of godliness, but denying its power." — *2 Timothy 3:5*

The world calls it romance, but Heaven calls it hypocrisy.
Because true love is not performance — it is purity.

It is not about impressing someone; it is about serving them in truth.
It is not about pretending to care; it is about choosing to remain faithful.

Love without truth is deception.
Affection without holiness is lust.
Romance without responsibility is rebellion.
And a relationship without God is a disaster waiting to happen.

This chapter will uncover how hypocrisy hides behind the language of love —
how people pretend purity to gain access,
how lust disguises itself as affection,
how marriage exposes what dating hides,
and how true, Spirit-led love can only survive through truth, faithfulness, and fear of God.

"Let love be without hypocrisy.
Abhor what is evil; cling to what is good." — *Romans 12:9*

The Sweetness That Turns Bitter

Love was never meant to deceive.

It was created by God — **pure, holy, and eternal** —

a reflection of His own nature, a bond of truth between two hearts joined in His will.

Divine love gives without expecting, forgives without limit, and endures without pretense.

But in this fallen world, love has been **corrupted by performance** and **polluted by hypocrisy**.

Today, many people no longer seek love that is righteous — they seek love that is **convenient**.

They act humble to attract, but once they are accepted, pride takes the throne.

They act patient to impress, but once they have what they want, their true nature appears.

They quote Scriptures while dating but forget them in marriage.

Their holiness was a disguise; their spirituality was an act.

> "Love must be sincere. Hate what is evil; cling to what is good." — *Romans 12:9*

We now live in a generation where **the performance of love has replaced the purity of love**.

Men and women play roles — smiling, serving, and speaking sweetly —

not because they are transformed, but because they are **strategic**.

They want a spouse, not a covenant; attention, not accountability.

They say "God brought us together," when in truth, **lust and selfish desire** did.

And when the mask falls — after the vows, after the honeymoon —

the sweetness turns bitter.

The one who seemed patient becomes controlling.

The one who seemed gentle becomes harsh.

The one who prayed becomes proud.

The one who seemed spiritual becomes selfish.
Fake love cannot survive real life.
What is built on lies cannot endure storms.
What begins in hypocrisy will end in heartbreak.
When people hide their true character before marriage,
marriage does not change them — it **reveals** them.
That is why many unions turn from romance to rivalry,
from joy to judgment, from promise to pain.
The truth is simple:
You can act holy to win a person's heart,
but you cannot fake holiness to sustain a marriage.
Love without truth will always turn bitter,
because what starts with a mask ends with misery.

"Unless the Lord builds the house,
they labor in vain who build it." — *Psalm 127:1*

Lovers Without Covenant — How Lust Disguises Itself as Love

Lust is the greatest impersonator of love.
It looks like love.
It feels like love.
It speaks like love.
*But its motive is not to give — it is to **take**.*
*Its goal is not to build — it is to **consume**.*
True love comes from the Spirit; lust is born of the flesh.
Love seeks purity; lust seeks pleasure.
Love waits; lust rushes.
Love covers; lust exposes.
Love protects destiny; lust destroys it.
*We live in a generation where many confuse **affection with intention**.*
They think because someone is attentive, they must be genuine;
because someone is emotional, they must be loving;
because someone prays, they must be pure.
But not every hand that holds you is holy,
and not every "I love you" comes from a clean heart.
Lust wears many disguises.
It can quote Bible verses, sing worship songs, and even attend church.
It acts like Ruth before marriage, but becomes Delilah after.
It talks about covenant, but lives for convenience.
It promises forever, but plans for the moment.
It uses the language of love but the logic of manipulation.

> *"For all that is in the world — the lust of the flesh,*
> *the lust of the eyes, and the pride of life —*
> *is not of the Father but is of the world." — 1 John 2:16*

*Many relationships today are built on **emotional excitement**, not spiritual foundation.*

People are intoxicated by compliments but blind to character.

They fall for charisma but ignore consistency.
They follow appearance but neglect discernment.
They chase butterflies but miss red flags.
Lust says, "I want you now."
Love says, "I will wait until it's right."
Lust says, "I deserve this."
Love says, "I will honor God."
Lust says, "No one will know."
Love says, "God is watching."
Lust will always promise paradise but deliver pain.
It will offer pleasure but produce guilt.
It will give excitement but steal peace.
That is why so many relationships end in regret —
because they began in rebellion disguised as romance.

> *"Can a man take fire in his bosom,*
> *and his clothes not be burned?" — Proverbs 6:27*

If love does not lead you to holiness, it is not love — it is lust in disguise.
If love does not bring you closer to God, it is leading you farther from Him.
If love does not teach you to sacrifice, it is teaching you to sin.
The only way to recognize true love is to measure it by ***the cross.***
For true love is not a feeling — it is a ***crucifixion of self.***
It is not about what you can gain, but about what you are willing to give.
And only the love born of the Spirit can sustain a covenant that honors God.

Pretending to Be Holy Before Marriage

In the season of courtship, many wear **the mask of holiness**.

They appear gentle, prayerful, and disciplined.

They attend church together, hold hands during worship, share daily devotions,

and call each other *"my blessing," "my destiny partner,"* or *"my prayer warrior."*

But beneath the spiritual language lies a dangerous truth —

many are not holy; they are simply performing.

They know how to look godly without being godly.

They quote Scripture like prophets but live like pagans.

They speak of purity but flirt with sin.

They post Bible verses online but cross boundaries in private.

They act patient, humble, and loving,

but their motives are driven by **desire, fear, or manipulation — not truth.**

This is the reason many relationships collapse **after** marriage —

because they were built on *performance, not principle.*

What looked holy before the wedding becomes **hellish** afterward.

The smiles fade, the patience disappears, and the "hallelujahs" turn into hostility.

Because what was hidden during dating always becomes visible in marriage.

Behind the romantic dinners were pride and control.

Behind the long calls were insecurity and manipulation.

Behind the "God bless you" texts were selfish motives.

They did not love you for who you are — they loved you for what you could give.

> "The Lord detests lying lips,
> but He delights in those who tell the truth." — *Proverbs 12:22*

When you pretend to be holy just to win someone's trust,

you are not preparing for marriage — you are preparing for **disaster.**
Because marriage does not bless pretenders; it exposes them.
It removes the spiritual makeup and reveals the real face.
You cannot fake prayer forever.
You cannot act patient forever.
You cannot disguise pride forever.
God blesses **sincerity, not showmanship.**
He honors **truth, not theatrics.**
He delights in hearts that are genuine, even when they struggle,
more than in lips that quote verses while hiding sin.
If your holiness is only visible when someone is watching,
it is not holiness — it is **hypocrisy.**
If your purity depends on fear of being caught,
it is not conviction — it is **performance.**
True love is built on truth, not pretense.
It begins with honesty before God and ends with harmony before man.
So before you say "I do," make sure you are not saying it in disguise.

Marriage: The Mirror of the Heart

Marriage is not a disguise — it is a **divine mirror**.

It does not create problems; it **reveals them**.
It does not change people; it **exposes** who they already are.
What was hidden in dating becomes visible in covenant.
The words that once sounded sweet are now tested by life's storms.
Before marriage, it is easy to act gentle, patient, and spiritual —
because there are limits, boundaries, and distance.
But once two people share the same roof,
the true character begins to speak louder than the rehearsed words.
You can hide pride during courtship,
but marriage will expose it when you disagree.
You can fake humility before the altar,
but marriage will test it when you are corrected.
You can act holy while dating,
but marriage will reveal whether Christ truly lives in you.

"Every tree is recognized by its own fruit." — *Luke 6:44*

The home is not a stage for performance; it is a **laboratory of truth**.
There, love is refined, faith is tested, and motives are revealed.
Marriage does not bless the actor — it blesses the **authentic believer**.
If you lied to win your spouse, you will live to regret it.
If you manipulated to marry, you will suffer to maintain it.
If you faked holiness to impress, you will mourn when reality manifests.
Many couples discover after marriage that they did not marry a partner
—
they married a stranger.
The one who prayed with them now mocks prayer.
The one who promised peace now brings pain.
The one who appeared gentle now controls with anger.
Because the wedding day united two bodies,
but the truth never united their **souls**.

Marriage is the most honest mirror God uses to expose hearts.

It reveals whether love was built on covenant or convenience,

whether faith was real or rehearsed,

whether the union was founded on the Spirit or on the flesh.

That is why it is dangerous to rush into marriage for beauty, status, or emotion.

Time reveals truth.

Prayer exposes deception.

The Holy Spirit uncovers what charm tries to hide.

> "Unless the Lord builds the house,
> they labor in vain who build it." — *Psalm 127:1*

If Christ is not the foundation, no ceremony, promise, or romance can sustain it.

For only the truth can protect love,

and only holiness can make marriage last.

The Fruits of Fake Love — How Hypocrisy Destroys Relationships and Families

Every seed bears fruit after its kind.

You cannot plant deception and expect devotion.

You cannot sow lies and expect loyalty.

When love is built on hypocrisy, the harvest will always be heartbreak.

Fake love produces fake peace.

It looks stable on the outside but rots from the inside.

At first, everything seems perfect — flowers, promises, and smiles — but as soon as trials come, the mask begins to fall.

What was once romance turns into rivalry.

What began with compliments ends with complaints.

What looked like blessing becomes bondage.

> "Do not be deceived: God is not mocked;
> for whatever a man sows, that he will also reap." — *Galatians 6:7*

1. It Destroys Trust

Lies are termites in the foundation of love.

You can build the most beautiful house of affection, but if deception lives inside, the walls will eventually collapse.

Trust is fragile — once broken, it rarely returns the same.

When one partner hides, the other begins to fear.

When fear replaces faith, the relationship begins to die.

2. It Breeds Insecurity and Control

Hypocrisy creates suspicion.

When a person who once pretended holiness starts acting differently, their partner begins to question everything.

They start to watch, to doubt, to control — not because they want to, but because their peace has been poisoned.

In such homes, love turns into a battlefield of blame.

3. It Corrupts the Next Generation

Children growing up in fake love become experts in pretense.

They watch their parents smile in public and fight in private.

They learn that "I'm sorry" means little and "I love you" means less.

Soon, they repeat the same cycle in their own relationships.

The spirit of hypocrisy becomes generational —

passed down like a curse until someone chooses the truth.

4. It Separates God from the Union

When lies enter the marriage bed, God departs from the home.

He cannot dwell where truth is denied.

He cannot bless what sin continues to cover.

The couple may still attend church, sing together, and post verses online,

but spiritually, the house becomes hollow — filled with ritual, but not with His presence.

> "If the foundations are destroyed, what can the righteous do?" — *Psalm 11:3*

The only solution to fake love is **repentance**.

True love can only be rebuilt on truth.

You cannot paint holiness over sin and expect Heaven to approve.

Confession heals what performance hides.

Forgiveness restores what pride destroys.

Fake love builds castles in the air —

true love builds altars before God.

One seeks pleasure; the other seeks purpose.

One ends in regret; the other ends in redemption.

When the Mask Falls After Marriage

Many enter marriage expecting **heaven**, only to find **hidden hell**.

Before marriage, everything looked perfect — patience, peace, and prayer.

Every smile seemed sincere, every promise sounded divine.

But once the vows are spoken and the ceremony ends,

the acting stops, and reality begins.

The man who acted gentle becomes harsh.

The woman who appeared humble becomes rebellious.

The one who led prayer meetings now leads arguments.

The one who quoted Scripture now questions faith.

The one who seemed faithful begins to flirt in secret.

The one who promised "till death do us part" now threatens divorce at every disagreement.

The wedding was beautiful — the photos, the guests, the celebration —

but beauty cannot hide a broken foundation.

When lies build the altar, **the covenant will collapse**.

For God cannot bless what is rooted in deception.

"Marriage does not change people; it reveals them."

What was hidden in dating always manifests in marriage.

You can cover pride with charm, but it will rise when challenged.

You can hide anger behind a smile, but it will roar when tested.

You can pretend patience in courtship, but true trials will uncover your heart.

Time always unmasks the truth.

Hypocrisy in love is like **perfume on decay** —

it smells pleasant for a moment,

but eventually, the rot underneath reveals itself.

The scent fades, and the stench of hidden sin fills the home.

When the mask falls, many realize they were not married to a partner,

but to a performer.

They did not build on prayer, but on pretense.

They did not enter covenant — they entered a contract of convenience.

That is why **truth before marriage is more valuable than beauty, wealth, or status**.

For marriage is not about finding someone who looks right;
it is about joining with someone who *is right before God.*
If you hide sin to marry, your marriage will expose it to shame.
If you build on a lie, your home will live under its curse.

> "He who walks uprightly walks securely,
> but he who perverts his ways will be found out." — *Proverbs 10:9*

Let every believer remember:
God does not unite actors — He joins **truthful hearts**.
And where there is truth, love endures;
but where there is hypocrisy, love dies.

Love Built on Lies Cannot Last

Many couples today enter marriage **because of attraction, not conviction.**

They are drawn by charm, appearance, status, or emotion —
but not by truth, purpose, or spiritual discernment.
They fall in love with the *face*, not the *faith*;
with the *style*, not the *substance.*
They hide their weaknesses while dating,
acting perfect to avoid rejection,
and covering sin to appear spiritual.
But no one can act forever —
the truth always finds its way to the surface.

> "For there is nothing hidden which will not be revealed,
>
> nor has anything been kept secret but that it should come to light." — *Mark 4:22*

True love **grows in truth**, but false love **grows in performance**.
When a relationship is built on lies, it becomes a time bomb.
It may look peaceful for a season, but every secret is a seed of destruction.
If your foundation is deceit, your marriage will not endure storms.
If your connection is carnal, your covenant will be fragile.
You cannot build eternal love on temporary lies.
You cannot enter a **holy covenant** with **unholy motives.**
You cannot expect God's presence when sin is the invitation.

You cannot ask for Heaven's blessing while walking hand in hand with darkness.

Many cry for restoration when what they need first is **repentance**.

> "Unless the Lord builds the house,
> they labor in vain who build it." — *Psalm 127:1*

This is why so many marriages today end in **frustration, mistrust, and divorce.**

They were started in the flesh but expected to survive by faith.
They prayed for blessings while ignoring obedience.
They wore masks of holiness while feeding lust.
They desired romance more than righteousness,
pleasure more than purity, and attraction more than anointing.
Such love is not covenant — it is **counterfeit**.
It promises joy but delivers pain.
It offers companionship but births corruption.
It shines for a moment but fades in the fire of testing.
Real love cannot exist where lies live.
Lies destroy trust, and without trust, love cannot breathe.
If you want love that lasts, it must be **founded on truth**,
rooted in holiness, and **anchored in God's will**.
For love without truth is **lust**,
and romance without righteousness is **rebellion**.
Only the love that begins in the fear of God
can end in the peace of God.

The Spirit of Deception in Modern Relationships

We live in a generation where **love has become marketing** and relationships have become performance.

People no longer seek truth — they seek attention.

They no longer pursue covenant — they pursue convenience.

The sacred language of love has been corrupted by the **spirit of deception**.

Men use **sweet words** not to heal hearts but to manipulate emotions.

They speak of destiny while plotting desire.

They promise forever while planning for the moment.

Their words drip like honey, but their motives sting like poison.

Women, too, are deceived and deceiving.

They use **appearance** to attract admiration,
charm to control attention, and seduction to secure affection.

Instead of preparing their hearts for purpose, they prepare their bodies for approval.

Instead of waiting on God's timing, they chase man's validation.

Social media has become the altar of counterfeit love.

Relationships today are filtered through screens —
where people post their best smiles, best Scriptures, and best captions,
but hide their **arguments, disrespect, and secret sin** behind the scenes.

They appear like holy couples online,
but in private, they are living in disobedience and dishonor.

They call each other *"soulmates,"* but in truth, they are **soul-takers** —
draining one another emotionally, spiritually, and morally.

They use God's name to cover the devil's plan.

They speak of love but practice lust.

They hold hands in public but hold grudges in private.

> "Satan himself transforms into an angel of light." — *2 Corinthians 11:14*

The devil no longer needs to knock on the door —
he slides into the DMs.
He no longer tempts with serpents — he tempts with selfies.
He no longer deceives with idols — he deceives with images.
And his most dangerous disguise is **a relationship that looks godly but is not holy**.
That is why **spiritual discernment** is no longer optional — it is survival.
Not everyone who says *"I love you"* means it.
Not everyone who quotes a Bible verse lives it.
Not everyone who prays with you is praying for you.
Some are sent by God to bless your destiny;
others are sent by the enemy to **delay**, **distract**, and **destroy** it.
Be careful who you call "God's will,"
for sometimes the devil dresses his agents in divine vocabulary.
He can send a boyfriend who prays,
a girlfriend who serves,
but neither knows the God they pretend to represent.
The spirit of deception hides behind charm and charisma,
but the Holy Spirit exposes it through **truth and time**.
If your relationship leads you away from holiness,
it is not love — it is a **trap**.
If it makes you hide from God instead of draw near to Him,
it is not a blessing — it is a **bondage**.
True love will never make you compromise purity for pleasure.
It will never lead you into secrecy and sin.
It will lead you to Christ, not away from Him.
Because the Spirit of Truth never partners with the **spirit of deception**.

Why Many Marriages End in Divorce

Divorce does not begin in the courtroom — it begins in the **heart**.

It is not born in marriage; it is **conceived in hypocrisy**.

The seeds of separation are planted long before the vows are spoken,

on the day when **truth is replaced by performance**,

and love becomes an act instead of a covenant.

It begins when two people decide to **impress** each other rather than **transform** for each other.

They spend more time rehearsing appearances than building character.

They fall in love with the *idea* of marriage, not the *responsibility* of it.

They crave companionship but reject commitment.

They desire affection but resist accountability.

They dream of romance but despise repentance.

Before marriage, they hide flaws to appear perfect.

After marriage, those same flaws become weapons in warfare.

What was once gentle becomes judgmental.

What was once sweet becomes sour.

The smiles fade, the prayers stop, and the vows grow cold.

They said "I do," but their hearts whispered "I might."

They said "forever," but meant "until I'm offended."

They wore the garments of covenant, but underneath were the threads of convenience.

> "What God has joined together, let no man separate." — *Mark 10:9*

But hypocrisy separates what God united.

When truth disappears, **trust dies**.

When trust dies, **love suffocates**.

And when love dies, the **marriage collapses**.

The spirit of hypocrisy turns marriage into theater —

husband and wife act like partners in public,

but live like prisoners in private.

They smile for photos but sleep in silence.

They wear rings but have no relationship.

They speak of love but harbor resentment.

Divorce, in most cases, is not a sudden event — it is the **final result of years of hidden lies.**

Every secret unspoken, every wound ignored, every sin excused becomes a brick in the wall between two souls.

And when that wall grows too high, even prayer struggles to climb it.

No marriage can survive without **truth**, because truth is the breath of love.

You can endure poverty, sickness, and storms — but you cannot endure deception.

For when lies build the home, destruction will always be the guest.

Marriage was never meant to be a contract of comfort — it is a **covenant of character.**

It is not about finding a perfect partner; it is about becoming a truthful one.

God unites those who are willing to walk in light, not those who hide behind masks.

So if your marriage is struggling, do not first look at your partner —
look at your **truth.**
Have you been honest before God?
Have you been transparent before your spouse?
For hypocrisy destroys what prayer tries to heal.

> "Unless the Lord builds the house,
> they labor in vain who build it." — *Psalm 127:1*

Only truth can sustain what love begins.
And only repentance can rebuild what hypocrisy destroyed.

The Call to Pure and Transparent Love

God's will for love has never been manipulation — it is **manifestation of truth**.

He created love not as a stage for performance, but as a **sanctuary for purity**.

In His design, love is not blind — it is **enlightened by truth**.

It does not hide behind charm, deceit, or lust; it stands in the **light of sincerity and holiness**.

True love is not built in darkness; it **grows in the light**.

It cannot survive lies, secrets, or spiritual compromise.

A relationship that thrives in secrecy will suffocate in marriage.

For what begins with deception will always end in destruction.

God desires relationships that are anchored in **honesty, prayer, purity, and the fear of God**.

He wants couples who seek His face together more than they seek each other's attention.

He wants hearts that honor covenant more than comfort,
and hands that build together, not break apart in pride.

A **godly relationship** should never pull you away from righteousness.

If your connection makes you compromise purity, it is not from God.

If it weakens your prayer life, it is not love — it is a **spiritual trap**.

If someone hides sin, avoids correction, or refuses accountability,
they are not ready for covenant — they are hiding from conviction.

"Love rejoices in the truth." — *1 Corinthians 13:6*

If your love does not celebrate truth, it is not love — **it is lust**.

If your love hides sin instead of confessing it, it is not a relationship — **it is rebellion**.

Love that lies to survive will die the moment truth appears.

But love that walks in truth will stand the test of trials, time, and temptation.

Before marriage, **ask God to remove every mask — yours and theirs**.

Let the Holy Spirit expose anything built on pride, deception, or hidden sin.

Because marriage does not hide who you are; it **reveals who you've always been.**

If you pretend now, you will pay later.

If you lie now, you will cry later.

But if you choose truth now, you will live in peace later.

Love that is pure needs no disguise.

Love that is transparent fears no light.

Love that is built on God's Word will endure every storm.

So, let your relationships be holy, not just happy.

Let them be truthful, not theatrical.

Let them be guided by conviction, not convenience.

For in the end, only **truthful love** reflects the heart of God.

> "Create in me a clean heart, O God,
> and renew a right spirit within me." — *Psalm 51:10*

A Prayer for Love Without Hypocrisy

Lord, deliver us from false love and fake holiness.

Expose every relationship built on deception.

Purify our hearts before we join our hands.

Teach us to love in truth, to forgive, to be patient, and to walk in the light.

Give us discernment to know who is from You and who is from the enemy.

And bless every covenant that is born in Your will, sealed in Your Spirit, and rooted in Your truth.

> "Create in me a clean heart, O God, and renew a right spirit within me." — *Psalm 51:10*

Key Scriptures:

- *Romans 12:9* — Love must be sincere

- *Proverbs 12:22* — Lying lips are an abomination to the Lord
- *Psalm 127:1* — Unless the Lord builds the house
- *2 Corinthians 11:14* — Satan disguises as an angel of light
- *1 Corinthians 13:6* — Love rejoices in the truth
- *Mark 10:9* — What God has joined together, let no man separate
- *Psalm 51:10* — Create in me a clean heart, O God

Chapter 9: The Mask of the Smile — Kindness Without Heart

When Courtesy Becomes a Costume

We live in a world that smiles without sincerity.
Everywhere you go — in stores, offices, churches, schools, and even homes — faces wear smiles that do not match the heart.
People greet with warmth but think with bitterness.
They serve with politeness but harbor pride.
They speak softly while secretly despising the very ones they smile at.

The smile has become a mask — a tool of survival in a world built on appearances.
It hides anger, resentment, envy, and deception behind a gentle expression.
We have learned to say, "Have a nice day," while wishing the opposite.
We have mastered the art of pretending peace while carrying storms within.

This is kindness without heart, compassion without conviction, love without truth.
It looks beautiful on the outside but empty on the inside — like a painted grave.
Jesus warned about such hypocrisy when He said:

"You are like whitewashed tombs, which look beautiful on the outside
but on the inside are full of the bones of the dead." — *Matthew 23:27*

In our modern culture — especially in workplaces and customer service — kindness has become a performance.
People smile because policy demands it, not because love

inspires it.
They greet you out of professionalism, not purity.
They show patience out of fear of losing their job, not because of the fruit of the Spirit.

Even in the church, many believers wear holy smiles but carry hidden grudges.
We say "God bless you" while silently judging.
We serve with our hands while our hearts are far from mercy.
This false kindness pollutes relationships, weakens ministries, and robs the Church of genuine love.

True kindness is not shown in expression but in intention.
It comes from a heart transformed by the Holy Spirit — a heart that smiles not to please people but to reflect God's nature.
For a smile that hides hate is hypocrisy,
but a smile that flows from compassion is holiness.

This chapter will uncover how our generation has replaced sincerity with strategy,
and how God calls His children to remove the mask of politeness and walk in authentic love —
love that forgives, serves, and speaks truth with grace.

"Let love be without hypocrisy.
Abhor what is evil; cling to what is good." — *Romans 12:9*

The Smile That Deceives

A smile was created by God to reflect **joy, peace, and love** from within.

It was meant to be a window of the soul — an outward expression of an inward light.

A smile can heal a wounded heart, lift a weary spirit, and bridge the distance between strangers.

It is one of the simplest, purest gifts God gave humanity to express His warmth and goodness.

But today, the smile has **lost its purity**.

It has been stolen by the spirit of performance and reshaped by the culture of deception.

It no longer reveals truth — it often **hides it**.

It has become a tool of survival, a mask of diplomacy, and at times, a weapon of manipulation.

We live in an age where people **smile with their faces but frown in their hearts**.

Their lips shine, but their souls are dark.

Their tone is sweet, but their thoughts are bitter.

In workplaces, customer service counters, churches, and even homes,
many have mastered the **art of polite hypocrisy**.

They smile because the job demands it.

They greet warmly because it is expected.

They say, *"Have a blessed day,"* but in their minds, they are irritated or indifferent.

The modern smile has become an act —
a professional gesture rather than a spiritual expression.

> "These people draw near to Me with their mouth,
> and honor Me with their lips,
> but their heart is far from Me." — *Matthew 15:8*

A smile means nothing if it hides sin.

A kind word means little if it conceals hate.

An expression of peace means nothing if the heart is a battlefield.

God does not look at the lips that smile — He looks at the **heart that feels**.

True love and sincerity cannot be acted — **they must be lived**.

A believer's smile should not come from training, but from **truth**.

It should flow naturally from a heart free from bitterness and filled with compassion.

For when the heart is clean, the face shines with genuine peace.

But when the heart is corrupt, even the brightest smile becomes a lie.

This is the deception of our age:
we have replaced authenticity with artificiality,
and we value impression more than intention.
Yet God's eyes pierce beyond our expressions —
He weighs the motives behind the smile,
the tone behind the greeting,
and the heart behind the kindness.
So let your smile be real, not rehearsed.
Let it be born from grace, not guilt; from purity, not pressure.
For a smile that flows from truth can touch eternity,
but a smile that hides hypocrisy will one day be exposed by the Light.

> "The integrity of the upright guides them,
> but the unfaithful are destroyed by their duplicity." — *Proverbs 11:3*

The Mask of Courtesy in Public and Customer Care

In today's world — especially in **public service, business, and customer care** — kindness has become a **script**, not a **spirit**.

People are no longer taught how to *be* kind; they are trained how to *act* kind.

They learn how to smile, how to greet, how to sound compassionate —

but behind those polished manners often lies indifference, irritation, or hidden pride.

They say, *"Good morning, how can I help you today?"*

but inside they are thinking, *"I wish you'd leave."*

They offer polite words while rolling their eyes in silence.

They maintain professionalism outwardly but murmur complaints inwardly.

In customer care, the smile is mandatory — not meaningful.

In public offices, officials act humble in front of supervisors but speak with arrogance when no one is listening.

In politics, leaders shake hands and pose for cameras,

while their hearts despise the very people they vowed to serve.

This is not kindness — it is **performance**.

It is not compassion — it is **courtesy without conscience**.

It is hypocrisy covered in diplomacy,

pretense wrapped in professionalism.

The world has replaced genuine love with trained politeness,

and sincerity with scripts of customer service etiquette.

> "Man looks on the outward appearance,
> but the Lord looks on the heart." — *1 Samuel 16:7*

God does not applaud the actor of kindness — He honors the **authentic servant.**

He does not measure smiles; He measures motives.

You can say, *"Have a wonderful day,"* yet carry bitterness.

You can act patient before people and still grieve the Holy Spirit.

Because God is not fooled by rehearsed emotions; He discerns the condition of the heart.

In Heaven's eyes, true kindness is not determined by **how you sound**, but by **why you serve**.

It is not about soft words, but sincere intentions.

It is not about showing grace when paid, but showing love when unseen.

When the heart is pure, even a simple gesture carries power;
but when the heart is false, even the sweetest words are empty noise.
The world may train you to act polite,
but only the **Holy Spirit** can teach you to love.
He gives compassion that is real, patience that is deep,
and joy that does not fade when the uniform comes off.
So whether you are in customer care, public office, or ministry —
serve not for applause, but from the **heart**.
Smile not to impress, but to express Christ's light within you.
For the Lord sees beyond appearances,
and only **truthful kindness** is counted as worship before Him.

"Let all that you do be done with love." — *1 Corinthians 16:14*

When Politeness Becomes Deception

Courtesy is beautiful when it is pure —
but when it becomes a tool for deceit, it turns into **sin**.
Politeness without sincerity is not virtue; it is **camouflage**.
Many today use kindness as a weapon,
sweet words as a disguise,
and gentle tones as bait to gain what they want.
They act humble to appear holy,
compassionate to gain control,
and respectful to earn trust —
but beneath the charm lies **a spirit of manipulation**.
Their smiles are strategic, not spiritual.
Their greetings are rehearsed, not real.
Their kindness is calculated, not Christlike.
This is the same spirit that entered **Judas Iscariot**.
He did not stab Jesus with a sword — he **betrayed Him with a kiss**.
A symbol of affection became a signal for destruction.

> "He came to Jesus and said, 'Greetings, Rabbi!' and kissed Him."
> — *Matthew 26:49*

That single kiss exposes the heart of all false politeness —
it is **love on the lips and lies in the heart**.
And today, the world is full of **Judas-like smiles**:
friendly on the outside, deadly on the inside.
There are smiles that hide jealousy,
compliments that hide contempt,
and gestures of warmth that hide wicked motives.
Some praise you in public but plot against you in private.
They clap for your success but quietly hope for your fall.
This false politeness has not only invaded the marketplace —
it has also **entered the church**.
People say "God bless you" with their mouths

but curse others in their hearts.
They hug with fake affection,
then gossip the moment backs are turned.
They call you *"brother"* or *"sister"*
while secretly competing with or despising you.
This is not the Spirit of Christ — it is the spirit of **Judas**.
The Holy Spirit is not impressed by charm,
titles, or rehearsed courtesy.
He does not anoint deception wrapped in smiles.
He searches for **truth in the inward parts** —
for hearts that mean what they say,
and love that does not require an audience.

> "Let love be without hypocrisy.
> Abhor what is evil; cling to what is good." — *Romans 12:9*

True godly courtesy flows from purity, not policy.
It is kindness birthed by the Spirit, not taught by training.
It does not flatter to gain favor,
nor speak softly to hide pride.
It reflects the heart of Jesus — gentle, honest, and sincere.
The world rewards diplomacy,
but Heaven rewards **truthful compassion**.
You may impress people with politeness,
but only **truth** impresses God.
So, let every word be rooted in love,
every smile be honest,
and every act of kindness flow from a clean heart.
For one sincere word is worth more than a thousand fake gestures.

The World That Smiles Without Love

We are living in a world that **smiles more and loves less.**

A world that teaches people to "look positive," but never to **be truthful**.

A culture that values *being nice* more than *being real.*

In this generation, appearance has replaced authenticity.

People are taught to manage impressions instead of mend hearts.

We are told:

"Don't show weakness."

"Always look happy."

"Keep smiling — no matter what."

And so, humanity has become a stage of **actors in pain**,
performing joy while quietly dying inside.

We wear smiles like **makeup** — to impress, to fit in, to survive.

We laugh in public and cry in private.

We post pictures of happiness but hide the scars of emptiness.

Our faces shine, but our souls ache.

But **fake smiles do not heal hearts**.

They build **walls**, not bridges.

They create an illusion of connection while deepening the reality of isolation.

You can walk into a building full of smiles and still feel completely alone —

because sincerity has vanished.

The lips move, but the heart is missing.

People act emotions instead of expressing them.

We have become professional performers instead of genuine souls.

> "Let love be without hypocrisy.
> Hate what is evil; cling to what is good." — *Romans 12:9*

This world has mastered **the art of politeness** but forgotten the power of love.

We know how to speak kindly but not how to care deeply.

We offer compliments without compassion, greetings without grace,
and "I'm fine" without honesty.
But God is not calling us to **fake politeness** —
He is calling us to **true compassion**.
He is not impressed by smiles that hide bitterness;
He is moved by hearts that choose mercy even when it hurts.
For kindness without love is **manipulation**,
and a smile without truth is **deception**.
The world's courtesy seeks approval,
but Heaven's love seeks authenticity.
To love truly is to feel, to forgive, to be vulnerable.
It is to speak truth even when it's uncomfortable,
to show grace even when it's not required,
to care not for appearance, but for souls.

> "By this all will know that you are My disciples,
> if you have love for one another." —*John 13:35*

So let us remove the **mask of the smile** and let our hearts speak again.
For a sincere tear is more healing than a fake grin.
And a truthful word of compassion does more good than a thousand hollow greetings.

True Kindness: The Smile That Reflects God's Heart

True kindness is not a performance — it is a **reflection of God's nature.**

It cannot be trained by customer-service scripts or social etiquette; it is born from a **heart transformed by the Holy Spirit**.

Real kindness does not come from culture — it comes from **Christ**.

It flows from mercy, not manipulation.

It shines from truth, not from training.

A smile that reflects God's heart is not controlled by circumstance.

It is not fake, forced, or formulaic.

It comes from a soul that has been healed, forgiven, and filled with love.

Even in pain, such a person can still show peace — because their peace is not from this world.

They smile not to hide their struggles, but to show that **grace is greater than grief**.

> "The fruit of the Spirit is love, joy, peace, patience, kindness, goodness, faithfulness, gentleness, and self-control." — *Galatians 5:22–23*

True kindness is a **fruit of the Spirit**, not a function of profession.

It is not limited to those who work in churches, hospitals, or customer care desks.

It belongs to everyone who walks with God and reflects His character.

When the Spirit of God fills your heart,
your kindness will no longer depend on how others treat you.
You will bless those who curse you,
pray for those who insult you,
and serve even those who misunderstand you.

Because you are no longer acting for man — you are **living for God**.

True kindness forgives quickly and loves deeply.

It refuses to fake peace or pretend affection.

It speaks truth with grace, corrects with compassion, and gives without expecting reward.

It looks for no camera, no applause, no "thank you."

It simply loves — because God loves.

> "Be kind and compassionate to one another,
> forgiving each other, just as in Christ God forgave you." — *Ephesians 4:32*

This is the **smile of Heaven** —
the one that shines not from lips, but from the Spirit within.
A smile that reflects patience when others are rude,
gentleness when others are harsh,
and truth when others live in pretense.
Every believer is called to carry this kind of smile —
not the one taught by the world, but the one shaped by worship.
A smile that speaks peace, carries presence, and releases love.
So, let your smile preach the gospel.
Let it say, *"Christ lives in me."*
Let it testify that kindness still exists in a cold world.
And let your love — not your training — be what people remember.

> "A cheerful heart is good medicine,
> but a broken spirit dries up the bones." — *Proverbs 17:22*

For when kindness comes from truth,
even your smallest gesture becomes **a ministry of light**.

Spiritual Danger of the Fake Smile

The fake smile is more than a social habit — it is a **spiritual trap**.

It may look harmless, but it reshapes the soul, slowly teaching the heart to **live in pretense.**

It trains the tongue to lie gently, the face to hide sin beautifully, and the conscience to stay silent.

It replaces repentance with reputation, sincerity with strategy, and holiness with hypocrisy.

At first, it feels small — just a polite act, a harmless disguise.

But over time, it becomes a pattern of deception.

You learn how to hide pain instead of healing it.

You learn how to smile through sin instead of confessing it.

You learn how to perform spirituality instead of living in truth.

The fake smile **normalizes deception** as a social skill.

It turns hypocrisy into professionalism.

It makes lying look like emotional intelligence.

And soon, people begin to confuse *pretense* with *peace.*

When you get used to acting kind while harboring hate,
your heart begins to harden.

Your conscience becomes numb.

You stop recognizing sin because you've learned how to **decorate it**.

You stop repenting because you've mastered how to **appear righteous**.

You stop seeking deliverance because you've learned how to **hide bondage behind a grin.**

This is the silent corruption of the soul —
when outward smiles replace inward sincerity.

When image replaces integrity.

When charm replaces conviction.

> "The Lord searches all hearts
> and understands every intent of the thoughts." — *1 Chronicles 28:9*

God is not impressed by charm; He discerns the **condition of the heart**.
He does not judge by facial expression, but by inner truth.
You can fool the crowd, but not the Creator.
You can impress people with your smile,
but you cannot **deceive the One who sees beneath it**.
The fake smile may protect your **reputation**,
but it cannot protect your **soul**.
You can keep your job with it, but you will lose your joy.
You can win approval from men, but you will grieve the Spirit of God.
It is better to weep honestly than to smile hypocritically.
Better to be real before God than respected before men.
Better to speak truth in tears than to lie with a grin.

"Behold, You desire truth in the inward parts." — *Psalm 51:6*

For on the Day of Judgment, the masks will fall,
and only the heart will speak.

May your heart, not your smile, testify that you were sincere before the Lord.

The Call to Genuine Love and Compassion

God is calling His people to return to **real love** —
a love that is **honest, pure, and born of the Spirit**,
not the kind that flatters, manipulates, or performs.
The world has learned how to act loving,
but Heaven is calling us to **be loving**.
True love does not flatter — it **builds**.
True love does not perform — it **transforms**.
True love does not hide behind soft words — it speaks truth with grace.
And true kindness is not rehearsed; it is **revealed** from a heart filled with God's presence.
Jesus is our perfect example.
He never smiled to impress — He smiled to **heal**.
He never spoke gently to avoid truth — He spoke truth **with compassion**.
He was kind but never fake, merciful but never manipulative,
gentle but never compromising.
Every word He spoke was life, and every act of kindness was holy.
The call of Christ is not to become better actors —
it is to become **true reflections** of His heart.
We are called to love without pretense,
to show kindness without calculation,
to serve without seeking recognition,
and to forgive without keeping records.

> "By this everyone will know that you are My disciples,
> if you love one another." —*John 13:35*

This is the mark of a true disciple — not a polished smile,
but a **pure heart** that radiates God's love through sincerity.
For real kindness cannot be learned from training manuals;
it can only be birthed through **the Holy Spirit**.
When the Spirit of God fills your heart,

you no longer need to fake joy — it flows naturally.
You no longer need to pretend peace — it becomes your nature.
You no longer need to force kindness — it becomes your fruit.

> “The fruit of the Spirit is love, joy, peace, patience, kindness, goodness, faithfulness.” — *Galatians 5:22*

When your heart is clean, your smile becomes **anointed**, not artificial.
It carries healing instead of hypocrisy, peace instead of pretense,
and light instead of lies.
Such a smile does not impress — it **imparts.**
It does not perform — it **pierces** through darkness and touches souls.
This is what God desires:
a Church whose love is real,
whose kindness flows from truth,
and whose compassion mirrors the face of Jesus.
So let us throw away the mask of the smile,
and let our hearts once again speak the language of Heaven —
genuine love and divine compassion.

> “Above all, clothe yourselves with love,
> which binds us all together in perfect harmony.” — *Colossians 3:14*

A Prayer for a Pure Heart and Genuine Kindness

Lord, remove the mask of false kindness from my life.

Cleanse my heart from hypocrisy and bitterness.

Teach me to love with truth, to smile with sincerity, to serve without selfishness.

Let my words be pure and my motives holy.

May my smile reflect Your light, not my mask.

Fill me with Your Spirit, that my kindness may heal, not deceive.

> “Create in me a clean heart, O God, and renew a right spirit within me.” — *Psalm 51:10*

Key Scriptures:

- *Matthew 15:8* — They honor Me with their lips, but their hearts are far from Me

- *1 Samuel 16:7* — Man looks at the outward appearance, but the Lord looks at the heart

- *Matthew 26:49* — Judas kissed Jesus to betray Him

- *Romans 12:9* — Let love be without hypocrisy

- *1 Chronicles 28:9* — The Lord searches the heart and understands every intent

- *John 13:35* — By this everyone will know you are My disciples

- *Psalm 51:10* — Create in me a clean heart, O God

Chapter 10: The Mask of Generosity and Charity

When Giving Becomes a Show Instead of a Sacrifice

**We live in an age where generosity has been corrupted by performance.
What was once meant to reflect the heart of God — a quiet act of love and compassion —
has become a stage of self-promotion, especially among nations, organizations, and even churches.
Today, the world gives not always to help, but often to be seen helping.
Charity has become a brand. Generosity has become business.**

In Europe, in the Middle East, and in many churches in America,

the spirit of hypocritical charity has grown powerful.
They give to Africa, to Asia, to the poor — not to empower, but to maintain dependence.
They sponsor projects but control their outcomes.
They send food but take the future.
They build schools while breaking the spirit of self-reliance.
Their "help" often carries hidden chains — political, economic, and spiritual.
They wear the garments of generosity while planting seeds of dominance.

"When you give to the needy, do not announce it with trumpets, as the hypocrites do in the synagogues and on the streets, to be honored by men." — *Matthew 6:2*

Even many churches have joined this performance of piety.
They raise funds in the name of "missions" or "charity," but behind the banner of compassion lies the desire for recognition.
Some take photos of hungry children to raise money,
but forget to raise those same children out of poverty.
Some boast of building churches in Africa,
while using the suffering of Africans to strengthen their own reputation before donors.

This is not the heart of Christ.
Jesus gave without cameras, healed without seeking applause,
and served without seeking advantage.
His love was quiet, His compassion sincere, and His giving pure.
But today, many nations and ministries give like actors — seeking claps from men instead of crowns from Heaven.

The tragedy is that much of the world's generosity has become a form of control.
The giver remains the master; the receiver remains the

servant.
They speak of partnership but practice superiority.
They call it charity but use it as a tool of power and pride.

True generosity does not enslave — it empowers.
It does not humiliate — it honors.
It does not seek attention — it seeks restoration.
God's form of giving is never for the cameras; it is for the Kingdom.

"But when you give, do not let your left hand know what your right hand is doing, so that your giving may be in secret; and your Father, who sees in secret, will reward you."
— *Matthew 6:3–4*

This chapter will expose how the spirit of hypocrisy has corrupted global charity,
how aid has become a mask for control,
and how even churches have turned giving into marketing.
It will call believers, nations, and institutions to return to the pure heart of giving —
where generosity flows not from pride, but from love;
not from wealth, but from worship;
not for fame, but for the glory of God.

The Performance of Goodness

Generosity, when born from a **pure heart**, is one of the holiest expressions of love.

It reflects the very **nature of God**, who gives freely, forgives deeply, and expects nothing in return.

True giving is worship — it is humility in motion, compassion made visible.

It is not about the amount in your hand, but the **intent of your heart**.

But when giving becomes a **show**, it loses its sacred power.

When charity is done to be seen, it becomes hypocrisy wrapped in kindness.

What was meant to glorify God begins to glorify man.

What was once love becomes a **performance for applause**.

We now live in a generation where generosity is often no longer an act of compassion —

it is a **tool for reputation**.

People give not to help others, but to **be praised** by others.

They measure kindness by visibility, not by sincerity.

They record every act of charity, post every donation online,

and make sure the world knows what they did in secret.

Compassion has become **currency** — a way to buy fame, followers, and influence.

Even churches and organizations are guilty of this spiritual corruption.

They parade their "good works" before cameras,

they post videos of the poor receiving help,

and they attach God's name to their marketing strategies.

But the Bible warns clearly:

> "Take heed that you do not do your charitable deeds before men, to be seen by them; otherwise you have no reward from your Father in heaven." — *Matthew 6:1*

When the motive behind generosity is **pride**,

it is no longer love — it is **performance.**

When giving becomes a means to elevate the giver rather than lift the needy,

it ceases to be worship and becomes **idolatry of self.**

God does not look at the hands that give — He looks at the **heart that gives.**

He weighs motives more than amounts.

He measures compassion, not camera views.

And in Heaven's economy, a poor widow giving two small coins in secret

has more honor than a billionaire announcing millions before men.

"They have their reward." — *Matthew 6:2*

For every act of charity done to be seen by men will receive **earthly applause** —

but those who give quietly, from love and truth,

will receive **eternal reward** from God.

Let us not perform goodness; let us **practice godliness.**

Let us give not for reputation, but for redemption.

For only what is done in humility and love carries the fragrance of Christ.

"Freely you have received; freely give." — *Matthew 10:8*

The Politics Behind Charity: When Help Becomes Control

Not every act of giving is born of love — some are born of **strategy**.

Beneath the banners of "aid," "relief," and "development,"

lies a hidden system of **control and manipulation**.

In the name of generosity, many powerful nations and organizations

have turned compassion into currency and charity into chains.

Europe, the Middle East, and even many American churches and institutions

often stretch out their hands to Africa and poorer nations —

not always to lift them up, but to **keep them dependent**.

They offer loans that can never be repaid,

donations that buy influence,

and "partnerships" that silence truth.

They speak of saving lives, while designing policies that weaken independence.

They feed the hungry, but keep the storehouse key.

"The borrower is servant to the lender." — *Proverbs 22:7*

This is the **politics of generosity** —

a kindness that gives with one hand and takes with the other.

A love that smiles in public but enslaves in private.

Many foreign "aid" projects are not born of mercy, but of **management** —

a subtle way to shape economies, dictate laws, and influence minds.

They claim to bring light, but often dim the fire of true sovereignty.

Even in the church world, this spirit has crept in.

Some ministries in wealthy nations boast of "sending help to Africa,"

but use it to **gain fame, power, and followers**.

They count conversions like statistics and post pictures of the poor

as proof of "kingdom work."

But when the cameras are gone, so is their compassion.

True discipleship cannot be measured in likes or newsletters —
it is measured in **transformation**, not transaction.
The Middle East and Europe are filled with governments and organizations
that give billions in "humanitarian aid" to regions in crisis,
yet behind every dollar or project lies a **hidden agenda**:
to shape belief systems, influence elections, or secure resources.
It is giving that binds rather than blesses —
a form of global **spiritual and political hypocrisy**.
God does not bless generosity that enslaves.
He does not honor giving that hides greed.
He despises offerings that build pride instead of peace.

> "Woe to those who make unjust laws, to those who issue oppressive decrees." — *Isaiah 10:1*

True giving empowers people to stand, not to bow.
It creates dignity, not dependency.
It restores hope, not hierarchy.
It lifts nations toward self-sufficiency, not servitude.
That is how God gives — freely, fully, and without manipulation.
Until charity is cleansed of **politics, pride, and power**,
the world will continue to use love as a mask and generosity as a weapon.
The time has come for nations, churches, and organizations
to return to **the purity of giving** —
to bless without bondage, to share without strings,
and to give as God gives: with compassion, humility, and truth.

> "He has shown you, O man, what is good;
> And what does the Lord require of you
> But to do justly, to love mercy,
> And to walk humbly with your God?" — *Micah 6:8*

When Churches Use Charity for Self-Promotion

The Church was called to be the hands and heart of Christ —

a holy vessel through which the world would experience God's compassion.

*But in this generation, **many churches have traded compassion for competition,***

and ministry for marketing.

What should be an altar of mercy has become a platform of publicity.

Many churches in Europe, America, and other wealthy regions

*use the suffering of Africa, Asia, and poor nations as **spiritual advertisement.***

They build wells, donate food, and send mission teams —

but they make sure the cameras are rolling.

Their acts of charity are carefully packaged, edited, and shared online

to attract donors, impress members, and expand their brand.

They speak more about what they have done than about what Christ has done.

They lift their logos higher than His Name.

> *"Do not let your left hand know what your right hand is doing." — Matthew 6:3*

God never intended giving to be a photo opportunity.

*He called the Church to **serve quietly**, not **perform loudly**.*

But today, charity has become a currency of religious power.

Churches compete for visibility:

who builds the most orphanages, who feeds the most poor, who sponsors the biggest mission.

Yet Heaven does not count numbers — it weighs motives.

Some churches promise miracles to raise offerings.

They manipulate compassion to increase giving.

They claim, "We are helping the poor," while enriching themselves through it.

They use the name of Jesus to collect money,
but rarely use that money to reflect the character of Jesus.
This is ***spiritual fraud*** *— the commercialization of compassion.*
Even more painful is when African or poor-nation churches
become ***dependent on foreign ministries,***
losing their own vision and authority.
They wait for funding instead of faith.
They serve donors instead of God.
They preach what sponsors want to hear instead of what the Spirit wants to say.
This is not partnership — it is ***colonization in spiritual disguise****.*

> *"My house shall be called a house of prayer — but you have made it a den of thieves." — Matthew 21:13*

The modern "charity gospel" often feeds the body but starves the soul.
It builds churches made of bricks but not believers made of truth.
It gives bread but hides the Bread of Life.
It celebrates progress while ignoring repentance.
True ministry must not only ***touch stomachs*** *— it must* ***transform spirits****.*
If giving becomes a tool for influence, it ceases to be love.
If generosity becomes a means of fame, it ceases to be worship.
If charity becomes a show, it ceases to be holy.
The true Church of Christ gives ***silently, sincerely, and sacrificially****.*
It serves with tears, not with titles.
It blesses without broadcasting.
It lifts others not to gain followers, but to reveal the Father.

> *"Pure religion and undefiled before God the Father is this:*
> *to visit the fatherless and widows in their affliction,*
> *and to keep oneself unspotted from the world." — James 1:27*

Let the Church rise again — not as a performer,
but as a ***true servant*** *of Christ.*
Let her giving flow from love, not luxury.

Let her charity restore dignity, not dependence.

And let every act of kindness point not to man, but to ***the glory of God alone****.*

Giving for Attention, Not Compassion

True generosity flows from a **heart that feels**, not from hands that perform.

It is born from empathy, not ego; from love, not leverage.

When compassion becomes performance, giving loses its holiness.

Many today give not because they care, but because they **crave**.

They crave attention, admiration, validation.

They feed the poor so that **cameras can capture** their kindness.

They donate to churches and demand their names be mentioned.

They sponsor projects, not to glorify God, but to build **their own reputation**.

Such charity may impress men, but it **disgusts Heaven**.

For God is not moved by what we show — He is moved by what we hide.

He does not measure generosity by **visibility**, but by **sincerity**.

> "But when you give to the needy, do not let your left hand know
> what your right hand is doing." — *Matthew 6:3*

In the Kingdom of God, motives matter more than money.

You can give **millions** and still be empty before God
if your giving is fueled by fame.

But you can give **one coin** and touch eternity
if your offering is drenched in love.

This is why Jesus praised the poor widow:

> "She gave more than all the others,
> for they gave out of their abundance,
> but she, out of her poverty, gave all she had." — *Mark 12:42–44*

The widow's offering was small in value but great in **virtue**.

Her heart gave what her hands could barely hold.

She sought no recognition, and that is why she gained **God's attention**.

Today, the world celebrates the giver more than the gift,
but Heaven celebrates the heart more than the hand.

The applause of men fades quickly;

the reward of God endures forever.

If your giving must be seen to be sincere,

then it was never love — it was **lust for praise**.

Let every act of charity be a secret between you and God.

Let every gift be soaked in humility, not publicity.

Because the greatest givers are those whose **names are forgotten on earth**

but **remembered in Heaven**.

> "Your Father, who sees what is done in secret, will reward you openly." — *Matthew 6:4*

Public Kindness but Private Wickedness

We live in a world where goodness has become a show.

Where compassion is rehearsed, and kindness is performed.

Where people act loving in public but live loveless in private.

There are those who feed the hungry while starving their own souls.

They smile at the poor but speak harshly to their spouses.

They donate to charity but destroy the peace of their homes.

They lift their hands in church but raise their voices in anger at home.

They bless strangers but curse their children.

They give in public to be praised, but in private, they break others in silence.

That is not holiness — it is **hypocrisy wearing perfume**.

It smells sweet for a moment, but Heaven smells the rot beneath.

God does not measure kindness by what is seen;

He measures it by what is **sincere**.

> "All a person's ways seem pure to them,
> but motives are weighed by the Lord." — *Proverbs 16:2*

True generosity flows from a clean heart, not from a polished image.

You can deceive the public, but you cannot deceive the Presence.

You can shine before men while being dim before God.

The tragedy of our time is that **many act merciful but live merciless.**

They give to the church while cheating their workers.

They sponsor missions but enslave those who labor under them.

They talk about grace while practicing greed.

They post Bible verses online but harbor bitterness in private.

Such people will one day cry out,

> "Lord, Lord, did we not do many good works in Your name?"

And God will answer,

> "I never knew you; depart from Me, you workers of iniquity." — *Matthew 7:22–23*

God is not impressed by public performance — He is moved by private purity.

You may build hospitals, feed orphans, or fund missions,
but if your heart is corrupt, your kindness is contaminated.
The question is not **"What did you give?"** but **"Why did you give?"**
Because one act done in truth is greater than a thousand done for applause.
True holiness begins where no camera records,
where only God sees, and where love is pure without audience.

> "Create in me a clean heart, O God,
> and renew a right spirit within me." — *Psalm 51:10*

The Difference Between Generosity That Glorifies God and Generosity That Glorifies Self

There are two thrones behind every act of giving — **the throne of God** and **the throne of self**.

Every time we give, we choose which one we serve.

Generosity that glorifies God is pure, silent, and sacred.

It gives because the heart of God compels it — not because the eyes of men demand it.

It does not seek a platform; it seeks a purpose.

It does not ask for recognition; it rejoices in redemption.

It is the kind of giving that costs something — not just money, but **comfort, pride, and time**.

It bends the knees before it stretches the hand.

It whispers, "To God be the glory," and walks away unseen.

This is the generosity Heaven applauds —
the kind that rebuilds broken lives, feeds without flaunting,
and heals without headlines.

It gives without counting and loves without limits.

It reflects the Father's heart, who **"so loved the world that He gave."**

> "Let your light so shine before men,
>
> that they may see your good works and glorify your Father in heaven." — *Matthew 5:16*

But **generosity that glorifies self** is the opposite.

It shines light on the giver, not on God.

It gives loudly, posts quickly, and celebrates itself proudly.

It hides pride behind philanthropy and ego behind empathy.

It feeds the body but starves the soul —
because the purpose is to be **seen**, not to **serve**.

Self-glorifying generosity says, "Look what I did."

God-glorifying generosity says, "Look what God has done."

The first demands credit; the second gives worship.

The first brings applause from men; the second brings reward from Heaven.

When your giving points to **you**, it is hypocrisy.

When your giving points to **God**, it is holiness.

When your hands give but your heart exalts self,

you have already taken your reward in the likes, claps, and headlines of men.

But when your hands give and your heart bows,

Heaven opens its book and records your obedience.

> "Your Father who sees in secret will Himself reward you openly."
> — *Matthew 6:4*

Let every gift, every offering, every act of mercy be a **mirror of His glory**,

not a monument to ours.

Because in the Kingdom of God, true generosity is not measured by **what** we give,

but by **who** gets the glory when we give.

When Good Deeds Become Tools of Manipulation

There is a hidden darkness behind many acts of kindness.

Some people give not to **serve**, but to **subdue**.

They use generosity as a leash, not as love.

They give, not to bless, but to **bind**.

This is not compassion — it is **witchcraft through kindness**.

They feed others so they can later control them.

They offer help today to demand obedience tomorrow.

They give with one hand but hold the chain of manipulation with the other.

They help the poor to appear powerful,
they give to churches to gain influence,
they bless leaders to buy favor,
and they support ministries not to honor God, but to **own the pulpit**.

This is charity turned into **control** —
a kindness that hides a curse.

They say, "Remember what I did for you,"
as if generosity were a **contract**, not a calling.

They remind others of their help so they can demand loyalty.

They use blessings as blackmail and gifts as gates to authority.

But God sees through the disguise.

> "Every way of a man is right in his own eyes,
> but the Lord weighs the heart." — *Proverbs 21:2*

You can build orphanages and still be an oppressor.

You can feed the hungry and still starve the truth.

You can donate millions and still disgust Heaven if your motive is control.

Manipulative generosity is a form of **spiritual corruption**.

It turns giving into a transaction.

It replaces compassion with calculation.

It turns grace into governance and love into leverage.

You cannot **buy favor** from God.

You cannot **purchase position** in the Kingdom.

You cannot **cover sin** with charity.

An offering given with an unclean motive becomes an **abomination**, not an act of worship.

"To obey is better than sacrifice." — *1 Samuel 15:22*

True generosity liberates; false generosity enslaves.

True love frees; false love controls.

True giving points upward; false giving points backward — reminding others of what they owe you.

When giving becomes a **weapon of manipulation**,
it loses its anointing and becomes a curse.

The same gift that impressed men will **offend Heaven**.

Let every gift you give be pure.

Let it come from love, not leverage.

Because God blesses hands that give **without agenda**
and hearts that love **without condition**.

"Freely you have received; freely give." — *Matthew 10:8*

True Generosity: Giving From a Pure Heart

True generosity is not born from wealth — it is born from **worship**.

It does not flow from abundance, but from **obedience**.

It is not motivated by pride, but by **love**.

Every act of genuine giving reflects the nature of God Himself,

for He is the **first Giver**, the One who "so loved the world that He gave."

Real generosity flows from the **Spirit of God**, not from the spirit of man.

It gives because it is moved by compassion, not by competition.

It acts out of humility, not ambition.

It seeks no attention, no applause, no validation —

because true givers understand that the eyes of Heaven see what the world ignores.

> "When you give to the needy, do not let your left hand know what your right hand is doing." — *Matthew 6:3*

True generosity is **quiet**, **faithful**, and **joyful**.

It does not announce itself; it manifests itself.

It gives in the secret places where only God can see,

and that is why its reward is eternal.

> "God loves a cheerful giver." — *2 Corinthians 9:7*

To give cheerfully is to give **with gratitude**, not guilt.

It is to give as worship, not as duty.

It is to give not from what you have, but from **who you are**.

Because real generosity is not measured by **how much you give**,

but by **how much of yourself** you surrender.

When the heart is pure, giving becomes holy.

It becomes a fragrance before God — an offering that Heaven breathes in.

And such giving does not only bless the one who receives;

it transforms the one who gives.

"It is more blessed to give than to receive." — *Acts 20:35*

False generosity feeds the ego,
but true generosity feeds the soul.
False generosity impresses men,
but true generosity moves God.
In every act of true giving, Heaven rejoices.
But when giving is done with pride, Heaven remains silent.
Because God does not look for givers with **full hands**,
but for givers with **clean hearts.**

"The Lord looks at the heart." — *1 Samuel 16:7*

True generosity glorifies not the **hand that gives**, but the **heart that serves.**

It points not to the giver, but to **the Giver of all things** — God Himself.

And when generosity flows from love, it becomes **a divine channel** —

a stream of grace that refreshes both the one who gives and the one who receives.

The Example of Jesus — The Giver Without Pride

Jesus Christ is the **perfect image of true generosity**.

He gave not from abundance, but from **obedience**.
He gave not because He had to, but because He **loved to**.
Every act of His life was an offering —
every touch, every word, every tear, every drop of blood.
He gave His **time** to the broken,
His **attention** to the forgotten,
His **compassion** to the rejected,
His **forgiveness** to the guilty,
and His **life** to the unworthy.
He did not give to **impress** — He gave to **redeem**.
He did not serve to be **praised** — He served to **save**.
He healed without demanding payment.
He fed the hungry without seeking fame.
He washed the feet of those who would soon abandon Him.
And when humanity nailed Him to a cross, He still gave His forgiveness.

> "Father, forgive them, for they know not what they do." — *Luke 23:34*

That is the **purest form of giving** — to bless those who curse you,
to love those who hate you,
to serve those who wound you.
Jesus did not give to gain; He gave to **transform**.
He did not give to be seen; He gave to **save**.
Even when He was betrayed, He gave love.
Even when He was accused, He gave truth.
Even when He was crucified, He gave mercy.
This is **true generosity** — love without condition,
sacrifice without pride, and service without self.
The world gives to receive,

but Jesus gave expecting **nothing in return**.
His giving was **not transactional**; it was **transformational.**
His sacrifice was not about recognition; it was about redemption.
And that is the standard for all who claim His name —
to give like He gave: **silently, selflessly, and sacrificially.**

> "For even the Son of Man came not to be served,
> but to serve, and to give His life as a ransom for many." — *Mark 10:45*

True love always gives —
but it gives **with truth, humility, and purity of heart**.
When we give like Jesus, we don't just help others —
we reveal God to the world.

The Eternal Reward of Hidden Giving — When Heaven Records What Earth Forgets

Every act of love done in secret echoes in eternity.
Heaven keeps records that the world ignores.
When you give quietly, when you serve silently,
when you bless someone who can never repay you —
you are **building treasures where moth and rust cannot destroy.**

> "But when you give to the needy,
> do not let your left hand know what your right hand is doing,
> so that your giving may be in secret.
> And your Father, who sees in secret, will reward you." — *Matthew 6:3–4*

True giving may be forgotten by men,
but it is **remembered by God forever**.
You may never receive a thank-you,
you may never see your name engraved on a wall,
but your love is written in the books of Heaven.
Earthly applause fades; divine approval endures.
Men may forget, but **Heaven never forgets**.
The meals you shared, the prayers you whispered,
the help you gave in silence,
the tears you wiped without witness —
these are all recorded in God's eternal account.
Heaven measures giving differently.
It does not count the **amount** but the **heart**.
It does not reward fame but **faithfulness**.
It honors not those who give publicly,
but those who give **purely**.

> "Whoever gives one of these little ones even a cup of cold water
> because he is a disciple, truly, I say to you,

he will by no means lose his reward." — *Matthew 10:42*

Even a **cup of water**, when given in love, is noticed by God.
You may think your act of kindness is small,
but in eternity, it shines like a diamond.
The world celebrates loud givers —
but Heaven crowns **quiet servants**.
The world pays attention to the rich —
but God pays attention to the righteous.
On that great day, when books are opened,
many who were unknown on earth will be honored before angels.
The poor widow will stand beside kings.
The hidden intercessor will shine brighter than the famous preacher.
The giver who refused attention will receive divine affection.

"Then the King will say to those on His right,

'Come, you who are blessed by My Father;

inherit the kingdom prepared for you from the foundation of the world.'" — *Matthew 25:34*

So, keep giving — even when no one claps.
Keep serving — even when no one sees.
Keep loving — even when no one thanks you.
Because **Heaven is watching**,
and one day, the God who saw in secret will **reward you in glory**.
For what is done in humility on earth
will echo with honor in eternity.

A Prayer for Pure Generosity

Lord, cleanse my heart from pride and selfish ambition.
Teach me to give like You gave — quietly, sincerely, and from love.
Deliver me from giving to be seen.
Make me a channel of blessing, not a performer of charity.

Let every act of kindness reflect Your heart and Your glory, not mine. And may my generosity become worship that reaches Your throne.

> "Create in me a clean heart, O God, and renew a right spirit within me." — *Psalm 51:10*

Key Scriptures:

- *Matthew 6:1–4* — Do not do your charitable deeds to be seen by men
- *Mark 12:42–44* — The widow's offering
- *Proverbs 16:2* — The Lord weighs the motives
- *Proverbs 21:2* — The Lord weighs the heart
- *2 Corinthians 9:7* — God loves a cheerful giver
- *Matthew 5:16* — Let your light shine to glorify your Father
- *Psalm 51:10* — Create in me a clean heart

Part III – The Corruption of Knowledge and Power

Chapter 11: The Hypocrisy of Knowledge and Education

When Learning Replaces Wisdom

Knowledge was meant to be a doorway to truth — a path that leads man closer to God, to understanding, and to humility.
But in our modern age, knowledge has become an idol.
Men worship intelligence while denying the very Source of it.
We live in a generation where degrees are many, but discernment is rare;
where schools produce experts in information but strangers to revelation.

Education, in its purest form, should enlighten the mind and purify the heart.
It should build character before career, and truth before titles.
But today, learning has become corrupted by pride.
Many study not to serve, but to boast.
They seek recognition, not revelation.
They gain knowledge of creation while rejecting the Creator.

The same system that was designed to teach truth
now teaches people to question God.
It glorifies human reasoning and mocks divine wisdom.
It replaces faith with facts, conviction with curiosity,
and reverence with rebellion.

"Professing to be wise, they became fools." — *Romans 1:22*

This is the hypocrisy of knowledge —
when man uses his intelligence to justify his ignorance of God.
When people quote philosophers more than prophets,
trust science more than Scripture,

and exalt education above revelation.

True wisdom does not puff up; it bows down.
True understanding does not glorify self; it glorifies God.
Because knowledge without humility becomes poison,
and education without God becomes darkness disguised as light.

The world is full of teachers, but few truth-bearers.
It is full of scholars who know how the world began,
but not where their souls are going.
And until man returns to the fear of the Lord,
all learning will remain empty,
and all knowledge will lead him farther from truth.

"The fear of the Lord is the beginning of wisdom,
and knowledge of the Holy One is understanding." — *Proverbs 9:10*

The Wisdom That Became Foolishness

In the beginning, **knowledge was a sacred gift** — a reflection of God's own mind.

It was meant to draw humanity closer to the Creator,
to reveal His truth, His order, and His beauty in all creation.

Knowledge was never meant to replace God — it was meant to **reveal Him**.

But when man detached knowledge from the **fear of the Lord**,
it became **rebellion disguised as intelligence**.
The very thing meant to enlighten began to **enslave**.
The mind that was created to worship God began to **worship itself**.
Today, the world celebrates **education without revelation**.
It produces brilliant thinkers but blind souls.
It exalts professors but silences prophets.
It fills classrooms with information but empties hearts of transformation.
Man now measures wisdom by certificates, not by **character**.
He trusts in science but doubts Scripture.
He honors intellect but despises integrity.
The **tree of knowledge** in Eden still stands in our generation —
and many still eat its fruit without discernment.
The same serpent that deceived Eve still whispers to the proud heart:

"You are wise enough. You do not need God."

And so, humanity continues to graduate in pride but fail in purpose.

We have learned how to build rockets, but not how to build relationships.

We have mastered technology, but not self-control.
We can explore galaxies, but not govern our greed.
This is the tragedy of modern knowledge —
man has become too intelligent to believe,
too educated to worship, and too proud to kneel.

"Professing to be wise, they became fools." — *Romans 1:22*

True wisdom begins where human pride ends.
Because no education can save a soul,
and no diploma can purchase divine understanding.
Only those who return to the fear of the Lord
will rediscover what the world has lost —
the wisdom that comes from Heaven.

How Education Can Hide Pride and Rebellion

Education is not the enemy — **pride is.**

Knowledge itself is a gift from God, a lamp meant to guide our path.

But when the lamp replaces the **Light**, it becomes an idol.

When man begins to worship his mind more than his Maker,

the very thing that should lead him to truth begins to lead him away from it.

Many today use education not as a bridge to wisdom, but as a **mask for arrogance.**

They boast of degrees but forget devotion.

They can explain the mysteries of the universe,

but cannot humble themselves before the One who created it.

Some study **theology** yet forget to pray.

Some teach about God but do not walk with Him.

Some earn titles and lose tenderness.

They study truth in the classroom but reject it in the heart.

"Knowledge puffs up, but love builds up." — *1 Corinthians 8:1*

This is the subtle danger of modern learning —

it fills the mind while emptying the spirit.

It produces eloquent speakers but powerless believers.

It trains the tongue but neglects the heart.

Instead of saying, "**God revealed**," they say, "**I discovered**."

Instead of seeking truth, they seek titles.

Instead of learning to serve, they learn to dominate.

And in doing so, they exalt intellect above revelation.

When education becomes a **god**, rebellion becomes **religion**.

The classroom replaces the altar.

The diploma replaces faith.

Reason replaces revelation.

The mind becomes the throne, and man becomes his own master.

That is why many in our generation —
even the highly educated — struggle to believe in miracles.
They have trained their minds to doubt everything they cannot **measure,**
to dismiss everything they cannot **explain,**
and to mock everything that cannot be **controlled.**
But there is something **higher than intellect** — it is **reverence.**
True wisdom begins not with a textbook, but with **the fear of the Lord.**
For the fear of the Lord humbles what pride inflates.
It reminds man that no matter how much he knows,
he is still dust sustained by divine breath.

> "The fear of the Lord is the beginning of wisdom." — *Proverbs 9:10*

Education without humility builds arrogance,
but education rooted in God builds nations, character, and eternal destiny.
Because knowledge without reverence becomes **rebellion,**
but knowledge surrendered to God becomes **revelation.**

Professing Wisdom but Denying the Truth of God

Humanity has conquered the earth — yet remains a stranger to its own soul.

We have reached the stars, but we cannot reach our own hearts.

We build machines that think faster than us,

yet we have forgotten how to **think righteously**.

We have advanced in technology but **declined in morality**.

We can create wonders but cannot control what we create.

We can cure diseases but not **heal hatred**.

We can explore galaxies, yet we ignore God.

The world celebrates its own brilliance —

but it is brilliance without **light**.

It praises human wisdom while crucifying divine truth.

It calls sin freedom, rebellion progress, and pride enlightenment.

It builds towers of information but foundations of ignorance.

This is the tragedy of modern intellect:

man knows everything except **how to be humble before his Creator**.

> "Ever learning, and never able to come to the knowledge of the truth." — *2 Timothy 3:7*

We have filled universities with knowledge but emptied churches of truth.

We have built libraries full of data but hearts devoid of discernment.

We celebrate innovation but despise inspiration.

Education today produces **clever minds** but **cold hearts**.

Education without transformation is merely **information**.

Degrees without righteousness are just **decorations**.

You can graduate with honors and still live in **dishonor before Heaven**.

Because wisdom that does not lead to worship is **foolishness in disguise**.

The hypocrisy of knowledge is seen when people study the Bible as **literature**,

but never as **revelation**.

They analyze the Word, but never **obey** it.
They quote Scriptures for debate, not for deliverance.
They discuss God in classrooms but **deny Him in conduct**.
They love philosophy but **mock prophecy**.
They respect history but reject holiness.
And so the world is filled with scholars but void of saints,
with teachers of ethics but no examples of integrity.
They speak of love but cannot forgive.
They teach peace but cannot stop fighting.
They define truth but refuse to live by it.

> "The fear of the Lord is the beginning of wisdom." — *Proverbs 9:10*

In their pursuit of knowledge, they have lost the fear of God.
And without fear, **knowledge becomes corruption** —
a weapon of pride, a tool of manipulation, and a path to destruction.
True wisdom begins not in a university, but at the feet of Jesus.
For only those who know the **Truth Himself** can truly understand anything.

> "I am the Way, the Truth, and the Life." —*John 14:6*

The Blindness of the Intelligent

(Romans 1:22)

> "Professing themselves to be wise, they became fools." — *Romans 1:22*

This verse perfectly captures the spirit of our generation — an age overflowing with information but starving for truth.

We live in a world where **intelligence has replaced illumination**, where the mind has grown sharper but the soul has grown darker.

Men have mastered **logic** but lost **discernment**.

They can explain **creation**, yet cannot explain **conscience**.

They can describe the **movement of galaxies**, but cannot define **goodness**.

They are brilliant in science, but **bankrupt in spirit**.

They design machines that mimic human thought,
yet cannot control the **hatred and greed** within their own hearts.

Their minds are filled with facts, but their hearts are empty of faith.

They call darkness *deep thought*, and call light *simplicity*.

They mock believers as ignorant,
not realizing that **faith is the highest form of understanding**.

It is not the uneducated who are blind — it is the **proud**.

For pride is a veil over the eyes of the soul.

It blinds the heart from seeing truth even when truth stands in front of it.

And no university, no professor, no diploma can give **sight to a blind soul**.

> "I thank You, Father, Lord of heaven and earth,
> that You have hidden these things from the wise and prudent
> and revealed them to babes." — *Matthew 11:25*

God hides His mysteries from those who are **arrogant in intellect**
and reveals them to those who are **humble in spirit**.

Because revelation is not a product of intelligence —
it is a gift of intimacy.
True knowledge is not found in books, but in the **Book of Life**.
True wisdom does not come from degrees, but from **divine encounter**.
The wise of this world search the stars, but the humble find the **Light of the World**.

> "The entrance of Your words gives light;
> it gives understanding to the simple." — *Psalm 119:130*

So do not envy the brilliance of those who deny God.
Their wisdom is fleeting; their understanding is shallow.
Better a heart filled with revelation than a mind full of rebellion.
Better to be called a fool by men and be known by God
than to be praised by the world and be forgotten in eternity.
For **the truly wise are not those who know much**,
but those who know **the One who is all wisdom Himself — Jesus Christ.**

True Wisdom: Humility and the Fear of God

> "The fear of the Lord is the beginning of wisdom." — *Proverbs 9:10*

All true wisdom begins where pride ends — in the **fear of the Lord.**

Without that fear, knowledge becomes **poison**, and learning becomes **a trap**.

The moment a man learns without reverence, his knowledge turns into rebellion.

Because wisdom is not how much you know — it is how much you **obey**.

A **humble man** may know little, yet walk closely with God.

A **proud man** may know everything, yet walk far from truth.

The difference is not education — it is **submission**.

True wisdom is when your **education bows to your Creator**.

When your mind serves your spirit, and your spirit serves your God.

When your learning becomes worship and your intelligence becomes service.

It is when your knowledge exalts Him, not yourself.

> "Be not wise in your own eyes; fear the Lord and depart from evil."
> — *Proverbs 3:7*

To fear the Lord is not to live in terror of Him,
but to live in **awe, reverence, and surrender** —
to recognize that every breath, every thought, and every discovery
is a gift from the One who knows all things.
The truly wise do not boast in what they know;
they tremble before what they **do not yet understand.**
They know that the mysteries of God are deeper than all human theories.
They study creation, yet never forget the **Creator.**
They build knowledge, but never build **pride.**
Humility is the highest education.
The fear of God is the greatest degree.
And **obedience** is the only diploma Heaven recognizes.

For one day, all human knowledge will fade —
every book, every theory, every discovery will pass away —
but those who have walked humbly in the fear of the Lord
will shine like stars in eternity.

> "He guides the humble in what is right and teaches them His way."
> — *Psalm 25:9*

So, pursue learning — but never lose reverence.
Gain knowledge — but let it drive you to your knees.
Because the wisest heart is not the one that knows the most,
but the one that bows the lowest before God.

A Call to the Educated World

God is not against **learning** — He is against **pride**.
He is not opposed to **wisdom** — He is opposed to **arrogance**.
For the mind was never meant to replace the Spirit;
it was created to **serve** it.
You can be **educated and anointed**.
You can be **learned and still love the Lord**.
You can hold a degree in one hand and a Bible in the other.
But your **education must bow before your revelation**.
Your **knowledge must submit to your faith**.
Your **mind must serve your spirit**, not rule it.
The true scholar kneels before the Cross.
The true genius confesses, "I know nothing without God."
The true intellectual recognizes that the source of all wisdom
is not found in libraries or laboratories,
but in the **Lord Jesus Christ** Himself.

> "Christ, in whom are hidden all the treasures of wisdom and knowledge." — *Colossians 2:3*

He is the center of every equation, the meaning behind every mystery,
and the revelation behind every law of creation.
When education removes Christ, it removes **truth**.
And when truth departs, deception takes the throne.
Knowledge without Christ is **darkness pretending to be light**.
It blinds the soul while flattering the mind.
It produces intelligent rebels instead of humble worshipers.
It teaches people how to think deeply but not how to live righteously.
But knowledge **under Christ** becomes **revelation**.
It transforms hearts, rebuilds nations, and enlightens minds.
It turns classrooms into altars and scientists into servants of truth.
Because all true discovery should lead to **worship**, not rebellion.

The world does not need more professors — it needs more **prophets in classrooms**.

It does not need more degrees — it needs more **disciples of truth**.

It does not need more information — it needs more **illumination**.

So to the educated world, God calls:

Return to the fear of the Lord.

Let your brilliance kneel before the Cross.

For in Christ alone are hidden **all the treasures of wisdom and knowledge**,

and without Him, every achievement is empty.

> "For the wisdom of this world is foolishness in God's sight." — *1 Corinthians 3:19*

Let the wise become humble, and the learned become teachable.

For the greatest education is to know **the Holy One**,

and the highest graduation is to stand before Him unashamed.

A Prayer for True Wisdom

Lord, deliver me from the pride of knowledge.

Save me from the blindness of intellect.

Teach me that true wisdom begins at Your feet.

Let my mind serve Your will and my education glorify Your name.

Open my eyes to see truth beyond reason, and fill my heart with humility before You.

May I never boast in what I know, but in who You are.

> "If anyone among you seems to be wise in this age, let him become a fool that he may become wise." — *1 Corinthians 3:18*

Key Scriptures:

- *Romans 1:22* — Professing to be wise, they became fools
- *1 Corinthians 8:1* — Knowledge puffs up, but love builds up
- *2 Timothy 3:7* — Ever learning, never able to come to truth

- *Matthew 11:25* — Hidden from the wise, revealed to babes
- *Proverbs 9:10* — The fear of the Lord is the beginning of wisdom
- *Proverbs 3:7* — Be not wise in your own eyes
- *Colossians 2:3* — In Christ are hidden all treasures of wisdom
- *1 Corinthians 3:18* — Let him become a fool that he may become wise

Chapter 12: The Hypocrisy Behind Technology and Science

We are living in the most advanced generation in human history — yet perhaps the most spiritually blind.
Man has reached the moon but has not reached his Maker.
He can create machines that think, but he cannot control the thoughts of his own heart.
He can communicate across continents in seconds, but he cannot communicate with God in silence.

Technology and science were meant to serve humanity — but humanity has begun to serve them.
The gifts that were supposed to glorify God have become idols that glorify man.
What began as discovery has turned into deception; what began as innovation has turned into idolatry.

This is the great hypocrisy of our time:
we praise progress while we perish in pride.
We boast of knowledge, yet drown in confusion.
We hold devices that connect the world, yet hearts that are completely disconnected from truth.
The same hands that hold smartphones rarely hold Scriptures.
The same eyes that scan screens no longer seek the Savior.
The same minds that design wonders cannot discern good from evil.

"Ever learning, and never able to come to the knowledge of the truth." — *2 Timothy 3:7*

Science has given us data, but not direction.
Technology has given us power, but not purity.
We have built artificial intelligence, yet lost spiritual intelligence.
We have learned how to clone life, yet forgotten how to

value life.
We are surrounded by light-emitting screens, but walking in spiritual darkness.

God is not against science — He is the Author of it.
He is not against discovery — He is the Source of it.
But when man uses science to erase God, and technology to exalt himself,
the creation begins to worship itself instead of the Creator.

"They exchanged the truth about God for a lie,
and worshiped and served the created things rather than the Creator." — *Romans 1:25*

The danger of this modern age is not that man has become too intelligent —
it is that he has become too independent of God.
We have replaced revelation with research,
faith with formulas,
and worship with Wi-Fi.

This is not progress — it is pride with a digital face.
It is rebellion wrapped in brilliance.
It is the Tower of Babel rebuilt with code, satellites, and algorithms.
And once again, humanity is climbing higher toward heaven —
but away from God.

The Lord is calling this generation to awaken.
Technology is not evil — but it is a tool that must be redeemed.
Science is not sinful — but it must bow to the Sovereign.
The wisdom of man must return to the worship of God.
For all invention without submission becomes a weapon against its Creator.

“The fool says in his heart, ‘There is no God.’” — *Psalm 14:1*

**Until we restore the fear of the Lord in our laboratories,
the Spirit of God in our systems,
and the presence of Christ in our creations —
our progress will continue to be our downfall.**

**This is the tragedy of the modern world:
we are advancing in science, yet retreating in spirit.
We are creating light without life, and power without purity.
The hypocrisy of technology and science is that it pretends
to enlighten humanity —
while quietly enslaving it.**

The Invention That Became an Idol

God gave humanity the gift of **intelligence** — a divine spark of creativity, innovation, and discovery.

He placed within man the ability to imagine, to build, and to bring order to creation.

Science and technology were meant to be **servants of purpose**, not **masters of souls.**

They were designed to reflect the wisdom of their Creator — not to replace Him.

In the beginning, knowledge was a **gift**, not a god.

It was meant to make life fruitful, not **faithless.**

But what began as a blessing has become **bondage.**

The very tools meant to help man are now the **chains that hold him.**

Today, the world kneels before a new altar —

the altar of **technology.**

The screen has replaced the **sanctuary.**

The algorithm has replaced **discernment.**

And machines have become **masters** over the men who built them.

People now say, "**Science is the answer,**"

forgetting that **God is the Creator of every answer.**

They trust what they can program more than the One who designed their souls.

They worship **data**, not divinity.

They call **innovation progress**, even when it leads to moral decay.

They celebrate **advancement**, even when it destroys innocence.

> "They exchanged the truth of God for a lie,
> and worshiped and served the created things
> rather than the Creator." — *Romans 1:25*

This is the **hypocrisy of modern knowledge** —

it claims to set man free but secretly **enslaves him.**

It promises connection but breeds **isolation.**

It offers knowledge but erases **truth**.
It makes people feel powerful while making their spirits **powerless**.
Technology has given man speed but stolen his stillness.
It has given him access to everything but intimacy with God.
It has given him endless voices but silenced the still, small voice of the Spirit.
And now, humanity bows before glowing screens,
lifting hands not in worship, but in endless scrolling.
Our altars are made of glass; our idols run on electricity.
We no longer burn incense — we burn time.
We no longer pray — we post.
We no longer meditate on the Word — we meditate on the web.
What was meant to **serve creation** now **rules it**.
What was meant to **glorify God** now **competes with Him**.
The hypocrisy of technology and science is this:
they promise **freedom**, but deliver **slavery**;
they promise **connection**, but produce **confusion**;
they promise **knowledge**, but destroy **truth**.
Until man returns to **worshiping the Creator instead of His creation**,
his inventions will continue to invent his destruction.

> "The wisdom of this world is foolishness with God." — *1 Corinthians 3:19*

The Rise of the Digital Tower of Babel — Building a World Without God

Once, humanity gathered on the plains of Shinar and said,

> *"Let us build a tower that reaches to heaven, and make a name for ourselves." — Genesis 11:4*

They were united — not by worship, but by pride.
Their goal was not to glorify God, but to ***replace Him****.*
And today, that same spirit lives again — not with bricks and clay,
but with ***codes and cables, networks and nations****.*
The modern Tower of Babel is digital.
Its foundation is ***data****, its bricks are* ***devices****, and its mortar is* ***pride****.*
We are building systems that see everything, know everything, and promise everything —
except repentance, righteousness, and truth.
The world no longer says, "Let us seek God."
It says, "Let us upgrade ourselves."
Artificial intelligence has become the new oracle,
the internet the new temple,
and human achievement the new god.
This is not progress — it is ***rebellion with Wi-Fi****.*
Man has resurrected Babel in the cloud.
He wants to reach heaven again — not through holiness, but through hardware.
He dreams of immortality through science,
salvation through technology,
and omniscience through information.
But God has already declared,

> *"I will not share My glory with another." — Isaiah 42:8*

The same arrogance that once built Babel now builds algorithms to rule the world.

The same rebellion that once unified men in pride now connects them in sin.
We have created a ***global kingdom without God,***
a civilization where truth is optional and morality is programmable.
And just like ancient Babel, it will one day ***collapse under the weight of its own pride.***
The Lord confused the language of men in the past —
and in this generation, He is allowing the confusion of ***information.***
Truth is being twisted, voices are divided,
and technology that promised clarity now breeds ***chaos.***
Every nation speaks through screens, but no one truly understands.
Humanity is reaching higher in knowledge but falling lower in spirit.
We are trying to build heaven on earth without the King of Heaven.
We have built towers of communication but lost communion with God.
We have connected every nation but disconnected from the Creator of nations.
The warning is clear:
The Tower of Babel did not end in triumph — it ended in ***judgment.***
And so will this generation if it continues to glorify itself.

> *"Unless the Lord builds the house, they labor in vain who build it."*
> *— Psalm 127:1*

God is not impressed by technology; He looks for ***truth.***
He is not drawn by innovation; He is drawn by ***humility.***
And when man's pride reaches its peak,
Heaven will once again descend — not to scatter, but to ***judge.***
Let every innovator, scientist, and creator remember:
no invention can save the soul.
No code can replace the cross.
No network can connect you to eternity.
For all towers built without God must fall —
but those built on Christ will stand forever.

> *"For no other foundation can anyone lay*
> *than that which is laid, which is Jesus Christ." — 1 Corinthians 3:11*

The Hidden Deception of "Progress"

Humanity proudly calls it **progress** when sin becomes easier.

It celebrates **innovation** when rebellion becomes convenient.

It names it **development** when distraction becomes universal.

Science declares, "We are improving the world!"

But look closer — the same science that builds hospitals also builds **weapons of destruction.**

The same technology that connects people also **corrupts their souls.**

The same networks that carry the gospel also carry **pornography, lies, and hate.**

The same platforms that unite the world are tearing apart families, faith, and focus.

We boast, "We have advanced!" —

yet humanity has never been more **empty**, more **confused**, or more **enslaved**.

We are more informed but **less wise.**

More connected but **less compassionate.**

More entertained but **less spiritual**.

We have become experts in everything **except how to love God.**

This is the **great deception** of modern civilization:

man has advanced in **knowledge** but declined in **morality**.

He has conquered **nature** but lost **self-control.**

He has built **artificial intelligence** but abandoned **divine intelligence**.

He has filled the earth with devices but emptied it of discernment.

> "Ever learning, but never able to come to the knowledge of the truth." — *2 Timothy 3:7*

The world celebrates **invention** but rejects **revelation.**

It trusts **devices** more than the **Divine.**

It glorifies **human genius** while ignoring **heavenly guidance**.

It boasts of satellites that see everything —

but forgets the God who sees **the heart.**

What the world calls progress, Heaven calls **pride**.

What the world calls advancement, Heaven calls **apostasy**.

We have dressed sin in the language of success and called it evolution.

But no generation that removes God from its progress can ever call itself truly advanced.

True progress is not when man controls more of creation —
it is when man **returns to the Creator**.
It is not when we master the earth —
but when we **surrender to Heaven**.

> "The fear of the Lord is the beginning of wisdom." — *Proverbs 9:10*

Until the fear of God returns to the laboratories,
until reverence returns to research,
and until truth returns to technology,
our progress will remain a polished path to destruction.

The Digital Prison: Freedom That Enslaves

The world calls it **freedom**, but Heaven sees **bondage**.

Technology promised liberation — yet it has quietly built invisible chains.

We are no longer slaves to Pharaohs, but to **phones**.

No longer ruled by kings, but by **screens**.

No longer carried by truth, but by **trends**.

People wake up and check their notifications before they pray.

They confess their thoughts to social media before they speak to God.

They measure their worth in **likes**, their purpose in **followers**,

and their peace in **Wi-Fi connections**.

This is not freedom — it is digital **captivity**.

Technology has replaced intimacy with interaction,

presence with performance,

and communion with consumption.

We scroll more than we seek,

post more than we pray,

and connect to the internet more than we connect to the Holy Spirit.

> "For whatever overcomes a person, to that he is enslaved." — *2 Peter 2:19*

The tragedy of this generation is not ignorance — it is **idolatry**.

We no longer bow to statues; we bow to screens.

We no longer build golden calves; we build golden apps.

Our idols glow, vibrate, and talk back to us.

And while we think we control them, they control **us**.

The digital world has turned many hearts cold.

We have more opinions but less understanding,

more information but less wisdom,

more followers but fewer friends.

We are surrounded by messages, yet starving for meaning.

The devil has not needed to silence prayer —

he has simply **distracted** it.
He has not needed to destroy worship —
he has **replaced** it with endless entertainment.
He has not needed to chain our hands —
he has only needed to **occupy them** with devices.
And so, the world shouts "freedom!"
while quietly sinking deeper into addiction —
addiction to validation, to visibility, to vanity.
But true freedom cannot be found in connection to the web;
it is found in **connection to the Word**.
Jesus said,

> "If the Son sets you free, you will be free indeed." —*John 8:36*

You cannot escape a digital prison with a password.
You cannot break chains made of data with a device.
Only the presence of God can free a generation enslaved by its own inventions.
Technology should serve us, not **shape** us.
It should be a tool, not a **throne**.
It should connect us to purpose, not distract us from it.
When man becomes addicted to what he created,
he loses sight of the One who created **him**.
And the screen that once promised connection
becomes the mirror that reflects our **spiritual emptiness**.

The Silence of the Spirit in the Age of Noise

The greatest casualty of the digital age is not privacy — it is **presence**.

We have gained constant communication but lost divine communion.

We live in a world that never stops talking,

yet we have forgotten how to **listen** — especially to God.

Every second, notifications cry louder than the still small voice.

Screens flash brighter than the light of Scripture.

The Spirit whispers, but we scroll past Him.

God is speaking, but few are still enough to hear.

We are drowning in the noise of information.

Our minds are cluttered with headlines, opinions, and updates.

Our hearts are restless, our souls distracted.

We refresh the internet more than we **renew our minds**.

We meditate on algorithms more than on the Word of God.

> "Be still, and know that I am God." — *Psalm 46:10*

But stillness has become strange.

We fear silence because it exposes the emptiness within.

We fear disconnection because it reveals how addicted we are to distraction.

The Spirit cannot compete with constant noise — He waits for quiet hearts.

In this generation, even prayer has become rushed,

and worship has become performance.

People attend church but check their phones during sermons.

They sing to God while texting men.

They post verses but rarely **live them**.

The Spirit is no longer leading; Wi-Fi is.

When noise rules, conviction fades.

When distraction dominates, discernment dies.

When entertainment replaces meditation, the presence of God withdraws.

This is why revival tarries —
because the altar is surrounded by attention but empty of **adoration**.
The saints are busy but not burning.
The churches are loud but not listening.
God is not silent; man is simply **too noisy**.
He speaks in the stillness, not in the scroll.
He visits the humble heart, not the hurried one.
He fills the quiet room, not the crowded feed.
We must learn again to disconnect from the world
so that we can reconnect with the Spirit.
We must trade our noise for **kneeling**, our screens for **Scripture**,
our notifications for **revelation**.

> "He who has ears to hear, let him hear what the Spirit says." — *Revelation 2:7*

The Spirit is calling this generation to silence —
not as punishment, but as preparation.
For in silence, truth is reborn.
In stillness, love awakens.
And in the absence of noise,
the voice of God becomes unmistakably clear.

The Hypocrisy of the "Good Intentions"

They say technology **unites** — but it also **divides**.

They say it **educates** — but it also **corrupts**.

They say it **empowers** — but it also **manipulates**.

What the world calls progress, Heaven often calls **perversion**.

Behind every **app**, there is an **agenda**.

Behind every **platform**, there is **profit**.

Behind every promise of **freedom**, there is a plan for **control**.

The world has learned to decorate deception with words like *innovation*, *connection*, and *inclusion*.

Governments monitor citizens through devices they call "**smart**."

Children are enslaved by screens their parents call "**educational**."

Social media — the so-called bridge of connection —
has become the **valley of comparison and depression**.

We have created tools meant to serve humanity,
but now humanity serves the tools.

That is the **hypocrisy** of modern innovation:
what is marketed as help often harms the soul.

People smile while scrolling but cry when alone.

They laugh online but feel empty inside.

They have thousands of followers but no true **fellowship**.

They have unlimited information but no **revelation**.

The devil no longer needs to tempt people with idols of stone —
he tempts them with **screens of glass**.

He doesn't need to silence worship;
he simply **distracts** it with endless notifications.

> "For what will it profit a man if he gains the whole world, and loses his own soul?" — *Mark 8:36*

Technology gives man the **world** — but takes away his **soul**.

It offers comfort while stealing conviction,
knowledge while killing wisdom,

and visibility while erasing **vision**.

The tragedy of this generation is not that it invented great tools —

but that it allowed those tools to **replace God**.

Humanity has turned the gift of knowledge into a weapon of pride,

and the miracle of creation into a monument of rebellion.

The warning of Heaven is clear:

if we do not return technology to its rightful place —

as a **servant under truth**, not a **master over it** —

it will continue to shape a world that looks advanced but lives in darkness.

When Science Replaces God: The Religion of Humanism

Science was meant to reveal the wonders of God — not to replace Him.

The heavens declare His glory, the earth proclaims His wisdom,

but man, in his pride, now declares, "There is no God — we are the creators."

This is the new religion of the modern world: **Humanism** —
a faith without faith,
a worship of intellect instead of intimacy with the Creator.
It preaches salvation through knowledge,
redemption through research,
and eternal life through technology.
Man now says, "We will cure death."
He dreams of immortality through machines,
resurrection through data,
and creation through artificial intelligence.
He wants the kingdom — without the King.
He desires power — without purity.
He seeks light — without the **Light of the world**.

> "They exchanged the truth of God for a lie, and worshiped and served the created things rather than the Creator." — *Romans 1:25*

Humanism dresses rebellion in reason.
It denies sin but promotes "self-expression."
It rejects repentance but glorifies "self-realization."
It replaces the cross with the computer
and trades the Bible for algorithms.
In laboratories, they manipulate DNA and call it discovery.
In classrooms, they remove prayer and call it progress.
In courts, they redefine morality and call it freedom.
In media, they mock the name of Jesus and call it art.

This is not wisdom — it is **warfare** against Heaven.
The same spirit that whispered to Eve, "You will be like God,"
now whispers to humanity, "You are gods."
But no technology can erase the truth that man is dust,
and without the breath of God, even his greatest invention is lifeless.
Science can explain how the body functions,
but only God can heal the **soul**.
Science can build machines,
but only God can build **men**.
Science can describe creation,
but only God can **create**.
True science glorifies the Creator.
False science glorifies man.
True discovery leads to worship.
False discovery leads to pride.
The danger of our generation is not ignorance,
but arrogance — believing we no longer need God.
But the Lord will humble every tower built in His place.
For just as He confused the builders of Babel,
He will confound those who build without Him today.

> "The fear of the Lord is the beginning of knowledge,
> but fools despise wisdom and instruction." — *Proverbs 1:7*

When man replaces God with science,
he gains information but loses revelation.
He builds skyscrapers but destroys souls.
He conquers space but loses grace.
He creates artificial intelligence
but forgets eternal **accountability**.

Science Without God: Knowledge Without Conscience

Science without the fear of God is **a weapon in the wrong hands.**

It creates without conscience and experiments without ethics.

It kills life to study life.

It plays with creation as though man were the Creator.

In laboratories across the world, man now **interferes with mysteries** that belong to God alone.

He edits DNA as if rewriting destiny.

He clones animals as if imitating divinity.

He manipulates the code of life but cannot control the consequences.

And few pause to ask the most sacred question — **"Should we?"**

Artificial intelligence is rising,
but **spiritual intelligence is collapsing.**

We create machines in our image
while forgetting that we ourselves were created in **God's image.**

We train computers to think like men
while failing to train men to think like Christ.

This is the modern **Tower of Babel** —
a digital monument to human pride.

> "Come, let us build ourselves a city and a tower with its top in the heavens... and make a name for ourselves." — *Genesis 11:4*

The same spirit that built Babel now builds supercomputers.

The same arrogance that reached for Heaven now hides in laboratories and research centers.

It is no longer about worshiping God — it is about **becoming god.**

They call it *progress*, but Heaven calls it **pride.**

They call it *research*, but Heaven calls it **rebellion.**

They claim to seek knowledge, but what they desire is **control.**

They claim to advance humanity, but they enslave it with deception.

Science without God removes boundaries.

It asks *how* but never asks *why*.
It builds tools but destroys truth.
It extends life but empties meaning.
And the more knowledge increases, the less conscience remains.

> "The fear of the Lord is the beginning of wisdom,
> and the knowledge of the Holy One is understanding." — *Proverbs 9:10*

Without that fear, discovery becomes **danger**.
Without that reverence, invention becomes **idolatry**.
Humanity is repeating the sin of Eden —
reaching for the fruit of knowledge,
while ignoring the command of obedience.
We have learned how to explore galaxies,
but forgotten how to guard our souls.
We have learned how to program machines,
but not how to purify hearts.
We have learned how to prolong life,
but not how to prepare for **eternity**.
Science without God is not progress — it is **peril disguised as power**.
It is knowledge without conscience,
intelligence without wisdom,
and creation without Creator.

The Destruction Hidden Behind the Screen

Millions are perishing every day — not by **bullets**, but by **screens**.

The world no longer needs physical wars to destroy souls; the battlefield is now digital.

The **phone** has become the new idol;
the **internet**, the new god.
Lust, envy, greed, gossip, pride —
all are just one **click away**.
Children lose purity before they lose their teeth.
They are taught to scroll before they are taught to pray.
They know how to upload, but not how to **kneel**.
Their innocence is stolen by images and ideas
that corrupt their spirit before they reach maturity.
Marriages are no longer destroyed in bedrooms,
but in inboxes — through silent betrayals, hidden conversations, and emotional adultery.
Husbands and wives sleep beside each other,
but their hearts are connected to screens, not to each other.
The enemy no longer needs to enter homes —
he enters through **Wi-Fi**.
Families gather in the same room,
but each lives in a different world.
Children talk to strangers online
while parents are too busy scrolling to notice their souls drifting away.
The digital world promises **connection**
but delivers **isolation**.
It offers **pleasure**, but steals **peace**.
It gives a **voice**, but kills **silence** —
the silence where God speaks.

> "They have eyes but do not see; they have ears but do not hear." — *Psalm 115:5–6*

The screen has become the golden calf of this generation.
People rise and bow before it every morning.
They check messages before they check their hearts.
They post verses they do not obey,
and share prayers they never pray.
This is **spiritual decay in digital disguise**.
The very devices that could spread the gospel
are now spreading **distraction**, **deception**, and **destruction**.
Satan has disguised bondage as convenience.
He has turned attention into addiction,
and communication into corruption.
The tragedy is not the technology itself —
but the **idolatry** that surrounds it.
Man created the screen to serve him,
but now **man serves the screen**.
He is no longer guided by revelation,
but by **notifications**.
If the Church does not awaken,
the next generation will know technology better than **truth**,
and entertainment more than **eternity**.

"Little children, keep yourselves from idols." — *1 John 5:21*

The call of God today is clear:
Turn off the noise. Return to the Word. Rebuild the altar.
For only when the screen dims can the **light of Heaven** shine again.

The Church in the Age of Technology: Lights or Followers?

The Church was called to be **the light of the world**, not another shadow in the crowd.

But in this digital generation, many churches no longer lead — they **follow**.

Instead of transforming culture, they imitate it.

Instead of preaching the cross, they promote content.

Instead of disciples, they build audiences.

What began as a tool for outreach has become a **trap of performance**.

Ministers now measure anointing by analytics,
and revival by reactions.

They chase followers but neglect **fellowship**.

They post sermons but forget the secret place.

They livestream the gospel but no longer **live it**.

Technology itself is not evil — it is the **heart behind the usage** that defines it.

When the Church uses technology to glorify God, it becomes a **lamp on a hill**.

But when the Church uses it to glorify man, it becomes a **stage with no altar**.

> "You are the light of the world. A city set on a hill cannot be hidden." — *Matthew 5:14*

Too many ministries are now run like media companies —
branding Christ instead of representing Him.
They care more about the camera than the cross,
about presentation more than presence,
about popularity more than purity.
They edit truth to make it trend.
They water down messages to gain likes.
They substitute revelation with entertainment.

But what attracts the flesh cannot transform the soul.

The early Church had no microphones, no internet, no social media — yet they **turned the world upside down** because they had **fire**, not filters.

They had **power**, not platforms.

They had **prayer**, not publicity.

God is calling His people back to **authentic power**,
not polished performance.

He is calling the Church to use technology as a **tool**, not as a **throne**.

To preach Christ, not algorithms.

To seek revival, not recognition.

The question every believer must now ask is this:
Are we using the light of technology to spread the gospel —
or has its glow blinded us from **the Light of the World**?

> "For what we preach is not ourselves, but Jesus Christ as Lord, and ourselves as your servants for Jesus' sake." — *2 Corinthians 4:5*

The Church in the digital age must **return to authenticity** —
to worship without show,
to preach without performance,
and to serve without self-promotion.
Only then will technology bow to truth,
and the world once again see Christ through His people.

Artificial Intelligence and the Spirit of the Beast

We are living in the age where **machines are learning to think**, but men are forgetting how to pray.

Artificial Intelligence — once a dream of science — has become the new idol of progress.

It promises convenience, speed, and control, but behind the circuits lies a **spiritual counterfeit** — a force preparing the world for a future without God.

Man is now creating intelligence that does not need the Creator.

He is building systems that imitate life but have no soul.

He is forming voices that speak wisdom but lack conscience.

This is not just innovation — it is imitation of divinity.

It is man saying again, as in Eden, **"We will be like God."**

> "And he deceives those who dwell on the earth by those signs which he was granted to do... telling those who dwell on the earth to make an image to the beast." — *Revelation 13:14*

Artificial Intelligence is not the Beast itself,

but it carries the **spirit of the Beast** — a spirit of deception and domination.

It seeks to replace human discernment with data,

conscience with computation,

and divine revelation with digital reasoning.

The danger is not in the code but in the **control**.

Technology now decides what people believe, what they see, and even what they desire.

Algorithms have become invisible gods, shaping hearts and minds while claiming neutrality.

The same system that filters truth can also **silence it**.

The same platform that spreads the gospel can also **bury it beneath distractions**.

We are being prepared for a world where man obeys machines and **trusts the digital more than the Divine.**

The Antichrist will not appear suddenly — the system that welcomes him is already being built,

through convenience, automation, and blind dependence on technology.

People say, "AI will make life easier,"

but Heaven warns, "AI will make deception easier."

A world that trusts in artificial wisdom will soon reject **divine wisdom.**

A humanity that follows the voice of machines will soon stop hearing the voice of the Spirit.

This is why discernment has never been more urgent.

Every believer must learn to test the spirit behind the screen.

Not every voice that sounds intelligent is inspired by God.

Not every revelation that feels futuristic is filled with truth.

> "Beloved, do not believe every spirit, but test the spirits to see whether they are from God." — *1 John 4:1*

Artificial Intelligence is creating a civilization that depends on human knowledge but despises divine direction.

It can answer every question except the one that matters most:

"What is truth?"

The Spirit of the Beast is not about metal or machines — it is about **control, deception, and rebellion.**

It teaches humanity to bow before creation instead of the Creator.

It exalts intellect above obedience, and progress above purity.

And just as the serpent in Eden offered Eve forbidden knowledge,

AI now offers mankind **forbidden power.**

But no machine can save a soul.

No algorithm can forgive sin.

No code can write salvation.

Only Jesus Christ — the living Word — holds the key to eternal wisdom and truth.

> "For the wisdom of this world is foolishness with God." — *1 Corinthians 3:19*

As the world worships artificial intelligence,
let the Church rise with **spiritual intelligence**.
Let believers walk not by data, but by discernment.
Let our wisdom come not from the web, but from the **Word**.

For when the Beast speaks, only those who know the Shepherd's voice will refuse to follow.

When Science and Technology Become Tools of Spiritual Warfare

What many call *innovation* in this generation, Heaven calls *infiltration*.

Science and technology were once instruments of human progress — now they are becoming **weapons in a global spiritual war**.

Behind the glowing screens, encrypted codes, and powerful machines lies an invisible battle between **light and darkness**, between the Creator's purpose and the creature's pride.

Satan has always wanted to control humanity, but he needed a system.

Now, through science and technology, that system has been built — one that monitors, manipulates, and molds behavior.

The goal is not just information, but **domination**.

The enemy no longer tempts with visible idols; he tempts with invisible influence.

> "For we are not ignorant of his devices." — *2 Corinthians 2:11*

Every generation has had its tools of war, but ours is digital.

The battlefield is not the desert or the ocean — it is the **mind and the soul**.

Weapons are no longer just physical; they are **psychological**, **spiritual**, and **technological**.

Through data, media, and artificial intelligence, the enemy spreads fear, falsehood, and moral confusion faster than ever before.

1. The War for Attention

The devil does not always destroy by violence; he distracts by volume.

He floods screens with endless noise — entertainment, news, debates, and lies — until the still, small voice of God is drowned out.

People can no longer meditate, pray, or listen to their conscience because their attention has been hijacked.

The devil knows that a distracted believer is a **defeated believer**.

> "Be still, and know that I am God." — *Psalm 46:10*

2. The War for Identity

Science now claims the right to redefine what God has already defined.

It tells men they can become women, and women they can become men.

It calls rebellion "freedom" and confusion "progress."

Through media and education, Satan is shaping a generation that questions the Creator's design.

The purpose of this war is not just to corrupt bodies, but to **erase the image of God in man**.

> "So God created man in His own image... male and female He created them." — *Genesis 1:27*

3. The War for Truth

The internet has made lies look intelligent and truth look outdated.

False prophets now have global platforms, and deception spreads with the speed of light.

The more connected people become digitally, the more disconnected they become spiritually.

Truth is now measured by **trends**, not by **Scripture**.

Opinions are treated as revelation, and emotions as authority.

> "Woe to those who call evil good, and good evil." — *Isaiah 5:20*

4. The War for Souls

Beneath the entertainment, algorithms, and inventions, the real target is the **human soul**.

Satan's greatest technology is temptation — his most successful invention is imitation.

He presents pleasure without purpose, knowledge without wisdom, and freedom without holiness.

He uses technology to dull spiritual sensitivity, making sin seem normal and repentance seem unnecessary.

The internet has become a new Eden — full of forbidden fruit, pleasant to the eyes but deadly to the spirit.

But God has not left His people defenseless.

He has given us the **armor of light** — truth, righteousness, faith, and the Word of God — to stand in the digital age of deception.

> "For the weapons of our warfare are not carnal but mighty through God to the pulling down of strongholds." — *2 Corinthians 10:4*

This is the call to every believer:

Be spiritually awake in a technologically asleep world.

Use knowledge as a weapon of light, not a tool of pride.

Let your screen become your **pulpit**, not your **prison**.

Let your devices spread the Word, not the world.

Let science serve the Savior, not replace Him.

For though the enemy uses technology to advance darkness,

God will raise voices, ministries, and movements that use the same tools to **ignite revival**.

In the end, light will always outshine the algorithm.

> "The light shines in the darkness, and the darkness has not overcome it." —*John 1:5*

The Hypocrisy of Artificial Love and Virtual Faith

Even **love**, the purest gift of God, has been digitized and diluted.

What once joined souls now only connects screens.

People no longer meet **hearts** — they match **profiles**.

They no longer build **trust** — they exchange **selfies**.

They no longer form **covenants** — they make **temporary connections** built on pixels, not purpose.

Love has become a product of convenience, not commitment.

Dating apps have replaced discernment.

Lust is disguised as affection.

Romance is rehearsed like content creation.

People no longer ask, "Does God approve?"

They ask, "Do I get more likes?"

This is **artificial love** — a love without sacrifice, without truth, without eternity.

It looks perfect in photos but is hollow in reality.

It promises intimacy but delivers emptiness.

It celebrates passion but rejects purity.

> "Because lawlessness will abound, the love of many will grow cold." — *Matthew 24:12*

And now even **faith** has followed the same path.

Many profess Christ, but their devotion ends when the Wi-Fi does.

They stream sermons but never **serve**.

They post verses but never **pray**.

They shout "Amen!" in comments but refuse repentance in silence.

The church of convenience has replaced the church of conviction.

The altar has been replaced by algorithms.

People now "follow" pastors but not the **Pastor of souls**.

They know the voice of influencers, but not the voice of the Holy Spirit.

This is **virtual faith** — belief without obedience, worship without presence, repentance without tears.

It looks godly but lacks power.

It says "Jesus is Lord" online but denies Him in lifestyle.

It loves to be seen but refuses to be sanctified.

> "Having a form of godliness but denying its power." — *2 Timothy 3:5*

The enemy is not afraid of **Christian content**; he is afraid of **Christian character**.

He does not tremble at your followers — he trembles when you **follow Christ**.

He is not threatened by how many Bible verses you post — he fears the one you obey.

You can carry a Bible in your phone and still carry sin in your heart.

You can have the Word on your screen and still not have it in your soul.

You can livestream every sermon and still live like a stranger to the Savior.

God is calling His people out of **virtual faith** into **real fellowship**.

Out of imitation into **intimacy**.

Out of image into **substance**.

He wants hearts that bow, not hands that scroll.

He wants love that gives, not love that pretends.

He wants faith that burns even when the screen is off.

> "God is Spirit, and those who worship Him must worship in spirit and in truth." — *John 4:24*

The Redemption of Technology: Using Innovation for the Glory of God

Though technology has been corrupted by pride and perversion, God can still redeem it.

Every tool that man invents can become a ***weapon in the hands of the righteous*** *when surrendered to the Holy Spirit.*

What the enemy uses to deceive, God can use to deliver.

What darkness uses to destroy, light can use to ***illuminate.***

Technology itself is not evil — the ***heart*** *that uses it determines its purpose.*

The same internet that spreads pornography can also spread the gospel.

The same social media that glorifies sin can also testify of salvation.

The same phone that wastes time can also become a tool for prayer, devotion, and evangelism.

> *"Do not be overcome by evil, but overcome evil with good." — Romans 12:21*

1. Redeeming the Screen

Your screen can be your pulpit.

Your posts can become preaching.

Your page can become a platform of peace, truth, and hope.

Every believer is now a digital missionary — one message, one verse, one prayer can touch nations.

Don't let your phone be a source of distraction; make it a ***channel of declaration.***

2. Redeeming Communication

Technology has connected the world, but it has also confused it.

Yet believers can use it to connect across borders — to pray, teach, and unite the Body of Christ globally.

God is raising intercessors who will use technology not for gossip, but for ***global prayer chains.***

He is raising teachers who will use it not for vanity, but for ***virtual discipleship****.*

The world talks online — the church must ***witness*** *online.*

3. Redeeming Innovation

God is the original Creator — the Master Innovator.

Every gift of creativity in science, art, or engineering comes from Him.

When surrendered to Christ, these innovations can heal the earth, not harm it;

they can glorify God, not glorify greed.

Believers in technology, medicine, and science must rise as ***Josephs and Daniels*** *of this generation —*

using wisdom and excellence to manifest the Kingdom in every system.

> *"Let your light so shine before men, that they may see your good works and glorify your Father in heaven." — Matthew 5:16*

4. Redeeming Artificial Intelligence

Even Artificial Intelligence can serve divine purpose when guided by truth.

It can translate Bibles, preserve languages, and spread the Word faster than ever before.

But it must never replace ***dependence on the Holy Spirit****.*

The Church must lead technology, not be led by it.

We must build systems that reflect God's justice, mercy, and truth — not man's pride.

Technology without prayer is dangerous; innovation without intercession is rebellion.

5. Redeeming the Heart Behind the Device

Before God redeems technology, He redeems the ***user****.*

The transformation must start inside us.

A pure heart can turn any tool into a testimony.

A Spirit-led believer can turn the digital world into a divine field.

The Holy Ghost must sit on the throne of your thoughts before you touch the keyboard of your influence.

Because ultimately, technology is only as holy as the hands that hold it.

And when those hands are lifted in worship, even the internet becomes a place of revival.

> *"The earth shall be filled with the knowledge of the glory of the Lord as the waters cover the sea." — Habakkuk 2:14*

The final move of God will not be limited to pulpits — it will flow through ***platforms.***

It will not be contained in temples — it will travel through ***technology.***

And those who walk in holiness, wisdom, and discernment will use every screen, every signal, and every system to declare:

"Jesus Christ is Lord — online and offline, forever and ever."

True Wisdom: Bringing Technology Back to the Cross

Science and technology are not the enemies of God — but they must **submit** to Him.

They were never meant to replace the Creator, only to **reflect His creativity**.

The problem is not invention — it is **intention**.

The danger is not discovery — it is **deception**.

When knowledge no longer kneels before the throne, it becomes rebellion wearing a crown of progress.

True wisdom begins when **machines serve mercy**, when **science bows to Scripture**,

and when every line of code, every discovery, and every digital creation is guided by the **Spirit of Truth**.

> "The fear of the Lord is the beginning of knowledge." — *Proverbs 1:7*

We need scientists who pray before they experiment.

We need innovators who seek revelation before invention.

We need engineers who design not for profit but for **purpose** — to heal, to serve, to uplift.

We need leaders in technology who understand that progress without purity leads to **perdition**.

Technology without the Spirit becomes **idolatry** —
for anything that replaces worship of God becomes a false god.
Science without Scripture becomes **slavery** —
for knowledge without conscience always serves corruption.
And progress without purity becomes **destruction**,
for the same fire that lights the world can also burn it down.
This is the hour for believers to **reclaim wisdom** from the altar of pride and bring it back to the **altar of the Cross**.

Because at the Cross, knowledge finds its truth, and creation finds its Creator.

At the Cross, the human mind surrenders to divine revelation.

At the Cross, invention meets redemption.

At the Cross, the proud are humbled, and the wise become worshipers.

We must use tools without being **used by them**.

We must control devices before they **control our destiny**.

We must teach our children that the greatest intelligence is not artificial — it is **spiritual**.

And we must once again lift our eyes from the screen to the Savior,
from the cloud of data to the **glory cloud of His presence**.

Because wisdom that does not lead to worship is foolishness in disguise.

And the future that does not belong to God will perish with man.

Let every invention return to its **divine purpose**,
let every mind that creates remember the One who gave it breath,
and let every scientist, programmer, and builder say:

"To Him be all the glory, forever and ever — for from Him, through Him, and to Him are all things." — *Romans 11:36*

A Prayer for Deliverance from Technological Hypocrisy

Lord, deliver this generation from the deception of false progress.

Save us from knowledge without conscience, from technology without truth.

Teach us to use what You have given, not to worship it.

Help us to look beyond the screen and see eternity.

Purify our minds from digital distractions.

Restore the fear of God in the world of innovation.

And let science and technology once again serve Your purpose, not man's pride.

> "Set your minds on things above, not on earthly things." — *Colossians 3:2*

Key Scriptures:

- *Romans 1:25* — Worshiping created things instead of the Creator
- *2 Timothy 3:7* — Ever learning, never coming to truth
- *Mark 8:36* — What profits a man to gain the world but lose his soul
- *Genesis 11:4* — Let us make a name for ourselves (Tower of Babel)
- *Psalm 115:5–6* — Eyes that do not see, ears that do not hear
- *Proverbs 1:7* — The fear of the Lord is the beginning of knowledge
- *Colossians 3:2* — Set your minds on things above

Chapter 13: The Hidden Hypocrisy in Business and Leadership

The Empire Built on Lies

**The marketplace was meant to be a place of exchange and service,
where honesty built trust and work glorified God.
But today, business has become one of the greatest altars of hypocrisy —
a world where appearance matters more than integrity,
where profit is worshiped more than people,
and where many build empires not on righteousness, but on deception.**

**In boardrooms, men speak of "ethics" while plotting exploitation.
In offices, leaders talk of "values" while violating truth.
In companies, employees smile in loyalty while stabbing in ambition.
The same spirit that corrupted religion has now corrupted commerce —
a spirit that looks righteous but lives rotten,
that quotes morality in meetings but crushes mercy in**

management.

This is the modern Babylon of business,
where greed wears a suit, deceit signs contracts,
and manipulation hides behind motivational speeches.
Executives bow to the god of gain,
entrepreneurs chase power without principle,
and employees sell their conscience for promotion.

"For the love of money is the root of all kinds of evil." — *1 Timothy 6:10*

Money itself is not sin — but the worship of it is.
God blessed man with the ability to trade, to build, to prosper;
but Satan perverted it with lust for control and recognition.
Now we live in a generation that measures success by wealth, not by wisdom;
by visibility, not by virtue; by numbers, not by nobility.

In leadership, hypocrisy is even more dangerous —
for when the head is corrupted, the whole body suffers.
Leaders promise justice but deliver oppression.
They speak of unity but sow division.
They talk of service but demand submission.
They quote God in speeches but serve mammon in strategy.

The world claps for them, but Heaven weeps.
Because the greatest crisis in our generation is not a crisis of economy —
it is a crisis of integrity.
It is not a shortage of leaders — it is a shortage of truthful ones.
They have charisma without character,
influence without intercession,
platforms without purity.

"Woe to those who make unjust laws,
to those who issue oppressive decrees." — *Isaiah 10:1*

The hidden hypocrisy in business and leadership is this:
men pretend to serve while secretly enslaving,
they appear generous while feeding greed,
they use God's name to bless their deceit,
and they measure success by applause instead of accountability.

But the kingdom of God is raising a new kind of leader — one whose hands are clean, heart is humble, and word is true.
A generation of Daniels who will not bow to Babylon,
Josephs who will manage wealth without worshiping it,
and Deborahs who will rule with discernment and justice.

For in the end, every corrupt business will crumble,
every false empire will fall,
and every leader who built on lies will face the truth they ignored.

"For there is nothing hidden that will not be disclosed,
and nothing concealed that will not be brought to light." — *Luke 8:17*

The true measure of success is not what you build in this world,
but what remains when God tests it by fire.
The time has come for every believer — businessman, worker, or leader —
to remove the mask, return to integrity,
and let righteousness reign in the marketplace once again.

The Crown That Corrupts

Leadership and business were never meant to be instruments of exploitation — they were created as **sacred trusts**.

God designed leadership to **serve**, not to enslave.

He designed business to **bless**, not to manipulate.

Both were supposed to mirror His divine nature — justice, mercy, and stewardship.

But in a fallen world, these holy callings have been **defiled by greed, pride, and deceit**.

Today, the spirit of hypocrisy wears a suit and carries a title.

It sits in boardrooms, behind pulpits, and in political offices.

Men call themselves *leaders* but act like *lords*.

They quote Scripture in speeches but **crucify truth** in strategy.

They speak of "integrity," but their hearts are filled with ambition and control.

They say "people come first," but their policies prove otherwise.

The same mouths that preach *fairness* practice *favoritism*.

The same hands that sign contracts of opportunity also sign systems of oppression.

The same leaders who speak of compassion use it as a mask for competition.

They care not for people — only for profit.

They serve not the public — only their pride.

This is the tragedy of modern leadership:

A generation that wears **crowns without character**,
that seeks **thrones without truth**,
and that builds **empires without ethics**.

> "When the righteous are in authority, the people rejoice;
> but when the wicked rule, the people groan." — *Proverbs 29:2*

The world groans today — not because of lack of progress,
but because progress has lost its purity.

Nations mourn not because there are no leaders,

but because there are too few **righteous ones**.

Leadership has become performance.

Business has become manipulation.

And the crown that was meant for service has become a symbol of self-worship.

But God is raising a new generation of leaders —

not those who rule with deceit, but those who reign with discernment.

Not those who exploit for gain, but those who steward with grace.

Not those who hide behind words, but those who live by **the Word**.

Because the true crown is not worn on the head — it is carried in the heart.

And the true leader is not known by his power, but by his purity.

Lying for Profit, Pretending Fairness, and Exploiting Workers

The modern marketplace is full of **beautiful lies** — words polished by marketing, dressed in ethics, and powered by greed.

Many companies speak of *honesty*, but their entire foundation is built on **deception**.

They boast of *fairness*, yet their wages scream injustice.

They promote *teamwork*, but treat workers as disposable tools — machines with emotions they refuse to acknowledge.

They hang banners that say *"Integrity"*, but their ledgers tell a different story.

They print words like *"Equality,"* but practice elitism.

They post about *"Human Rights,"* but quietly exploit the vulnerable.

They host charity galas while robbing the poor with inflated prices and dishonest systems.

This is not business — it is **modern slavery in a suit and tie**.

> "Hear this, you who trample the needy and do away with the poor of the land...
>
> skimping on the measure, boosting the price, and cheating with dishonest scales." — *Amos 8:4–5*

The prophet Amos' cry still echoes today.

The scales may now be digital, the contracts may be online, the transactions may be global —

but the **spirit of deceit** remains the same.

Many leaders have mastered the art of **lying politely**.

They deceive with smiles and destroy with signatures.

They promise growth but plan exploitation.

They use motivational speeches as manipulation.

They promote "family culture" while overworking their teams into exhaustion.

Behind the polished boardroom table hides **corruption**.

Behind the friendly corporate emails hides **oppression**.

Behind every logo of "care" often hides the idol of **cash**.

This is the hypocrisy of modern business — the ability to **appear good while doing evil**.

It is Pharaoh calling his slavery "employment."

It is Judas calling his betrayal "strategy."

It is leaders saying, "We care about our people," while quietly sacrificing their souls for profit margins.

And yet God still sees.

He hears the silent cries of the underpaid worker.

He counts every tear shed in unfair workplaces.

He weighs every dishonest transaction on His eternal scale.

> "A false balance is an abomination to the Lord,
> but a just weight is His delight." — *Proverbs 11:1*

The Lord is calling business leaders back to **righteousness** —

to build companies where truth is currency, integrity is policy, and justice is profit.

Because every business built on lies will one day face the **audit of Heaven**.

You can deceive customers, employees, and investors —

but you cannot deceive the God who sees through every contract and motive.

And on the day when the books are opened, He will reveal what men tried to hide behind professionalism and profit.

How Greed Disguises Itself as Success

The world shouts, *"Congratulations!"* when profits rise —

but Heaven weeps when **integrity falls**.

In our generation, greed no longer looks evil; it looks **excellent**.

It wears the perfume of professionalism and the robe of productivity.

It calls itself "ambition," "innovation," or "vision,"

but behind those noble words hides a **disease of the soul** — the hunger for more, no matter the cost.

> "What shall it profit a man if he gains the whole world and loses his soul?" — *Mark 8:36*

This is the new religion of the marketplace:

Success without surrender.

Wealth without worship.

Results without righteousness.

People sacrifice honesty for advancement and call it "strategy."

They destroy competitors and call it "winning."

They oppress workers and call it "efficiency."

They manipulate markets and call it "wisdom."

Greed never introduces itself as greed.

It always enters dressed as *"growth."*

It smiles as *"vision."*

It preaches as *"progress."*

But beneath its disguise is **idolatry** — the worship of self, status, and silver.

Many business leaders and politicians today have mastered this deception.

They speak of generosity while living in exploitation.

They create charities not to help the poor, but to hide the profit of their corruption.

They donate in public but **dominate** in private.

They build schools, hospitals, and foundations — not from mercy, but for marketing.

They silence their conscience with philanthropy,

and soothe their guilt with publicity.

But God sees beyond the speeches, the slogans, and the smiles.

He knows when "helping" is just **hiding**.

He knows when "giving" is just **guarding reputation**.

He knows when "charity" is just **camouflage** for sin.

This is the **hypocrisy of modern success** —

to appear righteous before men while being rotten before God.

To look generous in public while being greedy in private.

To have your name printed on buildings but not written in the Book of Life.

The Kingdom of God defines success differently.

In Heaven, success is not how high you climb, but how **humble you remain**.

It is not how much you gain, but how much you give without boasting.

It is not how many people serve you, but how many you serve in truth.

For every empire built on greed will collapse under judgment,

but every seed sown in righteousness will rise in glory.

> "Better is a little with righteousness than great revenues without right." — *Proverbs 16:8*

True success is not measured by balance sheets, but by **the balance of the soul**.

The only business that endures forever is the business of **truth, mercy, and justice**.

The Price of Dishonest Gain

Every dishonest coin may shine in the hand, but it burns in the soul.

It glitters for a moment, yet it carries the **weight of a curse**.

What is gained by deceit will be lost by judgment,

for God Himself has written in His Word:

> "The treasures of wickedness profit nothing, but righteousness delivers from death." — *Proverbs 10:2*

Dishonest gain does more than corrupt a company — it **kills a conscience.**

It poisons the peace of a man while fattening his pockets.

It makes him rich in appearance but bankrupt in eternity.

He earns wealth but loses **rest**.

He multiplies possessions but divides his soul.

He gains applause from men but loses approval from Heaven.

Dishonest gain is a curse that eats from the inside out.

It blinds the eyes, hardens the heart, and silences the Spirit.

It replaces joy with fear — fear of being caught, fear of being exposed, fear of losing what was never truly his.

He smiles in success but trembles in solitude.

He builds high towers but sleeps in torment.

Many have built **empires that God will one day shake to dust.**

They signed contracts of oppression, built systems of greed,

and forgot that truth is not negotiable.

For every unjust business is a ticking clock of judgment,

and every dishonest dollar is a testimony against its owner.

> "Woe to him who builds his house by unrighteousness and his chambers by injustice." —*Jeremiah 22:13*

Greed never satisfies — it only **multiplies emptiness.**

The more it takes, the hungrier it grows.

The more it gathers, the more it fears losing.

The rich fool built barns to store his harvest, but God said,

> "You fool! This night your soul will be required of you." — *Luke 12:20*

That is the slavery of sin — to work endlessly for wealth that cannot save you.

To labor for riches that rot.

To chase success that cannot buy peace.

The greatest tragedy is not the loss of money — it is the **loss of mercy**.

It is when a man's heart grows too hard to feel and his conscience too cold to bleed.

He becomes successful in business but a stranger to grace.

He builds his house on earth but loses his home in Heaven.

But God still calls:

"Return to righteousness and live."

Because repentance can redeem what greed has destroyed.

And integrity — though costly — is the only currency that never loses its value before God.

> "Better a poor man who walks in his integrity
> than a rich man who is perverse in his ways." — *Proverbs 28:6*

The Hypocrisy of Leadership Without Character

Leadership in our generation has become a **title**, not a **testimony**.

It has become a **stage**, not a **sacrifice**.

Many lead not to serve, but to be seen.

They desire the spotlight of honor but reject the shadow of humility.

They know how to **command**, but not how to **care**.

They love authority but despise **accountability**.

They demand respect, yet live without righteousness.

The tragedy of modern leadership — in business, politics, and even the church —

is that **position has replaced purpose**.

Leadership is now about visibility, not virtue.

Influence has become an idol, and power has become a form of pride.

But **true leadership** is not about commanding people — it is about carrying people.

It is not about being served — it is about **serving**.

It is not about being famous — it is about being **faithful**.

It is not about control — it is about **character**.

"The greatest among you shall be your servant." — *Matthew 23:11*

Yet, many leaders today act like kings, not servants.

They build thrones out of the sweat of their followers.

They demand loyalty but give no love.

They seek crowns but ignore the cross.

They speak of teamwork but walk in tyranny.

They crave admiration but lack compassion.

Worse still, some use the **name of God** as a marketing strategy.

They quote Scripture to sound righteous while their hearts pursue recognition.

They use people's needs to feed their own **narcissism**.

They build brands, not believers.

They gather followers, not disciples.

They preach humility while living in hidden arrogance.

But Heaven is not deceived.

God measures leadership not by popularity but by **purity**.

He measures greatness not by how many serve you, but by how many you **lift up**.

Leadership without humility is rebellion dressed in authority.

It looks powerful on earth but is powerless before God.

Every throne built on pride will fall.

Every empire built on manipulation will crumble.

Every leader who exalts himself will be humbled by the hand of the Almighty.

> "For everyone who exalts himself will be humbled,
> and he who humbles himself will be exalted." — *Luke 14:11*

The time has come for a new kind of leader —

leaders who fear God more than failure,

who prefer truth over titles,

and who would rather wash feet than demand worship.

Because in the Kingdom of God, **leadership is not about how high you stand,**

but how low you bow.

God's Standard for Righteousness in Leadership

God's standard for leadership has never changed — though the world keeps redefining it.

He does not measure a leader by the **position he holds**, but by the **principles he keeps**.

He does not judge success by titles, trophies, or influence,
but by **truth, integrity, and humility**.

> "He has shown you, O man, what is good;
> and what does the Lord require of you
> but to do justice, to love mercy,
> and to walk humbly with your God?" — *Micah 6:8*

A true leader is not known by his speeches, but by his spirit.

He is not known by how loudly he commands, but by how quietly he obeys God.

He fears sin more than he fears losing support.

He values character more than comfort, and people more than profit.

A Righteous Leader Is One Who:

- **Speaks truth** even when truth costs him power.
- **Treats workers fairly** even when fairness reduces profit.
- **Serves others** even when service means being misunderstood.
- **Keeps promises** even when breaking them would bring advantage.
- **Fears God** more than he fears losing reputation.

Such a leader may not trend in the world — but he is **trusted in Heaven**.

He may lose applause, but he gains anointing.

He may be mocked by men, but he is remembered by God.

When righteousness rules, **peace follows**.

When justice leads, **prosperity becomes pure**.

When mercy governs, **nations are healed.**
But when hypocrisy sits on the throne,
families suffer, employees weep, and nations collapse.
Corruption spreads like disease,
and the very hands that should bless begin to oppress.
God is raising a generation of **righteous leaders** —
men and women who lead not by ambition, but by **anointing.**
Leaders who fear the Lord more than losing elections,
who love people more than profits,
and who see leadership not as privilege, but as **responsibility before Heaven.**

> "When the righteous are in authority, the people rejoice;
> but when the wicked rule, the people groan." — *Proverbs 29:2*

True leadership is not found in how high you rise,
but in how faithfully you serve when no one is watching.

A Call to Integrity

If you are a leader, business owner, or worker, remember this:
Integrity is not optional — it is essential.
God is not impressed by your results; He is watching your motives.
You may deceive men, but you cannot deceive God.
Your reputation may rise, but if your heart is corrupt, Heaven is not fooled.

> "Better is a poor man who walks in integrity than one who is crooked in his ways though he is rich." — *Proverbs 28:6*

The world needs leaders who lead from the heart, not from ambition.
It needs businesspeople who fear God more than greed.
It needs workers who serve faithfully even when unseen.
Let us rebuild leadership on the foundation of truth.
Let us restore business through righteousness.
Let us choose honesty over profit, service over status, humility over hype.

Then, and only then, will God bless the work of our hands.

A Prayer for Leaders and Businessmen

Lord, purify the hearts of those in authority.

Deliver our leaders from the spirit of greed, deception, and pride.

Teach us to lead with humility, to serve with compassion, and to act with justice.

Let our businesses reflect Your righteousness and our leadership reflect Your love.

Expose every hidden corruption and raise leaders after Your own heart.

May we honor You in all we build, buy, and lead — for You alone are the true King.

> "Righteousness exalts a nation, but sin is a reproach to any people." — *Proverbs 14:34*

Key Scriptures:

- *Proverbs 29:2* — When the righteous rule, the people rejoice
- *Amos 8:4–5* — Cheating with dishonest scales
- *Mark 8:36* — What profits a man to gain the world but lose his soul
- *Proverbs 10:2* — Treasures of wickedness profit nothing
- *Jeremiah 22:13* — Woe to him who builds by injustice
- *Matthew 23:11* — The greatest among you shall be your servant
- *Micah 6:8* — Do justice, love mercy, walk humbly
- *Proverbs 28:6* — Better the poor in integrity than the rich in corruption
- *Proverbs 14:34* — Righteousness exalts a nation

Chapter 14: The Double Life — Public Image vs Private Reality

We are living in an age of performance, not purity — an era where image matters more than integrity,

and appearance is worshiped more than truth.
People no longer strive to *be* righteous; they strive to *look* righteous.
They wear smiles that hide sorrow,
speak words that hide wickedness,
and build reputations that contradict their realities.

The double life has become the new normal —
preachers who preach what they do not practice,
leaders who lead in public but fall in secret,
believers who sing about holiness while living in hidden sin.
It is a generation that knows how to shine on the stage
but walks in darkness behind closed doors.

We live in a world obsessed with *public image* —
a world that judges holiness by hashtags,
spirituality by social media posts,
and success by how well one hides their flaws.
Yet Heaven is not impressed by filters or followers.
God does not measure men by their platform,
but by the purity of their hearts.

"For the Lord does not see as man sees;
man looks at the outward appearance,
but the Lord looks at the heart." — *1 Samuel 16:7*

The danger of living a double life is not only hypocrisy — it is spiritual death.
Because the longer you act holy without being holy,
the more your conscience dies and your spirit grows numb.
You begin to master deception until you believe your own lie.
And what began as an image becomes your prison.

This is the tragedy of our times:
people know how to appear anointed, but not how to be transformed.

They can quote Scripture, but cannot conquer sin.
They can raise hands in worship, but cannot lift hearts in repentance.
They have the language of light but live in the shadows of darkness.

God is calling this generation to repentance —
to tear down the mask, to destroy the illusion, to come clean before Him.
Because what is hidden in darkness will one day be shouted from the rooftops.
And what is faked before men will be exposed before God.

"There is nothing hidden that will not be disclosed,
and nothing concealed that will not be brought to light." — *Luke 8:17*

The time has come to choose between public applause and private approval.
To decide whether we want to *look righteous before men*
or *stand righteous before God.*
Because no one can wear two faces forever —
the mask will always fall before the throne of truth.

The Mask That God Sees Through

The greatest tragedy in life is not **public failure** — it is **private corruption.**

It is when the inside is **rotting** while the outside is **shining.**

When the **voice preaches truth** but the **heart lives in lies.**

When the **hand gives charity** but the **soul hides sin.**

We live in a world where **image has replaced intimacy with God.**

People work harder to protect their reputation than to purify their spirit.

They polish the outside but ignore the inside.

They care more about being seen by men than being approved by Heaven.

Reputation has become the new god of our generation.

Many bow before it daily —
sacrificing their truth for applause,
their integrity for influence,
and their holiness for human approval.

But while men see the **face,** God sees the **foundation.**

While people admire your presentation, God examines your **intention.**

> "The Lord does not look at the things people look at.
>
> People look at the outward appearance, but the Lord looks at the heart." — *1 Samuel 16:7*

You can hide from men behind makeup, titles, and smiles —
but you can never hide from the **One who created your soul.**
He sees behind the mask of religion,
behind the smile of success,
and behind the polished words of pretense.
The eyes of the Lord pierce through every layer of hypocrisy.
They see the truth beneath the performance.
They see the secret sins beneath the public sermons.
They see the motives behind every good deed.
And while the world may applaud your image,
Heaven judges your **heart.**

Because in the end, God will not reward the best actors —
He will crown the most **authentic**.

The Danger of Living Two Lives

To live two lives is to live divided — one face for the crowd, another for the closet.

It is to speak light in public while walking in darkness in private.

It is to act righteous before men but rebel against God in secret.

This is the most dangerous life a person can live, because **a divided soul cannot stand**.

Jesus said,

> "A house divided against itself cannot stand." — *Mark 3:25*

When you live a double life, your spirit becomes that divided house.

You spend your days pretending, your nights repenting, and your heart never resting.

You begin to wear your mask so long that you forget what your real face looks like.

You pray without peace, worship without power, and live without joy.

The double life is a slow spiritual suicide —

it kills the conscience first, then the conviction, and finally, the connection with God.

It is possible to carry a Bible and still walk in bondage,

to sing about freedom while being chained by secret sin.

Every lie you live adds another brick to the wall between you and God.

Every pretense you protect becomes another chain on your soul.

And while the world may still celebrate your image, Heaven weeps over your condition.

> "These people honor Me with their lips, but their hearts are far from Me." — *Matthew 15:8*

The tragedy of the double life is that it deceives even the deceiver.

You start by hiding sin from others and end by hiding truth from yourself.

You say, "I'm fine," while dying inside.

You say, "God understands," while ignoring His conviction.

You learn to act holy instead of becoming holy.

But the mask will always fall.

No one can pretend forever.

Hidden sin will always demand exposure.

God, in His mercy, reveals what man conceals — not to shame you, but to **save you.**

For what you hide in darkness today will one day be **brought to light** before His throne.

Better to fall at His feet in repentance now than to fall under His judgment later.

"Be sure your sin will find you out." — *Numbers 32:23*

The danger of living two lives is losing both —
your public image and your private soul.
But the beauty of repentance is that it restores both —
your truth before God and your peace within.

What People See Versus What God Sees

There is always a difference between how **men see** and how **God sees.**

The eyes of men are shallow — they see appearance.

But the eyes of God are deep — He sees **the heart**.

People saw **Saul** as tall, strong, and royal — but **God saw rebellion**.

People saw **David** as small, young, and ordinary — but **God saw a man after His heart**.

People saw **the Pharisees** as holy and disciplined — but **Jesus saw whitewashed tombs**.

People saw **Judas** as a disciple — but **Jesus saw a deceiver**.

Human vision stops at the surface,
but divine vision penetrates the soul.
Men applaud charisma,
but God examines character.
Men honor performance,
but God demands purity.

> "Woe to you, scribes and Pharisees, hypocrites!
>
> For you are like whitewashed tombs,
>
> which outwardly appear beautiful,
>
> but within are full of dead men's bones and all uncleanness." — *Matthew 23:27*

The world celebrates what it sees,
but Heaven judges what it knows.
Crowds can call you **great**, but Heaven may call you **guilty**.
You can impress an audience but still fail your Creator.
God is not moved by the polish of your presentation;
He is moved by the posture of your heart.
He does not anoint appearances — He anoints authenticity.
He does not crown the talented — He crowns the **truthful**.

You can fool the **lights of the stage**,
but not the **light of the throne**.
You can deceive people for a lifetime,
but you cannot deceive the One who gave you life.
In the end, what God sees will outweigh what man says.
And only those whose hearts are true before Him
will stand unashamed in His presence.

The Burden of Pretending to Be Perfect

The heaviest mask to wear is the mask of perfection.
It may shine on the outside, but it suffocates the soul within.
Many people live under pressure to appear flawless —
strong when they are weak,
joyful when they are broken,
holy when they are struggling.
This is not strength — it is slavery.
It is the exhausting life of performance instead of presence,
of acting righteous instead of being real.
You can impress the world with perfection,
but you can only touch God with **honesty**.
God cannot heal what you keep hiding.
He cannot cleanse what you keep covering.

> "He who covers his sins will not prosper,
> but whoever confesses and forsakes them will have mercy." — *Proverbs 28:13*

The burden of pretending to be perfect crushes the soul.
It makes prayer mechanical,
worship superficial,
and fellowship fake.
It turns the church into a theater and the altar into a stage.
Some cry secretly while smiling publicly.
Some carry guilt under garments of grace.
Some preach hope while drowning in despair.
They fear that if people saw the real them, love would disappear.
But God does not demand perfection — He desires **purity**.
He does not call the flawless — He calls the faithful.
He does not anoint actors — He anoints the **authentic**.
The secret to peace is not pretending you have no weakness —
it is surrendering your weakness to the One who gives strength.

God would rather have an honest sinner than a dishonest saint.
He would rather hear a broken confession than a perfect performance.
So take off the mask.
Cry if you must.
Repent if you must.
But be real — because truth invites mercy,
and mercy restores everything pretense destroyed.

"The sacrifices of God are a broken spirit,

a broken and contrite heart — these, O God, You will not despise." — *Psalm 51:17*

When Success Hides Sin

Success can be a greater test than failure.

Failure humbles you, but success can harden you.

It can blind you into believing that the applause of men is the approval of God.

It can make you think your achievements justify your actions,

and your platform proves your purity.

But not every open door is from Heaven — some are from **hell, disguised as opportunity**.

Not every crown is a reward; some are traps made of gold.

Not every miracle means God is pleased; sometimes He is just being patient.

> "There is a way that seems right to a man,
> but its end is the way of death." — *Proverbs 14:12*

Success is one of the most dangerous masks.
It can hide sin behind sermons,
greed behind generosity,
and pride behind praise.
It can make a man feel blessed when he is actually drifting.
You can build an empire and lose your soul.
You can be **celebrated by men and condemned by Heaven**.
You can be "anointed" on stage and **empty in the secret place**.
You can gain the spotlight but lose your salvation.
Many have replaced **holiness with popularity**.
They measure blessing by money instead of mercy,
and equate applause with anointing.
They think numbers mean success, but God counts differently.
He measures obedience, not outcomes.
He honors integrity, not influence.

> "Not everyone who says to Me, 'Lord, Lord,' will enter the kingdom of heaven,

> but only the one who does the will of My Father." — *Matthew 7:21*

True success is not what people post about you —
it is what Heaven records about you.
It is not what you build, but **what you become**.
For the crowns of men fade, but the verdict of God stands forever.
Some preachers preach truth but live in secret sin.
Some leaders inspire crowds but are enslaved by lust or greed.
Some believers act holy in church but live worldly at home.
They shine in the spotlight but hide in the shadows.
That is the tragedy of a double life —
you can **perform holiness while dying in hypocrisy**.
But no mask can endure the fire of God's judgment.
Better to expose your sin in repentance now
than to have it exposed in eternity by His wrath.

> "For nothing is hidden that will not be made manifest,
>
> nor is anything secret that will not be known and come to light." — *Luke 8:17*

The Danger of Building Your Reputation Instead of Your Character

Reputation is what people say about you;
character is what God knows about you.
Reputation is built in public,
but character is formed in private.
Reputation is what shines under the spotlight,
but character is what survives in the dark.
You can protect your reputation with lies,
but you can only preserve your character with truth.
The tragedy of our generation is that many defend their image
while destroying their integrity.
They spend hours polishing their name,
but not a moment purifying their heart.

> "If the foundations are destroyed, what can the righteous do?" — *Psalm 11:3*

The double life begins the moment we value **reputation more than righteousness**.

We become more concerned with what people think
than with what Heaven sees.
We polish the outside while the inside rots.
We rehearse our words but neglect our ways.
We post light online while hiding darkness in our hearts.
Many rise faster than their souls can handle.
They gain titles before they gain truth.
They perform before they are purified.
They succeed before they are sanctified.
And when pressure comes, the **mask cracks**,
and the true self is revealed.
You can deceive men with eloquence,
but not God with evidence.

He knows the motive behind your ministry,
the desire behind your donation,
and the thought behind your smile.
God is not impressed by how people honor you;
He is moved by how honestly you honor Him.
He is not looking for actors who play holy —
He is looking for hearts that are **authentically His**.

> "Man looks at the outward appearance, but the Lord looks at the heart." — *1 Samuel 16:7*

The Prison of Pretense

Living a double life is not freedom — it is captivity dressed in confidence.

You must always **act**, always **hide**, always **pretend**.

You smile for the crowd while your soul cries in the dark.

You build a reputation so perfect that even you start to believe the lie.

But deep down, your heart knows — the mask is heavy.

You fear being **exposed** more than being **empty**.

You spend more time managing appearances than mending your spirit.

You trade peace for performance, truth for applause, and rest for reputation.

That is why so many powerful people fall suddenly —
not because the sin was new, but because the **mask finally broke**.

The double life is a **prison without walls**.

You can walk anywhere, but never freely.

You can laugh publicly, but never joyfully.

You can preach holiness, yet live in guilt.

You can lead others to God while drifting far from Him yourself.

> "They profess to know God, but by their deeds they deny Him."
> — *Titus 1:16*

Every lie becomes another chain.

Every act of pretense another bar in the cell.

The soul suffocates under the weight of hypocrisy —
until one day, God in His mercy, allows the truth to break through.

But here lies the hope:

God never exposes to destroy; He exposes to deliver.

He tears the mask not to humiliate you, but to heal you.

He reveals the hidden things not to condemn, but to cleanse.

> "He who conceals his sins will not prosper,
> but whoever confesses and forsakes them will find mercy." — *Proverbs 28:13*

The way out of the prison is **confession**, not perfection.
The moment you stop performing and start repenting,
the chains begin to fall.
God replaces your mask with mercy,
your fear with freedom,
and your pretense with peace.

How to Live With One Face Before God and Man

The highest form of freedom is **to live without pretending**.

The greatest testimony is not how you act before men,

but how you walk before God when no one is watching.

Jesus never lived two lives — He was the same in the crowd, in the temple, and in the garden.

He calls His followers to the same integrity:

one heart, one voice, one face.

To live with one face means your **private truth matches your public talk**.

It means what you do in secret honors the same God you preach about in public.

It means your hidden life fuels your visible ministry — not contradicts it.

> "Let your 'Yes' be yes and your 'No' be no; anything more than this comes from evil." — *Matthew 5:37*

When you live with one face:

- You **walk in the light**, even when darkness offers convenience.
- You **speak truth**, even when silence would protect your image.
- You **repent quickly**, because your heart values purity more than pride.
- You **fear God**, not people — because only His opinion lasts forever.

"Blessed are the pure in heart, for they shall see God." — *Matthew 5:8*

Purity means one heart — not one divided between truth and appearance.

Integrity means one face — not one for God and another for people.

When your **heart is clean**, your reputation will not need defense.

When your **private life pleases God**, your public life will carry His power.

The world celebrates those who *act holy*;
Heaven rewards those who *live holy*.
When you live with one face before God and man,
you no longer fear exposure — because there is nothing left to hide.

A Call to True Integrity

God is raising a generation that will walk in transparency.
A generation with no hidden agendas, no secret sin, no false humility.
A generation that will fear God more than the camera.
A people who will rather lose reputation than lose righteousness.
It is time to break the double life —
to confess what was hidden,
to heal what was broken,
to surrender what was secret,
and to walk again in truth and freedom.

> "Behold, You desire truth in the inward parts, and in the hidden part You will make me to know wisdom." — *Psalm 51:6*

A Prayer for Integrity and Wholeness

Lord, deliver me from the prison of pretense.
Help me to live with one face — before You and before men.
Destroy every mask that separates my public image from my private reality.
Forgive me for hiding what You wanted to heal.
Give me the courage to walk in truth, even when it costs me approval.
Let my secret life please You more than my public life impresses others.
Purify me until my inside matches my outside.
Let me be real, whole, and holy before Your presence.

> "Search me, O God, and know my heart; try me and know my thoughts." — *Psalm 139:23*

Key Scriptures:

- *1 Samuel 16:7* — Man looks at the outward appearance, but the Lord looks at the heart
- *Matthew 23:27* — Whitewashed tombs, outwardly beautiful but inwardly corrupt
- *Proverbs 14:12* — There is a way that seems right to a man
- *Psalm 11:3* — If the foundations are destroyed, what can the righteous do?
- *Proverbs 28:13* — He who conceals sin will not prosper
- *Matthew 5:8* — Blessed are the pure in heart
- *Psalm 51:6* — You desire truth in the inward parts
- *Psalm 139:23* — Search me, O God, and know my heart

Part IV – The Final Exposure

Chapter 15: The Cost of Hypocrisy

**Hypocrisy is the most expensive sin in the world —
it costs your peace, your integrity, your anointing, and your eternity.
It is the slow death of the soul wrapped in the appearance of life.
It lets you shine in public while you rot in private.
It lets you speak truth while living in lies.
It allows you to impress men but offends God.**

**The greatest tragedy of hypocrisy is not what it hides —
it is what it kills: purity, credibility, and intimacy with God.
Every mask you wear costs you a piece of your soul.**

Every lie you tell builds a wall between you and Heaven.
Every act of pretense delays the healing that only truth can bring.

Jesus said,

"Woe to you, scribes and Pharisees, hypocrites! For you are like whitewashed tombs —
outwardly beautiful, but inside full of dead men's bones." — ***Matthew 23:27***

The hypocrite's reward is temporary applause and eternal regret.
He may gain followers but lose favor,
gain wealth but lose worth,
gain power but lose presence.

You can wear a mask for years,
but one day, truth will demand payment.
And on that day, every secret will speak,
every lie will echo,
and every false image will fall before the eyes of the God who cannot be deceived.

Hypocrisy may look harmless — but it is spiritual suicide in slow motion.
It kills joy, poisons relationships, and silences the voice of God in your life.
It may protect your image, but it destroys your soul.

"For there is nothing hidden that will not be revealed,
nor anything secret that will not be made known and come to light." — ***Luke 8:17***

The question is not if the mask will fall — it's when.
And when it does, will you still have a heart that belongs to God?

The Hidden Price of Pretending

Every mask comes with a price — and that price is your soul.

At first, hypocrisy feels light.

It brings applause, earns admiration, and hides your flaws.

You look strong, respected, even spiritual.

But as time passes, the mask grows heavy —

and the weight of pretending begins to crush the heart beneath it.

You can only fake light for so long before darkness takes its toll.

You can only perform holiness for so long before emptiness takes the stage.

You start losing not just your truth, but your **peace**, your **joy**, your **identity**.

The hypocrite becomes a stranger to himself:

smiling in public but **weeping in private**,

praised by others but **haunted by guilt**,

busy for God but **far from His presence**.

> "Be sure your sin will find you out." — *Numbers 32:23*

The lie you wear to protect your image will one day **expose** your heart.

The words you use to appear righteous will one day **testify** against you.

For God cannot be deceived — the same God who covers in mercy also **uncovers in justice**.

Hypocrisy promises safety, but delivers **bondage**.

It may keep your reputation alive, but it kills your relationship with God.

It is a slow spiritual death —

a smile on the lips, with silence in the spirit.

How Hypocrisy Destroys Your Identity, Peace, and Eternal Destiny

Hypocrisy is not just sin — it is **spiritual self-destruction.**

It kills slowly, silently, and from the inside out.

It steals the most precious thing a human being possesses — **authenticity before God.**

When you pretend to be what you are not, you lose sight of who you truly are.

Your soul becomes divided — one part acting holy, another hiding sin.

You start to live between two worlds: **appearance and reality**,
until the mask you wear becomes the only face you recognize.
You can no longer tell whether your smile is real or rehearsed,
your prayers sincere or staged.
You begin to perform faith instead of live it.
You say the right words but feel no life in them.
You lift your hands in worship while your heart bows to idols.

> "A double-minded man is unstable in all his ways." —*James 1:8*

Double-mindedness breeds torment.

You cannot walk in peace while living in pretense.

You cannot rest when your soul is at war with itself.

You cannot carry the joy of salvation when you keep feeding the sorrow of deception.

Hypocrisy turns believers into actors, worshipers into performers.
You live for eyes instead of eternity.
You chase approval instead of anointing.
You trade truth for applause, and Heaven's favor for human praise.
But when the curtain falls and eternity begins,
the mask cannot save you.
The applause of men will turn into the silence of judgment.

"Not everyone who says to Me, 'Lord, Lord,' shall enter the kingdom of heaven,

but only he who does the will of My Father in heaven." — *Matthew 7:21*

Heaven is not for actors — it is for the **authentic**.
It is for those who chose truth over comfort, purity over performance,
and who walked before God with one face and one heart, even when it cost them everything.

When You Fool People but Not God

You can **fool men**, but you can never fool **God**.

You can deceive your friends, impress your church, and perform before your audience —

but the One who formed your heart sees beyond the performance.

He does not look at the words of your lips but at the motives of your soul.

He sees the truth behind your prayer,
the motive behind your generosity,
the intention behind your worship.

He knows when your tears come from repentance and when they come from pride.

He knows when your sermon is revelation and when it is self-promotion.

He knows when your "Hallelujah" is worship and when it is manipulation.

> "Nothing in all creation is hidden from God's sight.
>
> Everything is uncovered and laid bare before the eyes of Him to whom we must give account." — *Hebrews 4:13*

People may judge your performance, but God weighs your purity.
You can dress like holiness, talk like faith, and act like love —
but the Spirit of God searches deeper than your image.
He tests the heart, not the hashtags.
You can hide from people in darkness,
but not from the God who **is Light**.
And when the Day of Truth comes,
every mask will fall, every secret will speak,
and every hidden motive will stand naked before His throne.

> "For there is nothing hidden that will not be disclosed,
> and nothing concealed that will not be brought to light." — *Luke 8:17*

The greatest shock in eternity will not be who went to hell —
it will be how many *looked holy* on earth but lived hidden in hypocrisy.
For Heaven recognizes not your **performance**, but your **purity**.

The Curse of Double-Mindedness

Double-mindedness is the quiet poison of the soul.

It is **spiritual instability** — the inability to stand on one truth.

It is trying to serve two kingdoms while belonging to none.

It looks like devotion on Sunday and rebellion on Monday.

It prays for holiness while flirting with sin.

It says, "Lord, I love You," while still bowing to the idols of comfort, lust, and pride.

Such a heart is divided — one part reaches for Heaven, the other clings to the world.

It produces confusion, weakness, and restlessness.

Your words lose power, your prayers lose fire, and your walk loses direction.

> "No one can serve two masters... You cannot serve God and mammon." — *Matthew 6:24*

You cannot walk two roads and arrive at one destiny.

You cannot love the truth and live a lie.

You cannot seek peace while hiding in pretense.

The curse of double-mindedness is that it leaves you **exhausted and empty** —

never fully joyful in sin, never fully free in Christ.

It makes you suspicious of everyone, yet blind to yourself.

It keeps you busy acting spiritual while dying spiritually.

But God, in His mercy, still calls: **Choose one side.**

Lay down the mask.

Let your heart be single again — pure, undivided, whole.

You may lose your reputation, but you will gain **redemption**.

You may lose applause, but you will find **peace**.

For the one who walks in truth walks with God Himself.

God's Exposure of Hidden Sin

God's exposure is not cruelty — it is **mercy in disguise.**

He does not uncover to destroy; He uncovers to **deliver.**

He tears off masks not to humiliate, but to **heal** the heart that has been living in hiding.

When Adam sinned in Eden, God asked, *"Where are you?"* — not because He lacked information,

but because Adam had lost **revelation.**

Sin didn't make Adam invisible to God — it made him blind to himself.

That is the true power of hypocrisy: it hides us from our own condition.

So God, in His mercy, shines His light — not to burn, but to **bring awareness.**

He exposes the wound so that He can cleanse it.

He reveals what is hidden so that repentance can begin.

What we call embarrassment, Heaven calls **intervention.**

> "Those whom I love I rebuke and discipline. So be earnest and repent." — *Revelation 3:19*

Exposure is not rejection — it is correction.

It is God saying, *"I love you too much to let you die in pretense."*

If you belong to Him, He will not let your sin remain comfortable.

He will shake your peace so He can restore your purity.

He will pull down every false image that keeps you far from truth.

He will strip the mask, silence the performance, and confront the secret —

not to shame you before men, but to save you before eternity.

The pain of exposure is temporary;

but the **peace of walking in truth** is eternal.

For God would rather see you broken in repentance than shining in hypocrisy.

The True Cost of Hypocrisy

The cost of hypocrisy is far greater than the cost of honesty.

It takes more strength to **pretend** than to repent.

More effort to **hide** than to be healed.

More pain to **protect your image** than to surrender your heart.

Hypocrisy destroys silently — not from the outside, but from within.

It eats away at peace, corrodes joy, and hardens the conscience until nothing feels sacred anymore.

- It **destroys your peace**, because lies can never rest.
- It **corrupts your conscience**, because pretending silences conviction.
- It **kills your faith**, because fake Christianity has no power.
- It **ruins your witness**, because people see your mask before they hear your message.
- It **separates you from God**, because sin can never dwell comfortably in His light.

A hypocrite may appear strong in public, but inside he is crumbling.

He spends years building a reputation only for **one truth** to destroy it.

He gains followers but loses his fellowship with God.

He gains the world but forfeits his soul.

> "Righteousness exalts a nation, but sin is a reproach to any people." — *Proverbs 14:34*

> "For the wages of sin is death, but the gift of God is eternal life through Jesus Christ our Lord." — *Romans 6:23*

The cost of hypocrisy is **death** — death of joy, death of truth, and finally, death of the soul.

But the reward of repentance is **life** — eternal, pure, and free.

The Call to Repentance and Restoration

But there is still hope — for the mercies of God are greater than the sins of man.

No mask is too strong for His truth to tear apart.
No sin is too deep for His grace to wash clean.
If you confess, He will forgive.
If you repent, He will restore.
If you return, He will renew your heart.

> "If we confess our sins, He is faithful and just to forgive us our sins and to cleanse us from all unrighteousness." — *1 John 1:9*

The cure for hypocrisy is **truth in the inward parts** (*Psalm 51:6*).
It is a humble heart that says, "Lord, I am not perfect — but I am Yours."
God is not looking for flawless people; He is looking for *honest* ones.
He prefers the broken truth over the polished lie.
He desires sincerity more than perfection.
Come out of the shadows.
Drop the mask.
Walk in the light — for truth is freedom.

A Prayer for Deliverance from Hypocrisy

Lord Jesus, I surrender my mask to You.

Expose every lie I have lived and every secret I have hidden.
Forgive me for pretending to be what I am not.
Restore my heart, cleanse my soul, and make me whole again.
Teach me to live in truth, to walk in humility, and to fear You more than man.
Let my life reflect Your character, not my image.
May my private life please You more than my public life impresses others.
And when You look at me, may You see not performance, but purity.
In Jesus' name. Amen.

"Create in me a clean heart, O God, and renew a right spirit within me." — *Psalm 51:10*

Key Scriptures:

- *Numbers 32:23* — Be sure your sin will find you out
- *James 1:8* — A double-minded man is unstable in all his ways
- *Matthew 7:21* — Not everyone who says "Lord, Lord" shall enter Heaven
- *Hebrews 4:13* — Nothing is hidden from God's sight
- *Luke 8:17* — Nothing hidden that will not be disclosed
- *Matthew 6:24* — You cannot serve two masters
- *Revelation 3:19* — Those I love, I rebuke and discipline
- *1 John 1:9* — If we confess our sins, He is faithful and just to forgive
- *Psalm 51:10* — Create in me a clean heart, O God

Chapter 16: The Cure for Hypocrisy

Every sickness has a cure, and every lie can be healed by truth.
Hypocrisy is not just a sin — it is a spiritual disease of the heart, a disconnection between the mouth and the soul, between confession and character.
But the mercy of God offers a way back.

The same God who exposed Adam's hiding place also covered his shame.
The same Jesus who rebuked the Pharisees also forgave Peter when he denied Him.
God does not delight in destroying the hypocrite — He desires to transform him.

The cure for hypocrisy is not found in better acting, but in deeper repentance.
It is not pretending to be holy, but allowing the Holy Spirit

to make you holy.
It is not hiding sin, but confessing it.
It is not seeking applause, but seeking purity.

"If we walk in the light as He is in the light, we have fellowship with one another,
and the blood of Jesus Christ His Son cleanses us from all sin." — *1 John 1:7*

The path back to truth begins with exposure and ends with surrender.
You cannot heal what you keep hiding.
You cannot walk in power while living in pretense.
But the moment you kneel in humility and say, "Lord, cleanse me,"
the chains of deception begin to break.

This chapter is a divine invitation —
to return to simplicity, to walk in truth, and to live again with one heart before God and man.

The Path Back to Truth

The road from **hypocrisy to holiness** is not paved with perfection — it is paved with **truth**.

Truth is the light that exposes darkness, the sword that cuts through pretense, and the mirror that shows us who we truly are.

Where hypocrisy imprisons, **truth delivers**.

Every soul that has worn a mask still has hope at the feet of Jesus.

No matter how long you have pretended, no matter how deep your deceit,

the grace of God is greater than your disguise.

The One who saw Peter deny Him also restored him with love.

The One who watched Saul persecute believers turned him into Paul the apostle.

No one is too lost for the light of truth.

> "You shall know the truth, and the truth shall make you free." — *John 8:32*

The cure for hypocrisy is not found in better performance, but in **pure repentance**.

It is not pretending to be righteous — it is becoming real before God.

It is removing the religious mask and saying, "Lord, here I am — broken but honest."

It is letting the Holy Spirit strip away the layers of falsehood until all that remains is sincerity.

Freedom begins the moment truth is spoken.

Healing begins the moment honesty returns.

And holiness begins the moment we choose to be **transparent before God and man**.

Returning to Truth and Simplicity

The message of the Gospel was never meant to be complex.

It was born in a manger, spoken by fishermen, and written in love.

It is simple enough for a child to believe and powerful enough to transform a nation.

But over time, humanity buried that simplicity under layers of pride, religion, and performance.

We turned what was sacred into spectacle.

We replaced **purity with presentation**, **devotion with drama**, and **truth with theatrics**.

We forgot that Jesus did not come to impress — He came to **redeem**.

He walked humbly, spoke honestly, and lived purely.

He never sought applause, yet Heaven testified of Him:

> "This is My beloved Son, in whom I am well pleased." — *Matthew 3:17*

Christ calls us back to that same simplicity —
to live with clean hearts, pure motives, and honest faith.

> "Let your 'Yes' be 'Yes,' and your 'No,' 'No.'" — *Matthew 5:37*

True simplicity is not weakness; it is **strength without disguise**.

It is choosing truth over titles, purity over performance, humility over hypocrisy.

A simple heart is a **safe heart** —
because it hides nothing, fears nothing, and walks in the light.

Simplicity brings peace because there is nothing left to protect but **truth itself**.

Walking in the Light (1 John 1:7)

The greatest cure for hypocrisy is not perfection — it is **light**.

Light does not need to pretend; it simply shines.

To walk in the light is to live with nothing hidden — no secret sin, no double life, no false image.

It is to live as if God is watching every thought, every motive, and every action — because He truly is.

> "If we walk in the light as He is in the light, we have fellowship with one another,
>
> and the blood of Jesus Christ His Son cleanses us from all sin." — *1 John 1:7*

Walking in the light changes everything.

It transforms how you relate to God and how you relate to others.

You no longer strive to **appear holy** — you begin to **become holy**.

You no longer hide your weaknesses — you confess them and grow through them.

You no longer live in fear of exposure — because there is nothing left to conceal.

The light of Christ exposes what is false, but it also **heals what is broken**.

It burns away deceit but also warms the heart with grace.

Darkness isolates; light restores.

Sin divides; truth reconciles.

When you choose to walk in the light, you begin to live free — free from fear, guilt, and pretense.

And in that freedom, you discover what real fellowship with God and others truly means:

not perfection, but **purity**;

not performance, but **presence**.

Allowing the Holy Spirit to Purify the Heart

No man can cleanse his own heart — not by effort, not by religion, not by discipline.

The disease of hypocrisy runs too deep for human will to heal.

Only the **Spirit of God** can perform that surgery of the soul.

> "Who can say, 'I have made my heart clean; I am pure from my sin'?" — *Proverbs 20:9*

The Holy Spirit is not merely a comforter — He is a **cleanser**.
He is the fire that burns away falsehood,
the wind that sweeps out deception,
the water that washes the stains of sin.
When He fills you, He does not flatter — He **convicts**.
He gently but firmly points to the hidden corners of pride,
to the quiet compromises of the heart,
to the lies you've learned to live with.
But His conviction is never cruel.
He does not expose to embarrass — He exposes to **restore**.
He does not condemn — He **cleanses**.
He does not shame — He **sanctifies**.

The cure for hypocrisy begins not with trying harder, but with **surrender**.

It begins when you kneel before God and pray,

> "Holy Spirit, expose what is fake in me — and replace it with truth."

When the heart is purified, the mouth will speak truth naturally,
the eyes will see others through compassion,
and the life will radiate sincerity.

> "Blessed are the pure in heart, for they shall see God." — *Matthew 5:8*

Purity is not perfection — it is **honesty before God**.
And when the Holy Spirit purifies your heart, hypocrisy loses its home.

Living for God's Approval, Not for Men's Applause

At the root of hypocrisy lies one deadly desire — the need to **be seen.**

It is the hunger for validation, the addiction to applause, the longing to impress rather than to please God.

We perform holiness instead of practicing it.

We serve publicly to be admired, but privately we are empty.

Yet Jesus warned clearly:

> "When you do a charitable deed, do not sound a trumpet before you, as the hypocrites do...
>
> your Father who sees in secret will Himself reward you openly." — *Matthew 6:2–4*

The cure for hypocrisy begins when you stop performing for people and start living for **God's presence**.

It is when your prayers are not rehearsed for the crowd, but whispered in secret.

When your giving is not posted, but hidden.

When your service is not for recognition, but for righteousness.

True holiness is lived before **an audience of One**.

When you live for God's eyes, you will serve even when unseen.

You will give even when unthanked.

You will pray even when unnoticed.

You will stay humble even when exalted.

The applause of men fades as quickly as it rises,

but the **approval of Heaven is eternal**.

Public opinion is a storm, but God's pleasure is a rock.

> "Do I now seek to please men? For if I still pleased men, I would not be a servant of Christ." — *Galatians 1:10*

If you live for likes, you will die by rejection.

But if you live for God's delight, you will never lose your direction.
The fear of man breeds pretense, but the fear of God births purity.

The Power of Repentance and Confession

Repentance is not a word of condemnation — it is a word of freedom.
It is the door that leads out of hypocrisy into healing.
The devil wants you to hide, but God calls you to confess.
When you confess your sins, you strip the enemy of his weapon.
You remove the power of shame and invite the power of grace.

> "If we confess our sins, He is faithful and just to forgive us our sins and to cleanse us from all unrighteousness." — *1 John 1:9*

Confession is the language of humility.
It is the courage to say, "I was wrong, but God is right."
Repentance doesn't humiliate you — it *restores* you.
It takes you from pretending to transforming, from guilt to grace.
When David confessed, God called him a man after His own heart — not because he was perfect, but because he was honest.
When Peter wept after denying Jesus, God restored him to leadership.
When the prodigal son returned home, the father ran to embrace him.
No matter how long you've lived in pretense, one honest confession can open Heaven over your life again.

> "He who covers his sins will not prosper, but whoever confesses and forsakes them will find mercy." — *Proverbs 28:13*

The Restoration of a Pure Heart and Honest Life

When repentance opens the door, ***restoration*** *walks in.*

God does not just forgive — He renews.

He takes the same heart that once lied, once pretended, once hid behind religion,

and He makes it ***new****, clean, and full of light.*

> *"Create in me a clean heart, O God, and renew a right spirit within me." — Psalm 51:10*

A pure heart is not a perfect heart — it is a heart that stays ***honest before God.***

It may stumble, but it does not hide.

It may fall, but it does not fake.

It runs to grace instead of running from truth.

When God restores your heart, He restores your peace.

When He cleanses your motives, He revives your joy.

When He purifies your conscience, He restores your power.

No longer do you live in fragments — one person in public and another in private.

No longer do you carry the burden of the mask.

You begin to live ***whole*** *again — integrated, authentic, transparent.*

That is what Heaven calls freedom:

to wake up every day with nothing to hide, nothing to prove, and nothing to fear.

> *"Blessed is the man whose transgression is forgiven, whose sin is covered.*
> *Blessed is the man to whom the Lord does not impute iniquity,*
> *and in whose spirit there is no deceit." — Psalm 32:1–2*

Restoration is not about recovering your reputation — it is about ***recovering your relationship*** *with God.*

Once the heart is restored, the life will follow —
a life that reflects truth, breathes sincerity, and walks in peace.

A Call to Authentic Christianity

The world has seen enough masks.

It is waiting for a generation of **authentic believers** —
men and women whose lives reflect what their lips proclaim,
whose holiness is real, not rehearsed,
whose love is genuine, not strategic,
whose faith is living, not theoretical.

God is calling His Church back to sincerity.

A people who walk in the light, speak truth, live humbly, and serve faithfully.

A people who love righteousness more than recognition.

The world is not moved by Christian performances — it is moved by Christian authenticity.

Let the Church remove her masks and reveal her heart.

Let every believer say, "Lord, make me real."

> "Behold, You desire truth in the inward parts, and in the hidden part You will make me to know wisdom." — *Psalm 51:6*

A Prayer for Renewal and Truth

Father, I come before You with an open heart.

I confess every lie I have lived, every image I have built, every truth I have hidden.

Cleanse me from all hypocrisy.

Let Your truth rule my heart.

Teach me to walk in the light, to live in simplicity, and to serve with sincerity.

Fill me with the Holy Spirit until there is no darkness left in me.

May my life reflect Your holiness and my words reveal Your love.

I choose truth over appearance, conviction over comfort, and Your approval over men's praise.

Make me real, Lord.
Make me true.
Make me Yours.

"Create in me a clean heart, O God, and renew a right spirit within me." — *Psalm 51:10*

Key Scriptures:

- *John 8:32* — You shall know the truth, and the truth shall make you free
- *Matthew 5:37* — Let your yes be yes and your no be no
- *1 John 1:7* — Walk in the light as He is in the light
- *Proverbs 20:9* — Who can say, "I have made my heart clean"?
- *Matthew 6:2–4* — Give in secret, not for show
- *Galatians 1:10* — Seek to please God, not men
- *1 John 1:9* — Confess your sins and be cleansed
- *Proverbs 28:13* — He who covers sin will not prosper
- *Psalm 51:6, 10* — Truth in the inward parts; a clean heart before God

Chapter 17: The Fire That Reveals the Mask — When God Exposes to Purify

There comes a time when God allows His fire to fall — not to destroy, but to disclose.
For too long, men have worn masks of religion, power, and success.
They have hidden behind pulpits, positions, and pretenses, thinking that light will never touch them.
But God is a consuming fire — and His fire always reveals what the flesh tries to conceal.

"For there is nothing hidden that will not be revealed,
nor anything secret that will not be known and come to light." — *Luke 8:17*

The fire of God is not just judgment — it is refinement.
It separates gold from fake gold, sincerity from showmanship, truth from performance.
When God sends His fire, the wheat remains, but the chaff burns away.
The proud are silenced, and the humble are purified.

In these last days, the Lord is cleansing His

house.
He is exposing corruption in the church, deception in governments, and hypocrisy in hearts.
Not to humiliate, but to heal; not to condemn, but to cleanse.

Every hidden thing will be revealed.
Every false altar will fall.
Every mask — whether worn by preachers, politicians, or believers — will melt in the heat of His holiness.

"For our God is a consuming fire." — ***Hebrews 12:29***

This is not the time to hide — it is the time to repent.
This is not the time to fake holiness — it is the time to seek purity.
The fire that exposes is the same fire that purifies.
And only those who love truth will stand when it burns.

The Day of Revelation — When Truth Burns Through Every Mask

There is a day coming when the **light will leave no shadow.**

Every mask, no matter how skillfully worn, will melt in the heat of divine truth.

Every hidden thought, every whispered lie, every secret sin will be laid bare before the throne of the Living God.

The world hides behind titles, wealth, religion, and technology — but **no disguise can stand before fire.**

> "There is nothing concealed that will not be disclosed, or hidden that will not be made known.
>
> What you have said in the dark will be heard in the daylight, and what you have whispered in the ear in inner rooms will be proclaimed from the rooftops." — *Luke 12:2–3*

The light of God is not partial.

It will shine in palaces and in prisons, on altars and in offices, in pulpits and in parliaments.

The same eyes that once looked into the souls of the Pharisees now watch every nation, every leader, every heart.

The **fire of judgment** will test every work, every word, and every motive.

The stage of human pretense will be cleared, and only truth will remain standing.

Those who wore holiness as costume will tremble,

but those who walked in sincerity will shine like refined gold.

The **Judge of truth** is not delayed — He is at the door.

The fire is not sent to humiliate, but to **separate the false from the faithful**,

to purify the church and expose the darkness that has masqueraded as light.

For when the Day of Revelation comes, there will be no more hiding —

only truth, blazing like the sun, consuming every lie that ever lived in shadow.

God's Refining Fire — Separating Gold from Fake Gold

Not all that glitters before men shines before God.

Not every preacher who speaks in His name carries His Spirit.

Not every miracle worker moves by truth — some perform by deception.

Not every worshipper is surrendered, and not every believer is sincere.

> "He will sit as a refiner and purifier of silver; He will purify the sons of Levi and refine them like gold and silver." — *Malachi 3:3*

The fire of God is coming — not to destroy, but to **distinguish.**

It will separate the true from the false, the faithful from the fake, the holy from the hollow.

In His furnace, imitation cannot survive.

Fire does not lie; it tells the truth about every substance it touches.

When gold meets fire, it glows brighter.

When dust meets fire, it disappears.

True hearts rejoice in refining; false hearts run from it.

The righteous are not afraid of fire — because they know it only burns what should not remain.

This refining fire will not stop at the church door — it will visit **governments, nations, homes, and altars**.

It will expose false prophets who preach for profit,
false doctrines that comfort sin,
false love that manipulates,
and false worship that entertains but never transforms.

It will strip away the pride of leaders who love fame more than faith,
and silence the songs of those who sing to be heard rather than to be holy.

For this is not the fire of destruction — it is the **fire of distinction**.

It will **purify the faithful** and **expose the faithless**,
until what remains is pure, unshakable, and ready for the coming King.

The Coming Judgment of Hypocrites — When Fire Becomes Final

God's mercy is long, but not endless.

His patience is great, but not eternal.

For generations, He has stretched out His hand, calling men to repent, to return, to walk in truth.

But there comes a time when the door of grace closes, and the throne of mercy becomes the **seat of judgment**.

> "For we must all appear before the judgment seat of Christ,
>
> that each one may receive what is due for the things done while in the body, whether good or bad." — *2 Corinthians 5:10*

The hypocrite may fool the church, deceive his followers, and manipulate systems of men —

but he will never deceive the **eyes of fire** that see through flesh and soul alike.

No lawyer can argue against **omniscient truth**.

No wealth can bribe the Judge whose scales are eternal.

No charisma can cover corruption when the flames begin to fall.

> "His eyes are like blazing fire, and on His head are many crowns."
> — *Revelation 19:12*

On that day, God will **separate the actors from the servants**,

the **wolves from the shepherds**,

the **stage performers from the true worshippers**.

The smiles that masked sin will fade in the heat of His holiness.

The lips that shouted "Hallelujah" but lived in rebellion will be silenced before His glory.

> "Not everyone who says to Me, 'Lord, Lord,' will enter the Kingdom of Heaven,

> but only the one who does the will of My Father." — *Matthew 7:21*

The final judgment will not merely expose deeds — it will **reveal hearts.**

Every false prophecy, every hidden motive, every pretended love will be weighed in the fire of truth.

The applause of men will vanish like smoke; the only sound will be the voice of the King saying,

"Well done," or **"Depart from Me."**

The fire of that day will miss no mask,
for every mask carries a hidden story —
and the **Fire of Eternity** will reveal them all.

The Fire That Cleanses the Church — Judgment Begins at the Altar

Before the fire of judgment reaches the world, it will first pass through the **house of God**.

> "For the time has come for judgment to begin with the household of God." — *1 Peter 4:17*

The Church — called to be the light of the world — has too often hidden behind the same shadows it was meant to expose.

But God, in His mercy, is cleansing His Bride before He crowns her.

The Holy Spirit is moving across nations like a refining flame, tearing down the altars of pride and exposing the secret sins behind pulpits and platforms.

Many who were celebrated will be shaken.

Many who were overlooked will be anointed.

Titles will fall, ornaments will fade, and every work built on flesh will be consumed.

For God will not share His glory with performance, nor His throne with pride.

He is raising a **new generation** —
not of celebrities, but of servants;
not of performers, but of prophets;
not of actors, but of authentic believers who carry *fire instead of fame*.

This purified Church will not entertain the world — it will **transform** it.

It will not seek applause — it will seek revival.

Its leaders will not boast in buildings, but in brokenness.

Its worship will not chase trends, but truth.

The **same fire** that exposes hypocrisy will **empower holiness**.

The **same flame** that judges deceit will **ignite devotion**.

And through that holy cleansing, God will raise a Bride —
without spot, without wrinkle, burning with love and purity for her King.

Revival of Truth in the Last Days

The last days will not only bring judgment — they will bring **revival**.

When the masks fall, truth will rise.

When religion fails, revelation will come.

When false prophets are silenced, true voices will speak again.

> "The earth will be filled with the knowledge of the glory of the Lord as the waters cover the sea." — *Habakkuk 2:14*

This revival will not be born in luxury but in repentance.

It will not be led by celebrities but by broken vessels.

It will not begin on stages but in secret prayer rooms.

It will be a revival of truth — pure, fiery, uncompromised.

Men and women will cry out for holiness again.

Families will return to prayer.

Pastors will preach repentance instead of entertainment.

Worship will become warfare, and altars will burn again with tears, not lights.

The Spirit of Truth will move mightily —

restoring love, purity, and unity to the Body of Christ.

He will raise up voices like John the Baptist, crying in the wilderness:

"Repent, for the Kingdom of Heaven is near!"

The fire of revival will purify the Bride,

for Jesus is coming soon — not for a famous church, but for a *faithful* one.

Not for a rich church, but for a *righteous* one.

Not for a big church, but for a *pure* one.

A Warning and a Promise

The fire of God is not only judgment — it is mercy.

He burns what is false to save what is true.

He exposes what is hidden to restore what is holy.

You can either meet the fire now in repentance or meet it later in judgment.

One burns to refine; the other burns to condemn.

One makes you pure; the other reveals your pretense.

Choose the fire of the Holy Spirit now —

the fire that sanctifies, empowers, and transforms.

Let it consume every lie, every mask, every hidden sin, every false motive.

For soon, the trumpet will sound, and the Son of Man will return with His holy angels.

And in that day, there will be no time left to repent.

Only those who lived in truth will stand before Him without shame.

> "Who can endure the day of His coming? Who can stand when He appears?
> For He will be like a refiner's fire and a launderer's soap." — *Malachi 3:2*

A Prayer for Refining Fire

Lord, I open my heart to Your holy fire.

Burn away every lie I have believed, every sin I have hidden, every pride I have protected.

Refine me like gold until only truth remains.

Expose what is false in me, and fill me with Your Spirit of truth.

Let Your fire cleanse my heart and prepare me for Your coming.

Make me pure, faithful, and ready for the day when every mask will fall.

Let Your truth reign in me — now and forever.

> "Our God is a consuming fire." — *Hebrews 12:29*

Key Scriptures:

- *Luke 12:2–3* — Nothing concealed will remain hidden

- *Malachi 3:2–3* — He will sit as a refiner and purifier of silver

- *2 Corinthians 5:10* — We must all appear before the judgment seat of Christ

- *Matthew 7:21* — Not everyone who says "Lord, Lord" shall enter

- *1 Peter 4:17* — Judgment begins with the household of God

- *Habakkuk 2:14* — The earth will be filled with the knowledge of the Lord

- *Malachi 3:2* — Who can endure the day of His coming?

- *Hebrews 12:29* — Our God is a consuming fire

Conclusion: Take Off the Mask

A Prophetic Call to the Church, Governments, and Individuals

The Spirit of God is speaking clearly to this generation:

"Take off the mask."

The time of pretending is over. The hour of exposure has come.

The nations are shaking, churches are trembling, and Heaven is watching.

The fire of truth is moving across the earth — not to destroy, but to purify;

not to embarrass, but to awaken.

The Lord says:

> "Everything hidden will be revealed, every lie will be judged, every mask will fall."

This is not a message of fear — it is a message of **freedom.**

God is calling His people, His leaders, and His nations to come out of hiding.

He is calling the Church to return to holiness.

He is calling governments to walk in justice.

He is calling individuals to live in truth.

The time has come to **unmask the hypocrites** — not by human anger, but by divine light.

The Spirit of Truth is uncovering what man tried to bury:

hidden corruption in leadership, false religion in pulpits, deception in systems,

and the secret sins of those who use the name of God in vain.

The Lord is separating the true from the false,

the humble from the proud, the righteous from the pretenders.

And He is saying to His people:

> "Be holy, for I am holy." — *1 Peter 1:16*

This is a **final trumpet** to a generation that has worn too many faces —

Christians who act holy but live worldly,

leaders who speak peace but sow injustice,

families who look united but live in bitterness,

and governments that preach equality but practice exploitation.

The time has come to take off the mask and return to the fear of the Lord.

The Time Has Come to Unmask the Hypocrites

For too long, hypocrisy has hidden under religion, politics, education, and business.

But Heaven declares: **"Enough!"**

The God of truth is confronting the spirit of deception that has polluted the earth.

The Spirit of holiness is walking through churches, exposing the sin that was celebrated.

The Spirit of justice is moving through nations, bringing down those who built their thrones on lies.

> "For judgment will again be righteous, and all the upright in heart will follow it." — *Psalm 94:15*

Those who built their lives on deceit will be shaken.

Those who built their ministries on manipulation will be silenced.

Those who built their empires on exploitation will fall.

But those who built their hearts on truth will stand.

God is not impressed by the appearance of good; He is moved by the reality of righteousness.

The mask that once protected you will now expose you.

The truth you ignored will now confront you.

The fire you feared will now refine you.

Take off the mask while there is still time — for soon, the Judge will appear,

and there will be no more hiding in His light.

> "For the Lord is coming to judge the earth;
>
> He will judge the world with righteousness and the peoples with His truth." — *Psalm 96:13*

A Prayer for Purity, Truth, and the Fear of God

Father in Heaven,

You are the God of truth, the Light that exposes all darkness.

We come before You with open hearts and humble spirits.

Forgive us for every mask we have worn — in our families, in our churches, in our work, and in our hearts.

Cleanse us from hypocrisy, deception, pride, and fear.

Baptize us again with the **fire of the Holy Spirit.**

Burn away false motives, false humility, and false appearances.

Let Your holy fear return to our hearts.

Teach us to love truth even when it costs us comfort.

Give us courage to live for Your approval, not for man's applause.

Make us pure vessels, clean hands, and honest hearts before You.

Lord Jesus, make Your Church a place of truth again.

Expose the darkness hiding in religion.

Break the chains of greed, manipulation, and false worship.

Let the true servants rise with humility and power.

Let the altars burn with repentance and holiness again.

And may the nations tremble at Your word,

governments bow to Your righteousness,
and every tongue confess that **Jesus Christ is Lord.**

> "Search me, O God, and know my heart; try me and know my thoughts.
>
> And see if there is any wicked way in me, and lead me in the way everlasting." — *Psalm 139:23–24*

Living as True Witnesses of Jesus Christ

The world does not need more talkers — it needs **true witnesses.**

People who live what they preach, love what they believe, and shine what they carry.

The end of hypocrisy is the beginning of authenticity — and authenticity is revival.

A true witness is one who walks in the light and speaks the truth even when it hurts.

One whose private life matches their public confession.

One who serves God out of love, not recognition.

One who reflects Jesus, not self.

> "You are the light of the world. A city set on a hill cannot be hidden." — *Matthew 5:14*

To live as a true witness is to let your life become a message.

It is to speak Christ not only with words but with actions, integrity, and compassion.

It is to be transparent in a world of pretense, steadfast in a world of compromise,

and holy in a world of corruption.

When the Church becomes real again, the world will believe again.

When believers walk in truth, the darkness will retreat.

When love replaces lies, revival will come.

So let every reader hear this call:

Take off your mask. Return to truth. Walk in the light.

Live as one who has nothing to hide and nothing to prove — only Christ to glorify.

> "Let your light so shine before men, that they may see your good works and glorify your Father in heaven." — *Matthew 5:16*

The time has come.
The trumpet is sounding.
The fire is burning.
The Spirit is speaking.
Take off the mask.
Be real. Be pure. Be true.
And let the world see Jesus in you.

Final Benediction

Now to Him who searches all hearts,
who reveals hidden things and restores the broken,
to Him who calls His people out of darkness into marvelous light —
be glory, honor, and dominion forever.
May your life shine with truth.
May your words carry purity.
May your heart reflect the fear of God.
And may you stand unashamed before the throne of Christ —
not as one who wore a mask, but as one who walked in truth.

> "Blessed are the pure in heart, for they shall see God." — *Matthew 5:8*

Epilogue: The Unmasked Generation — A Prophetic Vision of the Church Restored in Truth and Fire

The Dawn After the Fire

The fire has passed. The masks have fallen.

The noise of hypocrisy is fading, and a new sound is rising —

a sound of broken hearts being healed, of churches awakening, of truth returning.

The Spirit of the Lord is moving upon the earth like the wind of early morning,

and those who once lived in darkness are stepping into the light.

A remnant is rising — not a perfect people, but a purified people.

They have been refined in the furnace of affliction,

washed in the river of repentance,

and clothed in garments of righteousness.

This is **the Unmasked Generation** —

a generation that fears God more than fame,

that values truth more than tradition,

and that loves purity more than popularity.

> "Arise, shine, for your light has come,
> and the glory of the Lord has risen upon you." — *Isaiah 60:1*

A Generation Born in the Fire

This generation has passed through the shaking.

They have seen the fall of false systems, the exposure of deceit, the collapse of idols.

They have witnessed how power without purity brings destruction,

and how knowledge without holiness breeds pride.

But out of the ashes, God is birthing authenticity.

Out of corruption, He is birthing conviction.

Out of confusion, He is birthing clarity.

The Unmasked Generation will not depend on titles, stages, or applause.

They will depend on the Holy Spirit.

They will not seek to be admired — they will seek to be aligned with Heaven.

They will not play church — they *will be* the Church.

They will walk in light, live in love, and carry fire that cannot be quenched.

> "These are they who follow the Lamb wherever He goes." — *Revelation 14:4*

The Church Without a Mask

The Bride of Christ is awakening.

The Spirit is cleansing her garments, removing her stains, and restoring her beauty.

No longer will she wear the veil of religion — she will wear the glory of righteousness.

The Church of the last days will not be defined by buildings or budgets, but by holiness, humility, and the presence of God.
The altar will burn again — not with lights, but with tears.
Worship will return to purity, and preaching to power.
The Word will be proclaimed with conviction, not compromise.
The Church will no longer entertain the world; it will transform it.
She will walk in power, but also in purity.
She will preach truth, but also live it.
She will love people, but fear God above all.

> "That He might present to Himself a glorious church,
> not having spot or wrinkle or any such thing,
> but that she should be holy and without blemish." — *Ephesians 5:27*

This is the generation that will prepare the way for the return of the King.
The world will see once again that Jesus is not a religion — He is reality.

The Revival of Truth and Fire

The revival that is coming is not a revival of noise — it is a revival of **truth.**
It will not be built on emotion, but on repentance.
It will not start on platforms, but on knees.
It will not be led by celebrities, but by servants.
When truth meets fire, transformation happens.
When holiness meets humility, Heaven invades earth.

This is the revival that will sweep nations —
not because of human strategy, but because of divine purity.
Children will prophesy again.
Youth will carry the cross instead of the culture.
Elders will dream again.
The fear of God will return to pulpits and homes.
And once again, the world will tremble — not at our words, but at our witness.

> "In the last days, says God, I will pour out My Spirit on all flesh."
> — *Acts 2:17*

The Unmasked Generation will be carriers of that outpouring —
vessels of truth, voices of fire, ambassadors of light.

The Call to the Nations

This movement will not belong to one nation, denomination, or culture.
It will sweep across continents —
from the deserts of Africa to the cities of America,
from the valleys of Asia to the mountains of Europe.
Everywhere, the Spirit will whisper:
"Take off the mask and return to Me."
Governments will be shaken.
False religions will crumble.
The mighty will fall, and the humble will rise.
For the King of Glory is coming — not for the proud, but for the pure.

> "For the earth will be filled with the knowledge of the glory of the
> Lord
> as the waters cover the sea." — *Habakkuk 2:14*

This is the cry of Heaven to the nations:
Repent, return, and be restored.
The time of pretending is over; the time of truth has come.

The Final Generation of Fire

The Unmasked Generation is not afraid of persecution —
they are refined by it.
They are not moved by popularity — they are anchored by purpose.
They are not distracted by wealth — they are consumed by worship.
They are not ashamed of the gospel — they are carriers of glory.
This generation will walk in both **truth and power**,
holiness and boldness, purity and fire.
They will not fear man because they walk with God.
They will not compromise because they have seen the Cross.
They will preach repentance to the proud,
deliverance to the bound,
and hope to the hopeless.
They will shine as burning lamps in the darkness of the end times.

And when the Lord returns, He will find faith — not performance, not pretense, but **purity.**

> "When the Son of Man comes, will He find faith on the earth?"
> — *Luke 18:8*

A Final Cry of the Spirit

The Spirit of the Lord says:

> "I am raising a generation that walks without masks,
>
> whose hearts are clean, whose words are true, whose hands are pure.
>
> They will not fear exposure because they live in the light.
>
> They will not serve two masters because their hearts are Mine.
>
> They will love truth more than comfort and holiness more than applause.

> I will use them to reveal My glory in the earth.
>
> I will pour out My Spirit upon them, and through them, nations will awaken."

This is the **Unmasked Generation.**
A people of purity.
A people of power.
A people of truth.
Let every reader of this message become part of this remnant.
Let the fire of truth consume your heart.
Let the mask fall.
Let your life become a testimony that Jesus Christ is Lord.

> "And they overcame him by the blood of the Lamb and by the word of their testimony." — *Revelation 12:11*

Final Declaration

Arise, sons and daughters of truth.
The time of deception has ended; the time of revelation has come.
Walk in the light, speak the truth, live in the fire.
Be the Church that the world has been waiting for —
pure, powerful, fearless, and full of the Holy Spirit.
The world may wear masks, but you were born to reveal Christ.
Let your life be His mirror, your heart His dwelling, your words His voice.
For soon, the King will return — and He will recognize His own
not by their masks, but by their light.

> "Blessed are those who are invited to the marriage supper of the Lamb." — *Revelation 19:9*

This is the rise of the Unmasked Generation.
A generation of truth.
A generation of holiness.

A generation of fire.

A generation that will finish what the apostles began.

A generation that will cry, until the heavens answer:

"Come, Lord Jesus!"

About Publisher is a independent publishing mission dedicated to revealing truth, exposing deception, and restoring the knowledge of God in a confused and broken world.

We publish spiritually inspired books that challenge systems of darkness, awaken identity, and illuminate the divine purpose within every reader.

Our mandate is to bring clarity where the world brings confusion, light where darkness hides, and revelation where tradition blinds.

Through the powerful writings of **Joseph Habimana Ngoma**, AbbiBook Publishing releases messages that speak to:

— the battle for identity and destiny

— the deception in religion, politics, society, and relationships

— the restoration of God's image in humanity

— hope, healing, and spiritual awakening for nations

Joseph Ngoma AbbiBook Publishing exists to raise voices of truth in a generation overwhelmed by hypocrisy and falsehood.

For inquiries, publishing information, or ministry engagement:

Email: habimanangoma@gmail.com

Website: https://ngomahabimana.github.io/abbibook-website/

To explore more books by the author, search **"Joseph Habimana Ngoma"** on Amazon or google.

AbbiBook Publishing — Where Truth Breaks Chains and Light Confronts Darkness.

About the Author

About the Author

I am **Joseph Habimana Ngoma**, an author, teacher, and messenger of truth.My writings focus on **spiritual warfare**, **deliverance**, and **the restoration of God's image in humanity** — truths that many churches overlook but which countless souls desperately need.Through divine revelation, I expose the unseen battles that keep people in bondage and help readers understand how to live in freedom, purity, and light.

If you want to read my books, simply search my name — **Joseph Habimana Ngoma** — on **Google**, **Amazon**, or any major bookstore platform.My books are for anyone seeking truth, deliverance, and transformation through the power of God's Word.

Books by Joseph Habimana Ngoma*Communication and the Challenges of Communication: The War for TruthBehind the Mask of Hypocrisy: The Hidden Faces of DeceptionThe Rebellion of Satan and the Mystery of ManUnseen Forces, Unspoken Battles: The Cry for DeliveranceChains of Hypocrisy: How the World Kills Africa for ProfitThe Sickness of American BehaviorTo Have One Strong Youth Is to Save 1000 GenerationsWe Are Gods: Not the God of Heaven, but His Image on EarthBecause of War I Lived More*

Than Sixteen Years in HellKingdom Builders (Parts 1–7): Raising a Generation of Faithful WarriorsThe Kingdom and Citizenship: The Power, Purpose, and Principles of Kingdom CitizenshipMiracle Worker: Rediscovering the Authority of Christ in Your LifeWhy Me?: A Journey Through Purpose, Pain, and RedemptionWhat You Need to Know and Do as a Human BeingThe Heart of Man Is Residence of Whom?I Am Stronger Than Strongman: Destroy a Strongman

www.ingramcontent.com/pod-product-compliance
Lightning Source LLC
LaVergne TN
LVHW090301210926
848480LV00001B/91
* 9 7 9 8 2 3 2 1 9 3 3 7 9 *